NEHRU'S FIRST RECRUITS

Other Books by the Author

The Great Game in Afghanistan:
Rajiv Gandhi, General Zia and the Unending War

NEHRU'S FIRST RECRUITS

THE DIPLOMATS WHO BUILT INDEPENDENT INDIA'S FOREIGN POLICY

KALLOL BHATTACHERJEE

HarperCollins *Publishers* India

First published in India by HarperCollins *Publishers* 2024
4th Floor, Tower A, Building No. 10, DLF Cyber City,
DLF Phase II, Gurugram, Haryana – 122002
www.harpercollins.co.in

2 4 6 8 10 9 7 5 3 1

Copyright © Kallol Bhattacherjee 2024

P-ISBN: 978-93-5699-751-6
E-ISBN: 978-93-5699-969-5

The views and opinions expressed in this book are the author's own and the facts are as reported by him, and the publishers are not in any way liable for the same.

Kallol Bhattacherjee asserts the moral right
to be identified as the author of this work.

All rights reserved. No part of this publication may be reproduced, stored in a retrieval system, or transmitted, in any form or by any means, electronic, mechanical, photocopying, recording or otherwise, without the prior permission of the publishers.

Typeset in 11.5/15.7 Bembo Std at
Manipal Technologies Limited, Manipal

Printed and bound at
Manipal Technologies Limited, Manipal

This book is produced from independently certified FSC® paper to ensure responsible forest management.

*For Mamoni and Babu—Smt. Amita Chakraborty and
Shri Keshab Kanti Bhattacharjee*

CONTENTS

Introduction: Finding the first recruits	ix
1. Military men, radio announcers, ICS officers	1
2. A friendship and a catalogue	54
3. 'Everyone's trying to make sense'	79
4. The outsider becomes an insider: The career of an IFS topper	95
5. Raj: The envoy for 'little nations'	115
6. Videsh Mantralaya: The man behind the term	140
7. The first evacuation of Indians in a foreign crisis	157
8. 'Wilfred must go'	186
9. Rebels and princes	211
10. The first women recruits: Leilamani and Vijaya Lakshmi	239
11. From Hanumannagar to Tashkent: Chandra Shekhar Jha	256
12. Mirza Rashid Ali Baig: The protocol chief who made all the difference	282
Acknowledgements	311
Notes	315
Index	331

INTRODUCTION
FINDING THE FIRST RECRUITS

FIRST CAME A DEEP TERRIFYING rumble from behind the hills, and we froze, leaving the football where it was. The tiny players looked towards the hills, expecting an angry dragon to raise its head. In the distance, the scary noise built to a crescendo. Within seconds, it no longer was at a distance but right at the feet of our little hill. It was time for the two football teams to show some courage, and we looked at each other hoping to find a solution to the rising fear as the sound seemed to be inching dangerously close. After a few minutes of tense arguments, it was my elder sister, Keya, who mustered enough courage to go to the edge of the hill and peer down. 'Tank!' she yelled as our teams trooped behind her, looking to find out more about the tank. To our collective amazement, the sound was not the result of a single tank, but dozens of hulking iron machines that were emerging in a single column from a garrison located in the hills.

How and where so many battle tanks were hiding in our hills for so long without us noticing their presence was a matter of animated discussion. The football was abandoned, and we children came down the hill to see the tanks that proceeded stoically. There they were, the hulking brown machines with a dome on top and a turret, each looking like a copy of the other and making that sound that shook everything around them as they marched ahead. These gigantic machines moved slowly, and as they moved, they left deep marks on the surface of our only lifeline—the Assam–Agartala Road that went through our town Kumarghat, one of the last Indian settlements on the border with Bangladesh.

Kumarghat was (and still is) a dreamland. Clouds hovered over it all day, creating elephants and cats in the sky that fell on us in large droplets of rain. At night, Longtorai hills came alive with fireworks from the homes where the tribals had been living for centuries. On the other side was the farmland and beyond that lay a foreign land. The hills and rivers were beautiful, but they also held secrets, we would learn later. We were told that our little hillock, where some of the accommodations housed families of government employees, came up in the previous decade when a big war was fought in 1971. Big machines were brought from abroad, and the hills were sliced overnight to build a passage for the military machines to fight in that war. We had not seen that war but were told of a great tumult that touched Tripura.

The rust-coloured column of tanks was among the residue of a war that was fought more than a decade earlier. Now, we were in peacetime. The epic violence had long passed. But the emergence of the roaring rusty-brown machines, as if from behind the cloud of time, next to the column of little children, was an image that was imprinted on my mind.

INTRODUCTION

Located in a distant corner of India, wedged between Southeast and South Asia, Tripura has witnessed many currents of history. In the south, it is separated from the Bay of Bengal by a sliver of land that forms Chittagong. Bangladesh, we were told by our grandparents, was the land of two big rivers—Padma and Meghna; it was the land where they were born and raised when it was still a part of British India. We had not seen those rivers, but our grandparents talked of them incessantly, building an image of an expanse of water that was endless. Padma was grey, and Meghna was dark, deep and dangerous. They often spoke of their past in that unknown land. The strip of Chittagong was so narrow that any storm that hit the vast mouth of Padma and Meghna nudged us. We were drenched by the rain that came from the oceans, and we prayed in the afternoon to the rain god to spare our daily football practice, which was the most important part of our daily activities. The cyclones of the Bay were, however, not the only elements that crossed the border to torment us occasionally.

I grew up on the tales of 1971 narrated to me by my parents and their parents, witnesses to a war that was accompanied by a huge humanitarian crisis involving nearly one crore displaced persons who came across the border and were provided safe refuge by India. Overnight, schools and government offices were converted into shelters to hold these people who poured into Tripura. The refugees wept and sought help from anyone willing to listen. Tripura had not experienced anything like that till then. The small state with its entire working population was mobilized to deal with the crisis. Government officials, including my father, were instructed to support the Indian armed forces. Soon, the bombing raids began, and fighter jets took off from Agartala and flew over the skies of Tripura. General Tikka Khan's forces were vanquished.

Every time we heard the story, our minds lit up with images of fireworks.

In my growing-up years, foreign affairs was not something that was part of an academic discussion. It was rather a part of daily life as we lived on a piece of land that had no option but to bear witness to some of the biggest changes that shook South Asia—in 1947 and 1971. Problems in the nearby areas overflowed, often affecting us. At times, our location gave us an autonomy that can only be experienced in marginalized geographies. The mighty Indian state did not care enough about what we watched on our TV screens or what was heard on our Philips radio sets, and for years we happily consumed the American programmes and news telecast from London and Dhaka.

Our location gave us a vantage point to observe the world, and sometimes, what happened nearby crossed the hills and rivers and flowed into our world. The news from Delhi would come home in print, a day later, and the news from the world reached us on TV in the evening. We would watch on TV American news footage that captured the civil war in Lebanon and the Israel–Palestine conflict. New Delhi was far away; Vietnam was nearer, and so we often saw it first through TV series like *M*A*S*H*, which centred on the war in Vietnam. *Movie of the Week*, Bangladesh TV's weekly film show, which telecast the best Hollywood films, introduced us to Elizabeth Taylor and Johnny Weissmuller long before we met Shatrughan Sinha or Rekha. We saw the black and white images of Arab mothers bidding goodbye to their sons as they went to fight Israel and heard and read the tales of violence in Iran. Doordarshan, the state-owned Indian TV network, had discussions on foreign affairs, but these were not available to us in Tripura, and the need for international news was thus met only by foreign news channels. There were no mediators or analysts on news programmes back in those days. There were not too many Saeed Naqvi-like analysts who travelled across the world and could hold forth on issues related to India. Occasionally, we would gather around the radio set to listen to All India Radio's programmes on foreign affairs. Then, eventually, Tripura was brought under the broadcast range of Doordarshan. It would be years before I realized what was 'their news' and what was 'our news'. This crucial distinction would come with the advent of *The World This Week* on Doordarshan, which started presenting world news from 'our' point of view. Yasser Arafat, Fidel Castro and George H.W. Bush were presented from our perspective to Tripura, and I, in my teenage years, finally understood that there was a distinctively Indian way to view the world and its leading actors. In the early 1990s, this distinction was ably narrated by our diplomats—serving and retired—who appeared on TV. Over the years, news evolved and created more space for analysis, introducing me to the first generation of Indian diplomats who would dissect news and explain the story behind it. But those appearing in the news were a tiny fraction of that vast body of diplomats who had participated in the iconic events that were part of the stories I heard in my childhood.

Diplomats with well-travelled pasts debuted on post-liberalization Indian TV in the 1990s and quickly gained popularity when NDTV, along with a few other TV channels, began to invite them to their TV studios. Diplomatic reporting is something that I had seen earlier in the American news capsules telecast from Dhaka, but now Indian diplomatic reporting took off in an impressive way. The first-generation Indian diplomats, with years of experience and foreign postings behind them, made a mark when they appeared on TV. They were articulate and impressed me with their clarity of thought. I was hooked to Indian diplomacy and diplomats. That is how the first-generation Indian diplomats came into my life. I did not anticipate at that point that they would go on to become a part of my profession as well.

Later, in the 1990s, I dialled the Afghan Embassy with a lot of trepidation and sought a meeting with the serving Afghan ambassador, Masood Khalili. Ambassador Khalili, then a plump ruddy Afghan, welcomed this young college student into his office and agreed to come to our college and talk about Afghanistan. It was the 1990s, and Afghanistan was under the control of the Taliban. New Delhi had not recognized the Taliban, and President Najibullah had been murdered recently. The talk turned out to be good, but I was too excited to focus on what he was saying. A few years later, I was shocked to read in the newspapers that Afghan Mujahideen leader Ahmad Shah Masoud was killed by a suicide bomber. At the time of the incident, Masoud was accompanied by a former Afghan ambassador, who turned out to be none other than Ambassador Khalili, who had once obliged us by being present at the weekly seminar in Kirori Mal College.

Ambassadors have tales to tell, and my belief in their lives was established. As I graduated into higher studies, it became clear that the Thursday seminar of our Centre for West Asian Studies in Jawaharlal Nehru University (JNU) had long made it a practice to invite serving and retired Indian diplomats to speak to students and researchers. Long before I became acquainted with the Indian way of diplomacy, JNU's seminar halls had been narrating and teaching the unique Indian tradition of *doing* foreign policy. My old beliefs were broken and repaired as I sat through the seminars of J.N. Dixit, A.K. Damodaran and other first-generation Indian diplomats. Indian TV news was late in catching up with the seminar culture of JNU. Here, away from the public eye, the doyens of Indian diplomatic thinking had been interacting for decades with researchers, teachers and young students of international studies.

It was here that I met the 'First Recruits' for the first time. Muchkund Dubey, Damodaran and Dixit were leading retired lives and were delighted to meet a seminar hall full of eager students willing to fill up their term papers with nuggets picked up from such seminars. They taught us to ask questions and reason, and most important of all, doubt the given truth.

The Indian or foreign diplomats who came to the JNU seminar halls were often not theoreticians, they were practitioners and had field experience, which made them a breed apart from the ones that the academic community presented. Their anecdote-rich accounts made for good sessions but also made them vulnerable to jibes from academics who had the gift of theorizing and could turn accumulated experiences into an academic exercise. With a hint of intellectual superiority, it was broadly indicated that professional diplomats were often overwhelmed by the details of real-world action while academics do the real thinking on international studies. But there was little doubt that the professional diplomats were unique—like foreign affairs reporters, they too dealt with the raw material for thinking about foreign affairs. In the university, I became member of a group of businessmen who interacted with foreign embassies in Delhi probably to scoop lucrative commercial contracts. In their company, I began my first free interactions with career diplomats—both foreign as well as Indian. These interactions with people who walk on the path of real-world international trade and diplomacy would prove to be helpful later when I began writing and reporting as a journalist.

As I transitioned into the life of a working journalist, I had to rely on my informal network. I had never gone to a journalism school and, with an inclination to write longish pieces for my term papers, was not particularly fit for writing for news magazines, where the reports were expected to be 'crunchy', anecdotal and substantive without weighing down the reader. The only foreign affairs-related people that I had known before this phase were the academics, student leaders who gave rousing anti-imperialist speeches on campus, and seasoned former diplomats like J.N. Dixit and Brajesh Mishra. My editors expected me to have the skills and wanted me to write about the foreign affairs of the Vajpayee and the Manmohan Singh governments, and the best I could do then was to consult my university teachers and the diplomats whom I met in the seminar circuit. Meetings with veteran diplomats helped me gain some grounding on foreign affairs writing and reporting. Here I reverted to my earlier circle of diplomats and businessmen who welcomed me back—this time as a journalist. Pot-bellied businessmen looking for export contracts invited me to be part of their occasional evening outings in Chanakyapuri, where they would introduce me to the foreign missions—helping me meet a much-needed requirement at that time for my profession.

It was only with my induction into *The Week* magazine's reporting team that I understood the importance of carrying the 'official version'. But there was a problem, as the official version always claimed to be the truth, and I as a journalist had the responsibility of providing as much correct information as I could distil from official and unofficial sources. Here I found that former Indian ambassadors were a great resource to 'test' the veracity of the facts handed over by the External Publicity Division—that ultimate repository of the Indian version. K. Natwar Singh, Chinmaya Gharekhan, Romesh Bhandari, Kayatyani Shankar Bajpai, Mira Sinha Bhattacharjea (also known as Mira Ishardas Malik) and—on days when he was available near his telephone—even the formidable Brajesh Mishra, all 'first recruits', always helped with their elephantine memories to verify and contextualize the claims made by the same Ministry of External Affairs that they served earlier. For every claim made by the successive governments of India over the past two and half decades, the 'first recruits' were ready with a comparison from the past. Mishra was tough to get through but generous in his post-retirement years till he passed away. Mira Sinha Bhattacharjea always answered the mobile warmly with that raspy voice that was her trademark. Over the years, these contacts matured. Once, when I wrote Bhandari's version for a cover story on Indira Gandhi for *The Week*, he bellowed, blaming me for ruining his upcoming autobiography. Of course, that rancour was not carried forward. These conversations would expose the gaps in official narratives and would help me get stories. I learnt an essential lesson in reporting foreign affairs. You can't write without the official version of events, but it was equally essential to put the official version through the test of experience, memory and the fire of arguments. That task was best conducted with the help of the 'first recruits' or those 'first recruits' who were still among us.

In 2006, the India–US civil nuclear agreement was the biggest development. Tall claims were made about it being the high point of India–US relations. Probing the claims soon led me to one of the 'first recruits' of the post-World War II US Foreign Service—John Gunther Dean. With generous help from John Gunther Dean and his Indian diplomatic partners, I dived into the story of high-tech collaboration between India and the US during the 1980s, in which an entire generation of his Indian contemporaries like Gharekhan, Bhandari, Triloki Nath Kaul, P.N. Haksar and K. Natwar Singh played their roles. While interviewing Dean, it became clear that there was something unique in the first generation of officials who joined the global profession back in the late 1940s and the 1950s. The old global order had ended, and a new generation of bureaucrats had emerged in the world dominated by two superpowers—unlike in any previous period in global history. Those were pre-internet days and diplomats had to come up with solutions pretty much on their feet, without getting dictated by their headquarters. The unique training that they underwent was supplanted by challenging assignments in the Cold War, which bolstered their legend. Dean, who was a contemporary of first recruits like Maharajakrishna Rasgotra and Chonira Belliappa Muthamma, explained that back in those days, a diplomat was pretty much his or her own boss and was driven by post-World War II values like freedom and equality. These factors had an impact not just on the first-generation American diplomats but also on their contemporaries in India in the Nehru era who championed decolonization and respect for sovereignty.

Indians had a unique responsibility, I realized, as they worked with a tight budget that was dictated by the Indian government's financial constraints.

Former ambassadors are a treasure trove of information, but as first-generation diplomats in a country that did not possess any foreign service worthy of the name before 1947, they became pioneers of the profession. I have been fortunate enough to know some of the 'first recruits' of Indian diplomacy, but most of them had already faded away long before I joined the profession of writing about foreign affairs. Yet, the few that I met left a deep impression on me about the extent of the institutional memory that they carried. Starting with the first years of the Indian republic, they pretty much had surveyed the entire growth story of India, which spanned the Nehru–Indira Gandhi years and covered the span of Cold War, ending with the Rao–Vajpayee–Manmohan Singh years. They indeed were the founders of a school of diplomacy that remains a model for developing societies.

1

MILITARY MEN, RADIO ANNOUNCERS, ICS OFFICERS

For seven hours on 31 January 1948, Indians sat near their radio sets as Melville de Mellow narrated the events surrounding the funeral procession of Mahatma Gandhi.

'The walls were white; the room was simply furnished. But these blue carpets contrasted with the white mattress upon which lay Mahatmaji. He was shrouded in spotless white khadi from his feet to his abdomen. His chest was bare. I could see the dark patches of the assassin's bullets against the skin of his frail body. His eyes were closed,' the legendary radio commentator said in his prophetic deep baritone.[1] Such was the power of de Mellow's words that the listeners sitting near small radio sets could almost walk beside the body of the Mahatma. Every word and every turn of phrase uttered by de Mellow brought Indians close to the epochal funeral, which took place in Delhi. Each Indian felt like they held the Mahatma in their arms as de Mellow proceeded to present the funeral like a magician of words.

India was divided before Independence, and the assassination of Mahatma Gandhi was a fresh attempt at deepening that division, but de Mellow's narration let India 'see' the man they loved deeply for one last time, and they realized, in the face of overwhelming odds, that they were part of one body. The next morning, the newspapers completed the picture with photographs and text.

The magic of words on airwaves and newspaper pages united India, which had been divided less than a year earlier. There was no way to undo the Partition, but the after-effects of the communal divide and hate had to be healed for the road ahead to emerge. Mass media was necessary for exactly that. It healed India's divisions as de Mellow presented the last journey of Mahatma Gandhi on radio. Villages, towns and cities echoed with de Mellow's narration as the power of radio was established in the largest country in South Asia. Assassinations, wars, communal riots and the shadow of the nuclear war loomed over the horizon but radio repeatedly reminded Indians that they were united and that they had a common destiny. The world that the new India was born into was moving towards television, but in India, radio had achieved its equivalent of the golden age with the speeches of Prime Minister Jawaharlal Nehru and the spectacular funeral procession of Mahatma Gandhi. Freedom was expected to produce a land of milk and honey, justice and equality. But it was not going to be easy.

The new India had to have new structures and traditions. But after a bruising fight with the fearful forces of history, India was exhausted. Yet, out of its best elements, the state had to start afresh. Modern mass media was, therefore, one of those elements where the finest of flashes of a modern India were visible. To negotiate the world outside that was merciless and unpredictable, Nehru's government had to create new pillars that would go on to support the free Indian state, and naturally, his ears and eyes would scan the radio waves and newspaper pages where he himself was one of the most prominent figures. From modern aircraft, which he saw in Europe with his daughter in 1927, to modern means of communication, Nehru now had the opportunity to materialize his fascinations, and building the Indian Foreign Service was one of those initiatives.

―

Celebrating rebellion was a major theme in Indian nationalism. Gandhi's rebellion was of the unarmed variety. But Indian nationalism thrived on the memories and tales of armed rebellion. Examples from the royalty of the past century—the Queen of Jhansi or teenaged Khudiram Bose—formed a parallel narrative of sacrifice that demanded accommodation. One such strand was inspired by violent revolutions in other parts of the world—most notably in Europe.

In 1914, a year before the return of M.K. Gandhi from South Africa to India, a group of youngsters tried to do the unthinkable. To this part of Indian society, the spread of English liberal philosophy and education ensured unprecedented access to European development. Ironically, greater awareness of western affairs cultivated a great sense of alienation in the country. For young people, the United Kingdom was the enemy and they looked for inspiration elsewhere—in India's past, and in western revolutionary movements that challenged the older colonial powers of Europe. Inspired by the revolutionaries of Europe like Giuseppe Garibaldi and Latin America's Simon Bolivar, young women and men in India's colleges and schools were planning bold moves to free India from colonial control. That the challengers in Europe—

Italy and Germany—could have colonial ambition as well, was of no significance to them. They viewed them as a support structure. Germany was the guiding star of their dreams.

The youngsters plotted a journey to Europe to obtain the support of the German government. A mysterious organization—the Indian Revolutionary Committee[2]—was formed in Berlin and this group became a nodal organ for transmitting messages from Berlin and the Indian revolutionaries in Europe. Germany's support for the planned Indian insurrection was to come in the form of money and arms.

A race against time had begun. The plan was to dislodge the British Raj from India. The opportunity was unique. For decades, disgruntled subjects of the Empire had been waiting for this moment. The hour of revenge was finally here. War drums had been playing in Europe for some time, and the revolutionaries in India felt coordinating the domestic uprising with events in faraway Europe would give them a better chance of succeeding. The vision was to launch a two-front attack on Britain. On the one front, the German war machine would overwhelm the United Kingdom, and on the other front, in India, with supply of weapons, the Indian fighters would overthrow the military-bureaucratic roots and branches of the British Empire. The revolutionaries required arms and ammunitions—lots of it. Clandestine meetings took place and Jatindranath Mukherjee was declared the commander-in-chief.

Accordingly, a messenger went to Berlin with a plan of smuggling arms into India. India's extensive and unmanageable coastline provided the point of vulnerability that the revolutionaries were looking for. The idea behind sending a messenger was that it would not be ideal for the cargo to be carried by the rebels from Germany personally. It was clear that they would prefer a neutral destination for taking charge of the delivery.

The rebels were not unique. They were indeed part of an emerging worldwide network of angry youth, which viewed assassins, militants and saboteurs as heroes necessary for ushering in a change. The waves of anger they felt and their youth produced a new kinship among youngsters across continents, nurtured by innocence and inexperience. Many of them were doomed to fail, but the shadow of such failure did not deter them. One such rebel, Gavrilo Princip, a radical Bosnian-Serb, stood at a street corner on 28 June 1914 and fired at Archduke Franz Ferdinand of the Austro-Hungarian empire. The assassination of the archduke, a popular figure in Europe, triggered a conflict that snowballed quickly. The violence was the last act in a series of tense developments that stretched back to the early years of the twentieth century and pitted the United Kingdom, France and Czarist Russia on the one side against Germany and Austria–Hungary on the other side. In the weeks following the assassination, events unfolded fast.

On 28 July 1914, Austria–Hungary declared war on Serbia. Russia stepped in to support the Serbians in the crisis. This happened almost simultaneously with Germany joining hands with Austria–Hungary. Caught between the fluid identity of nations and languages, Belgium had become a neutral country through the Treaty of London, in 1839. But that neutrality had little hope of surviving as resurgent Germans took to dominating the heart of Europe. Little Belgium's neutrality was bulldozed by Germany when it was attacked by Berlin's forces, as the control of Belgium was essential to fight the French forces. The violation of Belgium's decades' old shaky neutrality roused the anxiety of the United Kingdom, the preeminent imperial power in the continent at that time, which owned the largest foreign territorial possessions, including the bulk of South Asia, barring Nepal and Bhutan. In India, the anti-colonial movement closely tracked the unfolding war and the changing fortunes of European powers.

South Asia had been under complete British domination, starting with the 1857 mutiny, and there was a high probability that smuggling of arms from Germany through the eastern coast would be intercepted by the British Indian police and detectives. The plan was altered, and young rebels looked at India's south-east to the island named after millets, located in the vast archipelago under the control of the Netherlands—Java.

They reached Java, hoping to receive the consignment of arms from Germany. It was the first time that the land of millets, Java, and the Dutch East Indies were to emerge in the Indian public imagination. Despite the doomed first attempt, the revolutionaries succeeded in carrying out some of the most spectacular assaults on the colonial administration along the coast of Orissa that coincided with World War I, which left us with the legend of Jatindranath Mukherjee—also known as Tiger Jatin or 'Bagha Jatin'.

It was in this backdrop of wars and revolutions that Poonamalle Ramakrishna S. (P.R.S.) Mani was born on 14 February 1915.

The world changed dramatically by the time Mani learned to walk. M.K. Gandhi returned to India a month before Mani was born in Madras. The Russian revolution took place in 1917 and World War I would end in 1919. The shadow of revolutionary activities fell on Mani early in his life and, by his own admission, he was inspired by Garibaldi and Bolivar, like many other children born during that period. The hand of destiny works in curious ways and the two islands—Javadwipa and Suvarnabhoomi, also known as Java and Sumatra—that were known as the land of millets and the land of gold, would present themselves to Mani through a bloodbath. Mani grew up to be one of the many graduates of Madras University. His strengths were a confident and innocent personality and great writing skills, which made him a natural candidate for government jobs or journalism. But his restless life took interesting turns during World War II. Mani joined the Indian Army on 17 January 1944 and was sent to the Public Relations Directorate at the General Headquarters (GHQ).[3] He had his first experience of conflict when the GHQ promoted him to the post of Captain and dispatched him to the Battle of Imphal as an 'Indian Army Observer'. Here, he would report on the campaign in Imphal and the march into Burma. After a brief break in Madras, Mani would return to Burma with the troops where he would record the campaign by the 20th, 5th and the 17th Indian Divisions into southern Burma till the defeat of the Japanese forces in Yangon. From Yangon he moved to Singapore to witness the surrender of Japan in August 1945.[4] Unknown to him, Mani was being drawn to the finale of all colonial wars in Southeast Asia.

In the autumn of 1945 Mani landed in Jakarta, which was then known as Batavia, capital of the Dutch East Indies. The war in North Africa and Europe had ended, and Mani sailed with the rest of the British–Indian troops towards Southeast Asia. At the end of the brutal campaign in Southeast Asia and Europe, many of the young men were hoping for a new beginning. But dark clouds of war lingered in patches over South and Southeast Asia. From Batavia in western Java, they were ordered to proceed to Surabaya in eastern Java.

A clear and windy morning greeted Mani in Surabaya on 26 October 1945. On the previous day, he had landed in the scenic port city along with the Indian troops. The campaigns in the North African desert and the forests of Burma had ended up freeing British Indian troops from action against the Axis powers of World War II. There was war fatigue among the troops, and they wanted to return home. They did not have a clear idea about why they were being sent to Java, which they had known to be part of the Dutch Indies.

Behind the extraordinary natural beauty of Java, and its happy, alcohol-filled bars, there were dangers lurking which would soon erupt, engulfing the Indian soldiers.

As their ship arrived in the harbour of the city, the word that greeted them everywhere was 'Merdeka'—Freedom. Behind the red and white Indonesian flags were an impatient people waiting for far too long to break free. To Mani, the slogans sounded like the faint clap of a distant thunder. With every move and every step that he took, it became clear that the storm was coming nearer. But it would take some time before Mani would realize that something had gone terribly wrong in Surabaya.

The first sign of trouble surfaced one day when Mani was driving, with his English colleague Lt Tony Cardew of the Royal Navy in an open-top jeep. Mani was thirty and with his striking smile and intelligent eyes looked like a military version of the dancer Uday Shankar, but he noticed that his friendly *salamat pagé* (Good Morning) greetings were drawing rude responses from the people on the streets. It was shocking but a necessary wake up call. It took no time for Mani to realize that the locals had identified the British Indian soldiers as the 'vanguard of Dutch imperialism'. Many Indians had settled in Surabaya for decades, and some of them now cautioned Mani that the local Indonesians viewed the presence of the soldiers as an attempt to sabotage the freedom that they had announced just two months earlier on 17 August.

Just days before that, Emperor Hirohito had announced the surrender of the Empire of Japan. Within forty-eight hours,

Indonesia, formerly Dutch Indies, declared independence. The celebration was far from complete when the Indian troops of the 49th Infantry Brigade arrived. The Indian soldiers consisted of Jats, Marathas and Rajputs primarily, but they also had representation from many other parts of India. Muslims, Tamils, Anglo-Indians were all there. The words that they read on the walls of the jetties were 'Freedom or Bloodshed'. The arrival of the British Indian forces to Java made little sense either to the Indian soldiers or the Indonesians. The Indian soldiers who participated in the war in Europe and Southeast Asia were aware that they fought despite stiff domestic public opposition to their involvement in the war. The war had ended in Europe months earlier, and they should have returned home by now. On the other hand, the war in Southeast Asia had also ended with the dropping of the atomic weapon on Japan on 6 and 9 August. Ideally, the Indian soldiers should have returned home afterwards, and the Indonesians should have got on with their free existence. But that did not happen. Instead, the British Indian forces that were homebound were steered towards Java. The curious situation soon turned suspicious as the Indonesians found the arrival of the Indian soldiers under the command of British officials antithetical to their interest. The matter escalated with each passing hour. It was increasingly clear that Britain was bent on helping the Netherlands to re-establish its colonial rule over Java, in a complete turnaround from the defence of liberty, which it had championed while fighting the Axis powers till a few months ago. The Indian soldiers began to ask their commanding officers if they were now expected to fight the Indonesian nationalists. The disaster began to unfold one episode at a time.

Sensing growing tension among the local population, Brigadier Aubertin Walter Sothern Mallaby, commander of the 49th Indian

Infantry Brigade, tried to assert the authority of the British forces and declared before the governor of Surabaya, 'I am the ruler of this city.'[5] These proclamations would soon turn out to be disastrous for the soldiers as well as for Mallaby, drawing the world's attention to the unbelievable situation that had emerged in the Southeast Asian region just weeks after the end of World War II. Surabaya was a last-ditch attempt to resurrect the dying colonial era and prevent the birth of decolonization. Mallaby and others in his team had been warned about the volatile nature of the situation in Surabaya, where a vast number of locals had armed themselves during the previous few years. Apart from the freedom fighters, the local population also had a good number of communists, who were close to the Soviet Union and were viewed suspiciously by the British commanders. While the central leadership of Indonesia led by Sukarno conducted itself with great poise, the local forces were often more enthusiastic and at times violent in achieving the goal of freedom. The Indians would find out in the days to come that there were at least 15,000 trained Indonesian troops in Surabaya, and that apart, there were the trained irregular fighters. As news of the Indonesian irregulars taking up position to stop the movement of Indian soldiers went out, the Royal Air Force Spitfires started dropping leaflets across town demanding that the fighters lay down arms. This demand effectively set fire to the already volatile situation. Local Indians, out of concern, reached out to the soldiers and alerted them about growing public anger. But it was too late.

On 28 October 1945, Mani and his colleagues spent the day in anticipation, and finally the attack began when the hotel that served as their residence came under fire from multiple directions. The fighting continued till late evening and then stopped, only to resume the next day when they were overpowered, forcing them to take shelter in the attic of the large building. The ferocity of the battle can be measured by the fact that on the first day itself, the Allied powers dropped 500 bombs on Surabaya to suppress the rebellion.[6] But by the evening of the second day soldiers began to die as bullets came from all directions, including through the roof of the hotel. Indian soldiers divided themselves into multiple groups, and in one case, took refuge in a cavernous cinema hall, which was burnt down by the guerrillas, killing all of them. With no help forthcoming, P.R.S. Mani and his colleagues surrendered and were taken to a local prison, marking a landmark in the history of the Indonesian freedom struggle. In the twenty-first century, the Kalisoesoe or Kalisosok prison of Surabaya was converted into a low-income housing project, but back in 1945, it presented Mani and his colleagues with a nightmarish situation, which would last for several hours.

News of the killing of a large number of Indian soldiers who had been sent to Surabaya just three days earlier began to spread. On hearing this, President Sukarno rushed to the city to help restore calm, along with Information Minister Amir Sharifuddin. In the meanwhile, hours passed and during dinner time, the Indian guests were served rice with 'foul-smelling meat' and black coffee.[7] With the end of the war in Southeast Asia, Allied soldiers who spent time in Japanese captivity had begun to allege that the Japanese practised cannibalism in certain regions under their control.[8] The practice was also alleged to be imposed on captives, who were made to serve as slave labour to the Japanese war machine as a means of terrorizing them. Probably because of this context and the recent Japanese presence in the region, Mani and his colleagues feared that the meat offered to them was the flesh of their slain colleagues. Sensing this fear, the Indian soldiers only accepted the black coffee.[9] The harrowing experience ended abruptly after Sharifuddin came in and freed the captives. They were taken to the residence of the governor where Sukarno welcomed them and everyone apologized, indicating that the Indonesian nationalists valued their relations with the Indians as they both were on the same side of the war against colonialism.

The biggest tragedy of those fateful days of October–November 1945 was the needless loss of lives of scores of Indian soldiers and the murder of Brigadier Mallaby, who was shot and killed on 30 October when a ceasefire was being finalized between the British Indian troops and the guerrillas of Surabaya. The battle of Surabaya is remembered as one of the most violent phases of struggle for Indonesian independence, and the battle remains remarkable because it was not part of World War II but took place months after the war ended. Nearly 40,000 Indonesians died in the uprising, which lasted three weeks. The Indians were deeply conflicted by the experience, and most of them fought to subdue the rebellion. But many Indian soldiers refused to fight the Indonesians, and around 800 joined the rebels. Mani's sympathy was wholly with the Indonesian side. The bloody battle of Surabaya deeply impacted Mani, whose work both during his brief career as a journalist and later as a diplomat would be suffused with sympathy for the Indonesian cause for freedom and India–Indonesia relations.

The journey of Poonamalle Ramakrishna S. Mani, which began at the beginning of World War II, was representative of the importance that modern forms of communication media had in the affairs of the modern state. The post of army observer was however not the first job that Mani held.

He began in October 1939 as a publicity assistant and announcer in All India Radio, Madras. World War II was also fought on radio, where conflicting narratives collided, and it was necessary to stay ahead on that front as it shaped public opinion. Mani's job at that time included surveying radio reports to assess public opinion from Berlin and Moscow.

A year later, he joined Kalakshetra of Rukmini Devi Arundale to look after the commercial affairs of the famous centre for the arts. It was on the prompting of Rukmini Devi that Mani joined All India Radio in Delhi in 1942 as World War II was at its peak.

The 'Battle of Surabaya' was Mani's first introduction to Southeast Asian conflicts, and he was hooked. He quit the military and returned to India for a few months before the mysteries of Java called him back in March 1946—this time as a journalist with *The Free Press Journal* of Bombay. He would continue with his career in media from 1946 till India attained independence. During his journalistic stint in Indonesia, he earned the friendship of the leading stars of Indonesia's freedom struggle like Ahmed Sukarno, Mohammad Hatta and Dr Sutan Sjahrir. P.R.S. Mani's application to join the Indian Foreign Service brings out for us the early trends in the recruitment of Indian diplomats.

Mani first got to know Nehru as part of his journalistic assignments. He exchanged letters with him and accompanied him as a reporter for *The Free Press Journal* when Nehru visited Malaya in 1946. Later, while applying for the Indian Foreign Service, Mani remarked that Nehru appreciated his work and focused on Indonesia as his core competence in his application, saying, 'Indonesia has been my interest ever since I landed on her shores and I can justly claim considerable understanding of her people and her problems as I have watched the growth of the Republic ever since its birth, rather from a close angle.'[10]

In Indonesia, he saw the rebuilding of a unique country and its equally fascinating leaders. Mani was fascinated by the cultural mix that guided the Indonesian leaders. The 1945 Constitution of Indonesia gave the principle of 'Pantja Sila' or the five principles. For an Indian raised on the legends of the Mahabharata, the idea of the five principles seemed striking. Mani discovered that Sukarno, born of a Balinese Hindu mother and a Muslim father, was deeply influenced by his mother's side. The five principles for Sukarno were reminiscent of the Mahabharata, which Mani had heard of in his childhood. Sukarno talked often of the 'Pantja Pandawas'/Pancha Pandavas and how he identified with Dhananjaya, the other name of Arjuna. For centuries, mothers in India and Bali had been narrating the tales of Arjuna and the Pandavas, and Mani sensed that the powerful Sukarno who was named after the eldest, disinherited prince Karna of Kurukshetra in the same epic was, unlike his namesake, finally set to rule over a realm. The 1945 Constitution of Indonesia introduced the 'Pantja Sila', the five jewels. Nationalism, humanism, sovereignty of the people, social justice and belief in God were the five principles that were to guide Indonesia. Mani witnessed, two years before India was to become independent from colonial rule, the formation of a modern nation state in the vast archipelago spreading from the Indian to the Pacific Ocean. In declaring its fundamental principles, Indonesia shone a light on the struggle for freedom that had continued across the ocean in India. Sukarno referred to Mahatma Gandhi and said his people should be cautious about preventing the degeneration of nationalism into chauvinism and quoted the Mahatma, who had said, 'I am a nationalist, but my nationalism is humanity.'[11] The freedom of Indonesia had a different trajectory from India's as the Japanese conquered the archipelago, displacing the Netherlands as the ruling power. On 9 March 1943, Indonesia was granted the Central National Organisation (Peasant Tenega Rajkat, or POETARA) under Japanese control. In June, Japan's

Prime Minister Hideki Tojo visited Indonesia and promised self-rule. Behind the promise was, however, the Japanese aim to mobilize resources and ensure winnability in the war against the Allied forces. The POETARA whipped up pro-Japanese passion, but it was led by President Sukarno and Mohammad Hatta, who also fuelled nationalist sentiment in Indonesia.

By the end of the battle of Surabaya, P.R.S. Mani had acquired an idea of the challenges that a new country like Indonesia or India would face in the coming days. Indonesia, for example, required technological support to ensure the uninterrupted flow of rubber and oil into the world market. At the same time, it was apprehensive of the attitude of the former Allied powers, which had won the war and could very well create trouble for the Sukarno–Hatta–Sjahrir trio, who had worked with the Japanese earlier. To deal with the set of challenges, Indonesia required new friends, especially from India, which was fast emerging from colonial rule. P.R.S. Mani correctly assessed the web of relations and friendships that were required for Indonesia and India to support each other. It is a matter of record that the Indonesian struggle for freedom had been closely followed in India by leaders like Nehru and revolutionaries, as was evidenced by the early twentieth-century attempts at armed insurrections on India's east coast, but the close coordination between the leaders of the two countries in the immediate aftermath of World War II was definitely helped by two factors—the decision of the United Kingdom to send its military forces to Java and the presence of P.R.S. Mani among them.

In a letter to Nehru written on 19 August 1946, Sukarno argued that there was a hand of destiny in the way the two countries were reintroduced to each other in the mid-1940s.[12] Indonesia was a land of magic, rituals and mystery and the idea that some unseen supernatural forces were behind this phase suited the beliefs of the leaders of this ancient land. The hand of destiny in this case manifested in the form of P.R.S. Mani.

It is believed that ancient Indian agriculture traders from the kingdom of Kalinga (Odisha) landed in Probolingga or Purba Kalinga on the northern coast of East Java. The massive islands of Indonesia were famous even back in those days for their rich harvest, and it was this that would once again help India. Odisha marks the memory of its ancient entrepreneurs every year during the festival of 'Bali Jatra', when paper boats are set afloat on the sea in memory of those traders. Such cultural ties had substantial appeal and Mani probably sensed the opportunity for an alliance.

The war had disrupted the supply of rice from Burma to India and the bulk of the domestic produce was diverted to the troops on the frontline. The result was a man-made scarcity of essential food items, which ultimately led to the famine in Bengal. By the time of the end of the war, the food crisis was deepening, and the shadow of famine lingered over the rest of India. On 29 September 1945, the Allied commander had granted de facto recognition to Indonesia. The bonhomie generated by that gesture was dented by the Battle of Surabaya which also showed that the Indonesian people supported self-rule. P.R.S. Mani was aware of the agricultural situation back home and saw that Java and Sumatra had no agricultural crisis comparable to India. During a conversation between Dr Sutan Sjahrir and P.R.S. Mani, the latter suggested the Indonesian 'republic' could consider exporting the much-required rice to India, helping the country in its hour of crisis, in exchange for Indian textiles and medicines. Mani had known since childhood that 'Java' meant millets and the Dutch Indies were to him synonymous with agricultural abundance. Mani recorded Dr Sjahrir's response to his honest suggestion:

MILITARY MEN, RADIO ANNOUNCERS, ICS OFFICERS 17

For once Sjahrir's face showed more than a boyish smile; his face lit up in a broad gleam; he closed his eyes for a minute and kept silent for a further two. Then expressing his sympathy for the Indian people, he generously offered half a million tons of rice for them. He wanted India to arrange ships to take them. He pointed out that Java had just had bumper harvest and enough to spare. There was a shortage of textiles in Indonesia and if India could help with them, they would be welcome.[13]

The proposal for the supply of Java rice as a gift to India was mooted at a time that accentuated the sense of drama of the period. Nehru had been in prison from 9 August 1942 to 15 June 1945 along with the rest of the Congress working committee. His release from prison was followed by intense political consultation with the British rulers, who had sent the Cabinet Mission to India to plan the transfer of power. The proposal of Java rice from Dr Sjahrir provided a distant view of the future of decision-making in free India. With one proposal, Dr Sjahrir blew away the economic blockade that the Dutch had imposed on his country because the rice was a goodwill gesture for India, an ancient partner who appeared promising for modern Indonesia. The Netherlands could not strengthen the blockade, which was weakened greatly by the rousing pro-Indonesian public opinion among the Indian masses in the spring of 1946. On 8 April, *The Free Press Journal* of Bombay published a banner headline carrying the offer of rice supply to India. Mani hit a scoop that made his name famous among the decision-makers. He also became a talking point among the Dutch and British authorities in Indonesia and India who were curious about his activities and ideology. The interim government of India would be formed on 2 September 1946 and Nehru would be the vice president of the Executive Council in charge of External and Commonwealth Affairs. But several months before India got an interim government, the Nehru–Sjahrir duo, with generous support from an unconventional journalist with a military past, had achieved a breakthrough by agreeing to receive Java rice that redrew the rules of regional interactions between South and Southeast Asia. The historic first barter trade of rice and textiles between the two Asian giants announced the end of colonial economy and rule in the region. The agreement over Java rice remains the singular instance of economic diplomacy that suited mutual interest perfectly. At the end, India received the rice at a time when it was most required and Indonesia's troubled new government, which a few months earlier was a Japanese front, received legitimacy from the nationalists of India. It's noteworthy that India was the first major country to recognize Indonesia, which thereafter received recognition from other members of the decolonized group, including the members of the Islamic bloc. On 17 June 1946, a grateful Nehru wrote to Mani, 'Some of our friends in Bombay have offered 200 bales of cloth as a free gift to Indonesia. I have communicated this offer to the Government of India and asked them to make arrangements for despatch to Dr Sjahrir.'[14]

Mani soon left journalism and joined the fast-growing body of official diplomats that the Nehru government was recruiting. Just two months after India's Independence, he became the press attaché with the Indian Diplomatic Mission in Jakarta. According to Mani's personal papers, he began working for the government of newly independent India from 8 October 1947, when he joined as a press attaché to the consul general of India to Indonesia.[15]

The *History of Services*, the first directory of professional diplomats in India, however, records his date of joining the IFS as 6 June 1949.[16] It appears Mani probably joined government service in October 1947, but the confirmation and the official process of joining the IFS took till June 1949. The appointment triggered a fast-paced race as the date of the announcement of the Indian Republic was approaching. On 26 January 1950, with the bonhomie between India and Indonesia at its peak, Ahmed Sukarno, the pragmatic leader from Jakarta, became the first head of state to be the 'guest of honour' of the Indian Republic Day parade. Mani's energetic intervention, first as a media professional and then as a diplomat, had reached its pinnacle with the arrival of Sukarno as the chief guest in the first Republic Day celebrations in Delhi. The India–Indonesia warmth would linger for a full decade till the Bandung summit of 1955. But the example that P.R.S. Mani had set would be difficult even for him to replicate, though he would continue to be in diplomatic service for another twenty-three years, retiring in 1973. The episode involving rice from Indonesia and the establishment of political relations between New Delhi and Jakarta were among the first diplomatic successes that the Nehru government attained. This success was not a product of a structured foreign service cadre but was a blend of Mani's youthful activism, Nehru's willingness to take new people on board and ancient cultural links between the people and leaders of Indonesia and India.

Mani was the second radio professional to have made it to the IFS as the Nehru administration picked up people from diverse professions to curate a service that hitherto did not exist.

On 4 March 1949, Ranbir Singh, an English newsreader and programme announcer, was appointed in the Junior Scale of the IFS, on probation. P.R.S. Mani, Ranbir Singh and Ascharj Ram Sethi[17] were the three former All India Radio staff members who joined India's diplomatic service in the early years of the republic. Apart from the three who joined the IFS-A, there was also Samuell Verghese who joined IFS-B. Given the power of radio and newspapers, it is not a surprise that three top-level diplomats were recruited from All India Radio backgrounds. Out of the four, it was the 1909-born Verghese who was the eldest. All three—Mani, Singh and Sethi—went on to serve in important locations. Mani grew in the service and in the mid-1950s served in post-war Bonn in West Germany as counsellor in the Indian consulate. On 12 December 1995, the Government of Indonesia decorated P.R.S. Mani with the First Class Star of Service, the highest honour in that country, during a ceremony held at the Indonesian Embassy in New Delhi. The other two who were awarded with the First Class Star of Service were Mohammed Yunus, a contemporary IFS recruit of Mani who served as the attaché in the Indian consulate in Jakarta from October 1947 to June 1949. On 4 July 1949, P.R.S. Mani succeeded Mohammed Yunus as the Indian consul in Jakarta.[18] The third person to be awarded the same honour that day was Biju Patnaik, who personally flew an aircraft on several occasions and acted as an emissary of Prime Minister Nehru during the tense confrontation with the Dutch authorities and the British forces. Weeks before Indian Independence, Nehru asked Patnaik to fly the Indonesian leaders to India. Patnaik flew a Dakota and brought Vice President Hatta to New Delhi for a visit that was kept secret for a few days. During his visit, Hatta sought India's recognition of Indonesian independence. According to the protocol, an Indian national or an organization had to propose the idea. Nehru gave that honour to P.R.S. Mani. At the same event, the late Nehru was honoured with the First Class Star of the Republic of Indonesia.[19] The year 1995 was also significant from the regional point of view as India became a 'dialogue partner' of the Association of South East Asian Nations (ASEAN), of which Indonesia is the largest member.

MILITARY MEN, RADIO ANNOUNCERS, ICS OFFICERS 21

Professionals with radio and newspaper backgrounds were a significant part of the officials who joined India's diplomatic wing. There were many others who came in representing other parts of the erstwhile colonial administration.

Being a prolific writer and editor himself, Nehru of course was aware of the power of the written word, and there were a good number of officials who came from a newspaper background. Frederick Marion De Mello Kamath came from *The Times of India*, Bombay, where he had worked during 1932–33, followed by a stint at the Oxford University Press, Bombay. He became editor of *The Indian Listener*, All India Radio in Delhi, during 1938–39. His exposure to the media also involved the agriculture sector, as he served as the editor of *Indian Farming* in ICAR for five years—1939–44. Kamath was among the first wave of diplomats even before the adoption of the Constitution. Two months after Kamath joined the IFS on 1 May 1949, Purshottam Lal Bhandari joined on 1 July 1949. But even before Bhandari and Kamath, Uma Shankar Bajpai, a former journalist and the son of Secretary-General Girja Shankar Bajpai, had found space for himself on probation in the Junior Scale of the IFS on 9 January 1948. All three—Bajpai, Bhandari and Kamath—were part of the IFS group A as were their AIR counterparts, barring Verghese. Indian diplomats had the task of narrating the story of new India to the world, and ex-media professionals with their command over multiple mediums of communication were necessary.

The power of the media at the moment of the birth of India was explained by *The Times of India* in the early 1950s when it said, the most important weapon in the world is the radio.

We seem unable to perceive that today it is a matter of linked survival and that unless we make every effort to unravel the tangled anarchy of ideas, we shall all perish. Somewhere, someone is fighting someone now. We call it war, an incident or a revolution—but always it is one group against another. And all wars begin with ideas, which in their turn beget words to convey those ideas to other men. The most powerful medium that deals with words today is radio.[20]

To deal with the world of ideas, diplomats of new India had to be proficient with the workings of the new information world, of which the radio and the newspaper were among the biggest influencers.

It was thus the necessity of the age that made the Indian Foreign Service recruit people from the world of radio and newspapers, and ever since, information, ideas, policy discussions and at times combative articulation have been part of India's foreign policy establishment's evolution. Times have changed, but the interaction between the media and the Ministry of External Affairs (MEA) continues even in the twenty-first century.

This tradition strikes every Thursday in the twenty-first century when around 250 journalists receive an invite on their hand phones. These are journalists located mostly in the National Capital Region of India who are cordially invited to come to the media briefing room in the MEA. That message triggers a journey that's worth watching as dozens of journalists from different parts of the Indian capital can be seen strolling across the India Gate lawns or driving through the central grid of New Delhi to the office of the joint secretary, External Publicity Division. By afternoon, a good number of them turn up and wait patiently for an hour of briefing, followed by sumptuous snacks and tea. Many of the guests have been performing this routine for decades, and for them the blue sofas and microphones of the briefing hall are as essential as the notebook in their pockets.

At the prescheduled time, the Indian state comes alive as the spokesperson speaks. The ritual appears imperious as the official speaks while his retinue of assistants scurry across the hall carrying the microphone to facilitate the question-and-answer session. The official spokesperson is on paper just the spokesperson of the Ministry of External Affairs but in fact, he becomes the voice of the Indian state. Over the years, the location of the 'weekly briefing' has shifted, but the ritual has remained uninterrupted.

Conventionally, the privilege of speaking for the Indian state goes to the political leadership—the Prime Minister, the President and the council of ministers. The official spokesperson, the foreign secretary and the secretaries of the Government of India, from time to time, have the singular privilege of speaking to the world at large regarding the foreign policy of India.

Given the unique requirements of India's diplomacy, a significant number of the foreign service officers are expected to be in proximity to the political leadership. This rare access to the levers of policy making has, over the decades, endowed the foreign service officers with a unique position in the affairs of the state. They are privy to national security priorities, international diplomacy, economic and political secrets of the kind that other members of the civil service are generally not allowed to access.

P.R.S. Mani stopped being active in the social circles with the advent of the twenty-first century. He was last remembered on 3 September 2011, when the then Foreign Secretary Ranjan Mathai sent a letter of condolence to Mani's sister, Girija Karthikeyan, after Mani passed away quietly at the age of ninety-six.[21] With the passing away of P.R.S. Mani, who belonged to the very first batch of the IFS officers recruited by Prime Minister Nehru, an era truly came to an end. However, the story of the 'first recruits' was not over. A few of Mani's juniors, who, unlike him, were recruited through competitive examination, were still shaping the foreign and security vision of India in the twenty-first century.

A 1951 recruit, Brajesh Chandra Mishra was a baby-faced youngster when Mani and others formed the senior ranks of the IFS. He grew into a diplomat known for his eternal all-knowing smirk. Admired by his colleagues and family as a brilliant mind and a fierce nationalist, Mishra dominated the news headlines as the undisputed 'national security czar' in his position as the national security advisor, or NSA, to Prime Minister Atal Bihari Vajpayee. Jyotindra Nath Dixit (IFS 1958), a tough-talking, pipe-smoking former foreign secretary joined the IFS in the tenth year of the service, at the height of Nehru era. The prime of his and Mishra's careers braced the Cold War period, but both played a crucial role in helping the Indian foreign policy establishment complete the journey from the Cold War-era global politics to the post-Cold War international reality.

The year 1998 unleashed a terrifying summer across north India. Gurudwaras set up large containers of iced water and Roohafza to help exhausted people. An intense hot wind swept across the plains. Home Minister L.K. Advani had planned a trip to Lakshadweep, which he knew would take him away from the capital's heat for a few days. But suddenly the trip was called off. Advani rushed to a meeting with Prime Minister Atal Bihari Vajpayee. One of the journalists who was to accompany Advani sensed some palpable tensions around 5, Race Course Road, with a large number of vehicles racing in and out of the Prime Minister's residence. He sensed something was afoot and found from his sources that the countdown had begun for a nuclear test, which was to take place the next day, on 11 May. Jayanta Ghoshal, the journalist, rushed to his bureau and broke the astounding news, which his editors then accepted with great reluctance. The next morning, *Bartaman*, a Bangla daily from Kolkata, published the news by Ghoshal; the editors then waited to witness the outcome of their gamble. Some time after lunch, the news turned out to be true when Prime Minister Vajpayee took out his glasses and read a statement without smiling. India had tested a thermonuclear weapon in the deserts of Pokhran, he announced on the lawns of his official residence as the members of the media forgot all professionalism for a few seconds and raised patriotic slogans. With the single announcement that was telecast on live TV, Vajpayee's government blew away the carefully laid out nuclear ambiguity that India had practised for decades. As Vajpayee announced the momentous development, behind him stood his private secretary Shakti Sinha and cabinet colleague Pramod Mahajan, but no one had any doubt about the fact that the shadow of Brajesh Mishra also loomed in the background. For the young IFS officer of the 1950s, along with Jaswant Singh, was in charge of nuclear diplomacy. A few minutes before the announcement, Mishra and Singh had in fact consulted the scientists who carried out the nuclear tests in Pokhran and drafted the statement that Vajpayee read to the media.[22]

The IFS recruits of 1948–58 had covered all the major disruptions—from the import of Java rice, which broke the last band of imperial resistance against Asian countries, to the 1998 Pokhran nuclear tests. Eight years earlier, the Soviet Union was swept away in the tides of history, and the ripples of that great event were felt in South Asia. Soon, the 1990s felt like the

1940s of Mishra's youth. City after city—Mumbai after Kanpur, Bhagalpur after Calcutta, and Guwahati after Hubli—were washed in the colours of hate and violence. In India, communal riots are often followed by wars, and the communal violence unleashed in the early years of the 1990s was quickly followed by the Kargil war of 1999. Half a century had passed since Mishra joined professional diplomacy, but the more India changed, the more India had remained the same. Yet, in that backdrop, a new political opening was emerging, which would give Mishra the biggest break of his career, years after he had retired from service.

Mishra was twenty-three in 1951 when he joined the Indian Foreign Service as India headed to its first election. His early career coincided with his father Dwarka Prasad Mishra's soaring political trajectory. Mishra was instrumental in securing support for Indira Gandhi within the ranks of the Congress party and ultimately enabled her to establish her authority in it. Soon thereafter, it is said, they fell apart. Though there is no evidence, it is widely believed that a part of Brajesh Mishra's career fell under the shadow of the turbulent political relationship between his father and Indira Gandhi, who was unwilling to acknowledge the senior Mishra's contribution in building her profile.

Mishra's formal training was in sync with the prevailing sentiments. He served as the third secretary in the Indian High Commission in Nairobi between 1955 and 1956 and went on to be appointed the first secretary in the Indian Embassy of Brussels in 1957.

His first brush with high-stakes diplomacy came rather unexpectedly when Foreign Secretary Triloki Nath Kaul and Parmeshwar Narain Haksar—who served in the secretariat of Prime Minister Indira Gandhi, initially as the secretary and later on as the principal secretary—were planning India's response to the fast-unfolding political storm in East Pakistan, where explosive tensions were building up between the Sheikh Mujibur Rahman-led Awami League and the ruling military-political elite of West Pakistan. The Awami League, with the bulk of its support base in East Pakistan, would go on to win the general election of 7 December 1970 but was not allowed to take charge. Indira Gandhi had built a close working relation with the Soviet Union already, and Haksar and Kaul helped firm up the Indo-Soviet Friendship Treaty of August 1971, which would help India win the war against Pakistan in December that year.

The liberation of Bangladesh was still far away on 1 May 1970 when Mao Zedong stopped by at the May Day celebrations in Beijing and reached out to Mishra, who was then the chargé d'affaires of the Indian Embassy in Beijing. Before being posted to Beijing, then known as Peking, Mishra was posted in the Permanent Mission of India at the United Nations in New York. In 1968, the permanent representative of India, G. Parthasarathy, visited Delhi for consultation and returned to ask if Mishra would be willing to be the chargé d'affaires of the Indian Embassy in Beijing.[23] It was a challenging posting as India and China had a frosty relationship and did not have full diplomatic relations with ambassadors in each other's missions as a result of the bitter war of 1962. Despite the bitterness between New Delhi and Beijing, a hint of a new beginning was being felt in world affairs. The period between 1968 and 1969 was important for the evolution of the Cold War as the Soviet Union, China and the United States were all calibrating long-held positions at this juncture. In 1968, Czechoslovakia was invaded by the combined military of the Soviet Union, Poland, Hungary and Bulgaria—the Warsaw Pact countries. This was followed by the Sino-Soviet conflict over Ussuri river and Damansky island. The clashes, which lasted for seven months, left a permanent imprint on China's attitude towards the communist superpower in Moscow. In response, Mao famously declared, 'We have friends everywhere in the world,'[24]—a clear sign that communist China was trying to wean itself away from the Soviet Union. The appointment to Beijing was, therefore, an opportunity for Mishra to participate in the unfolding international realignment. It was in this backdrop that Mishra, along with his wife, went to attend the May Day celebration in Beijing in 1970. Remembering the exchange between Mishra and Mao, Bollywood filmmaker Sudhir Mishra, nephew of the late diplomat, said that occasion marked a defining part of his uncle's career. Brajesh Mishra was the elder brother of Sudhir's mother.

On 1 May 1970, when Chairman Mao attended the grand celebration, he walked to every head of mission waiting for him on the ramparts of Tiananmen. He began by greeting the Albanian envoy who was the dean of the Diplomatic Corps in the Chinese capital. Mishra was nearly at the end of the row. As Mao came near Mishra, he noticed the *bindi* on the forehead of Mrs Mishra and stopped to say, '*Indu*,' denoting that he had recognized her as being Indian. Before Brajesh Mishra could say anything, Mao said, 'How long are we going to keep quarrelling like this? Let us be friends again. My greetings to the President of India and Prime Minister Gandhi.'[25] These were the friendliest remarks that Indian diplomats had heard in nearly a decade from the Chinese leadership, and it was obviously a watershed moment. The grand celebration continued with a generous serving of Maotai, but Brajesh Mishra's focus was now on sending the message from Mao to Delhi as soon as possible. The Mishras thus quickly wrapped up their engagements, and Brajesh Mishra rushed to the embassy to send a telegram to New Delhi bearing the message of friendship from Mao.[26] Over the subsequent decade, 'Mao's smile' became part of the legends associated with Brajesh Mishra.[27] Over the years, several versions of the remarks from Mao to Mishra were carried forward, primarily because of Chinese records. However, Mishra's own version of 'Mao's smile' included a reference to a growing impatience in Mao's tone. Mao's emphasis on 'how long' had clearly signalled Beijing's growing political will to rebuild ties with India.[28] Mishra's apparent excitement about Mao's remarks, however, was not unreasonable, as it matched the mandate that he was given in New Delhi. After being sounded by G. Parthasarathy—who was the last ambassador of India before the 1962 war disrupted ties—about a possible posting in Beijing, Mishra, on 1 February 1969, left New York, where he had served as the deputy permanent representative of India to the UN. In Delhi he was granted a rare meeting with Prime Minister Indira Gandhi. During the conversation Indira Gandhi said, 'We are in a box, in our relations with China. I want to get out of that box.'[29] Sensing turbulence in international dynamics, on 1 January 1969, Indira Gandhi had made a similar argument about Sino-Indian relations, though not so directly. Mishra reached Beijing in April that year and, following Indira Gandhi's instructions, began holding dialogues with the Chinese Foreign Office once or twice a month, 'pushing for normalisation of relations'. It is clear that Mishra had held several rounds of meetings with various Chinese interlocutors by the time the famous 'Mao's smile' moment took place. 'It was of course much more than a smile,' Mishra said in an interview in 2006.[30]

Nearly eight years had passed since the bitter setback of the 1962 war and India and China were far from re-establishing talking terms, and it would be several years before an Indian ambassador would return to Beijing. Mao's overture to Mishra, therefore, was an intriguing development that was loaded with meaning.

In the backdrop of the frozen hostilities between India and China and the uncomfortable comradeship between the USSR and China, an interesting development had taken place on 1 August 1969. Some time before that, President Richard Nixon was advised by French President Charles de Gaulle saying, 'It would be better for you to recognise China before you are obliged to do so by the growth of China.'[31] Nixon began a world trip, code named 'Moonglow', and flew to the South Pacific to welcome the returning Apollo XI astronauts. He then arrived in Pakistan for a stopover that lasted twenty-two hours. During the stay, Nixon urged his host President Yahya Khan to serve as an intermediary between him and the Chinese leadership. After his stay in the country, Nixon flew to Romania to meet President Nicolae Ceauşescu and urged him to open a channel of dialogue with the Chinese. Pakistani author Fakir Syed Aijazuddin has argued that Nixon informed Ceauşescu because he anticipated that the Soviets would be briefed by the Romanian dictator about the American interest in China (thereby muddying the waters of the Soviet–China friendship). What, however, is not mentioned is that the Soviets could have also shared that intel with Prime Minister Indira Gandhi's ambassador in Moscow, D.P. Dhar. That alone explains why Haksar and Kaul gave Mishra a cold shoulder when he came to Delhi to brief them about his May Day exchange with Mao. Sudhir said that Mishra did not write his own version of events, where he played a role, and that probably will be the reason that evaluation of Brajesh Mishra's career will never be free of speculation. After Brajesh Mishra's meeting with Haksar and Kaul, he was met by Prime Minister Indira Gandhi who appeared cautious but nevertheless asked him to 'draft something'. However, the note did not move further as Brajesh had insisted on getting a written communication from the Prime Minister's Office. In a rare interview that he gave, for the October–December 2006 issue of *Indian Foreign Affairs Journal*, Brajesh Mishra stated that as per his assessment, the Chinese were more concerned with their fast-eroding friendship with the Soviet Union which had prompted them to start secret dialogue with the US. This policy was best evident in Mao's slogan: 'We must have friends everywhere in the world.'[32] Mao's overture to India did not lead to a concrete outcome, as developments on the India–Pakistan front overtook everything else. In July of 1971, Henry Kissinger made the landmark trip to China that led to the 1972 China visit of President Nixon, marking a decisive shift away from the Soviet Union. Mishra's assessment of Soviet–China tensions proved to be correct as the Soviet Union got closer to India, signing the landmark Indo-Soviet Friendship Treaty in August 1971, and the Nixon administration started shifting towards Beijing. With his friendship with Moscow gone sour, and a big beginning with the US around the corner, Mao maintained an enigmatic silence on the topic of Chinese borders with India during the Indo-Pakistan war of 1971. China finally moved away from the Soviet axis by opening doors to the United States.

Mishra belonged to a generation of diplomats who were shaped by widespread economic and political disruptions. But that was in the past. Now circumstances demanded that India carry out a reorientation and convince the sole superpower, the United States, about why Vajpayee wanted an active nuclear deterrence. Sudhir Mishra says, despite the show of might that the nuclear testing entailed, his uncle was neither a hawk nor a dove, nor was he a right-wing Hindu nationalist. 'He was someone who liked to see the bare facts as they really are without any ideological colour and that he always conveyed through his smirk,' Sudhir said during an interview, adding that his uncle was someone who did not look kindly at long-winded arguments. Brajesh Mishra lived at a time when grand ideological constructs moved people and their destinies, but he preferred to walk through the clutter to find clarity. 'People in India had [an] ideological position on the issue of apartheid in Africa, but he liked to know all the facts on the ground even if they were unpleasant for the anti-apartheid side too. For him the whole truth was necessary before he made up his mind,' Sudhir said. He was a pragmatic practitioner of diplomacy. International relations for him were a fluid, uncertain domain where relations tend to wax and wane depending on circumstances. He was from the generation of diplomats from the era of non-alignment when Prime Minister Nehru gave the call of equidistance from Cold War blocs but had come to believe that equidistance was not always possible.

'India must act with caution and wisdom to safeguard its own security and other interests. This is not to say that our relations with the other countries have to be equidistant or of equal closeness or equal detachment. Some relationships are bound to be closer than others,' he once said.[33]

Sudhir also recollected his uncle's intervention in the UN in January of 1980, when he presented the Indian position on the Afghan peace process at the global body as a lasting contribution. Indeed the 'Afghan-led and Afghan-owned' peace process that India has championed since Mishra first placed it on the floor of the United Nations has remained the only viable solution to the Afghan crisis. The shadow of his father's career continued to fall on Mishra as long as the Congress era lasted, and there is still some doubt about whether he would have got the opportunity to be the first national security advisor of India had the Congress era continued, undisturbed by the rise of the Hindu right in India.

Mishra had entered the life of the ruling Bharatiya Janata Party (BJP) at a point when the world was emerging from the shadow of the Cold War. In 1991, he joined the ascendant party, which took a hard line on responding to Pakistan effectively. Soon, it was he who handled national security-related questions from the media for the party. By the time he became the principal secretary to Prime Minister Vajpayee, Mishra had transcended diplomacy and had become a visionary of security for the National Democratic Alliance (NDA) government. The Vajpayee–Advani duo was for the rise of BJP; the Vajpayee–Mishra duo was for ensuring the cautious navigation of the BJP-led government amid global currents.

What distinguished him was the longevity of his diplomatic career, which he reinvented after retirement by joining the BJP. By the late 1990s, most of Brajesh Mishra's contemporaries had retired from government service as well as public life. Upon his passing away, which happened at a time when political temperament was turning away from the soft Hindu nationalism to Hindutva of the Narendra Modi variety, Natwar Singh described him as someone who 'never played to the gallery'.[34] Singh, who was two years younger than him, said that the creation of the post of the national security advisor was an 'unprecedented' development.[35]

Apart from him, Jyotindra Nath Dixit and Natwar Singh often appeared in the newspapers and on TV channels speaking on foreign affairs during the Vajpayee–Manmohan Singh years.

J.N. Dixit was the youngest of the lot featured in the 'census' of foreign service officials conducted in the 1950s.[36] He had joined the Indian Foreign Service in 1958. Natwar Singh, a Jaat from the erstwhile Bharatpur state, gifted with an elephantine memory and shrewd sense of politics, had created a space for himself within the

Congress fold after leaving the foreign service in 1984. Unlike Mishra, who operated from the shadows of the South Block, Singh had debuted in politics after winning the Lok Sabha seat of Bharatpur in 1984. J.N. Dixit, IFS of 1958, sharpened his diplomatic acumen through a series of tough postings that included Bangladesh, Sri Lanka and Afghanistan. Most of the decade from 1996 to 2006, quite correctly, was dominated by Mishra, but not to be left behind by their senior, Singh and Dixit caught up with him in the twenty-first century and for a brief while, Dixit became the successor of Mishra in the Manmohan Singh government after 2004, before his tragic demise, and Natwar Singh joined the same government to serve as an outspoken external affairs minister in 2004.

These three were the most prominent remnants of a generation of diplomats who were first to serve post-1947 India—the first direct recruits. Apart from the three, there were several of that generation like Kayatyani Shankar Bajpai and Muchkund Dubey who lived quiet retired lives, occasionally commenting on the affairs of the state. But the most prominent of them was the triumvirate of Mishra, Dixit and Singh who continued to hit the headlines because of their roles in politics and national security. Despite their prominence, they were the end of a once majestic comet that streaked across the sky of free India in its first decade between 1948 and 1958.

The first recruits covered a vast age bracket, and most of them had retired and faded into oblivion by the late 1980s. The former veteran ICS who dominated the first two and half decades had long left the scene. Y.D. Gundevia (1963–65), Chandra Shekhar Jha (1965–67), Rajeshwar Dayal (1967–68), Triloki Nath Kaul (1968–72) and Kewal Singh (1972–76)—all foreign secretaries at the peak of their careers—were the last of the colonial-era ICS to be absorbed in the Indian Foreign Service. For a brief period, Jagat Singh Mehta and Ramchandra Dattatreya Sathe—two diplomats who had started their careers as military men—became foreign secretaries. But it was ultimately M.K. Rasgotra who, in 1982, was the first of the directly recruited IFS officers to become the foreign secretary. By that time many of the first recruits to Indian diplomacy had either retired or were close to retirement. The few of those from the first decade of the IFS, who remained active after that period, were able to find places for themselves in a fast-changing world purely on the basis of their personal initiative and socio-political relevance. An entire generation of diplomats and support staff slowly faded away from the public sphere as India moved into the era of liberalization post-1991.

A defining moment in the fading away of that generation was the now infamous press conference of 1987. Prime Minister Rajiv Gandhi had taken charge after the assassination of his mother, Prime Minister Indira Gandhi. He won the next election in December 1984 and launched an ambitious foreign policy agenda trying to befriend the United States while dealing with a hostile Pakistan and cold China.

Ayilam Panchapakesa Venkateswaran, an IFS officer of the 1952 batch, was appointed to the post of the Foreign Secretary (FS). This foreign secretary had joined the service when the future Prime Minister was a child in the house of his grandfather Jawaharlal Nehru at the Teen Murti Bhavan. As the FS, Venkateswaran thus did not take Rajiv Gandhi seriously, and his colleagues found him 'light-hearted' towards the PM.[37] There were ample hints that the FS belonged to an 'older' generation while the PM represented a bold, new, emerging future of India. The young diplomats of the first decade of free India were fast approaching the end of their tenures during the twilight of the Cold War, and the new younger generation of politicians found them unfit. But not everyone from the first-generation diplomats would fit the impression they had, and Mishra, Singh and Dixit proved the cynics wrong by staying on in the corridors of power for many more years.

Already the more outgoing among them, Natwar Singh, for example, had made unconventional career choices and joined the political class.

Days before her tragic assassination, Indira Gandhi had a brief meeting with Natwar Singh on the stairs of South Block. To convey his political mood, Singh dressed in white kurta pajama, the dress code of the Congress workers. Elections were around the corner, and Singh wanted the PM to know about his aspirations. Singh then verbally shared his future plans with Indira Gandhi and said, he had attained the highest point in his career with the Padma Bhushan that came his way after he successfully organized the 1983 Non-Aligned Movement (NAM) summit in Delhi. Natwar Singh, who was from the 1953 batch of the IFS, had already become a minister for fertilizers when A.P. Venkateswaran, his senior, became the foreign secretary in 1986. Sensing better possibilities in politics, Singh had resigned, five years before his formal retirement, to start a political career.

With J.N. Dixit becoming the foreign secretary under Prime Minister Narasimha Rao in December 1991, the entire IFS batch from Nehru's first decade entered their retired lives. Legend had it that they belonged to another era and that having served during the Cold War years, they probably would not succeed in handling post-Cold War years successfully. But as Mishra showed, the youngest of the first recruits could bring their experience to good use even many years after the end of the Cold War, as they too had witnessed the emergence of a new world order at the end of World War II.

The first recruits are a distant memory now. Diplomacy is now often on social media and diplomatic incidents are often on public platforms. Yet there are traditions and precedents, from protocol to the relation with major powers and India's links with the neighbourhood, that indicate a past where it all began. Unlike in the past, diplomacy in the twenty-first century reaches prime time TV, but the noise of media cannot hide the rich beginning made by the 'first recruits', the Indian diplomats who were hired in the first decade of independent India's existence.

Dixit's pinnacle of success came with the arrival of the Manmohan Singh government in 2004, when he succeeded Mishra to the post of national security advisor. His untimely death put an end to an illustrious career. J.N. Dixit, Brajesh Mishra, Natwar Singh and Chinmaya Gharekhan, a batchmate of Dixit who served as a special envoy of Manmohan Singh to the West Asian region, will be remembered in history as the first generation of Indian diplomats who continued to play a public role well into the twenty-first century. But they were also the youngest of that generation because they belonged to the section of diplomats who were the direct recruits—officers fresh out of graduate courses.

The bulk of the 'first recruits' were decades older than direct recruits like Mishra and Dixit. In both these NSAs, twenty-first century India, therefore, saw just the faint end of a generation that dealt with Richard Nixon, Chou En-lai, John F. Kennedy and Ho Chi Minh among many others.

During the first two decades of the twenty-first century, career diplomats of India more or less displaced political appointees, who once used to form a regular feature of India's diplomatic human resource. Today, the formal inductees occupy all the important diplomatic positions across the world in Indian missions and any and every diplomacy related posting in the Prime Minister's Office, the Ministry of Defence and other offices where India's foreign interests are involved. Over the years, these officials have begun to articulate their opinions on domestic issues such as education, agriculture, culture, religion and a vast number of topics that usually are dealt with at the level of the Indian provinces or Indian society. Indian diplomats can be seen talking about Indian 'values', culture, civilization, Yoga as well as defence purchases, space exploration and India's global campaign against cross-border terrorism—and that makes them as much political as any service could ever aspire to be.

Earlier, in 2022, the Ministry of External Affairs held a press conference where professional diplomats spoke at length about India's growing diplomacy with Israel, the United States and the United Arab Emirates where agriculture—a state subject—featured prominently. When asked about the participation of farmers in this new grouping titled I2U2—Israel, India, the UAE and the USA—an official said that the farmers were not taken on board yet.[38] Agriculture is, however, not the only area where the career diplomats of modern India are involved. Like many of their counterparts in major economies in the contemporary world, they routinely steer policies about energy, human rights, education, digital and physical infrastructure far more frequently than they did previously. Indian diplomats are no longer just articulating the Indian position to the world, they also tell India about what they should think on various issues of global importance. Indian diplomats have indeed come to represent a think tank that articulates policy for the citizens. In doing this, they are very much a part of a tradition that Indian Foreign Service officials have followed from the early days of India's post-colonial existence, when food, energy, industrialization and even education were part of India's diplomacy.

Apart from economic and social indicators, the professional diplomats of India are increasingly the most visible and one of the vital parts of peace building and peace maintenance in India's neighbourhood. This adds a special quality to India's diplomats, considering the present Indo-Pak hostility.

Around 11.45 a.m. on 29 November 2016, Official Spokesperson Vikas Swarup asked media persons to rush to the media briefing hall in Jawaharlal Nehru Bhavan in the heart of the Indian capital. After a brief introduction, he passed the microphone to the director general of military operations, Lt General Ranbir Singh, who announced that Indian commandoes had sometime earlier carried out an audacious 'surgical strike' within Pakistani territory. The announcement, and the dramatic manner in which it was delivered, had the potential of triggering a fresh conflict with Pakistan. Therefore, the announcement was framed with a bit of ambiguity.

While announcing the surgical strike, Singh did not clarify if the strike was carried out 'across' or 'along' the Line of Control with Pakistan. No official explained why the announcement kept the word 'along' in the text, though it was obvious that this subtle word play gave India a public relations' advantage while reducing chances of escalation. Sources later shared that the language was considerably toned down by the MEA officials to ensure that the announcement did not sound like a call for war against Pakistan, which had been caught in a spiral of tension since the first week of January because of terror strikes that the Government of India had blamed on violent elements inside Pakistan. India's professional diplomats thus were a continuous presence while framing policies for maintaining peace in South Asia, or for better production of millet in India or in augmenting India's pharmaceutical and vaccine-related strength to defeat the COVID-19 pandemic.

Starting with Jawaharlal Nehru, who had Girja Shankar Bajpai as his secretary-general in the Ministry of External Affairs, all Indian Prime Ministers have had professional diplomats in their teams but the nature of the professional diplomats serving in the PMO of India have been changing gradually since 1947. Parmeshwar Narain Haksar or P.N. Haksar practised law at the Allahabad High Court and was a friend of Congress leader Feroze Gandhi. He joined the Ministry of External Affairs as an officer on special duty in October 1947. Two decades later, it was he who would become the centre of authority in the PMO of Indira Gandhi.

In Rajiv Gandhi's PMO, Ronen Sen was the young Turk who led Rajiv's diplomacy in total secrecy. During the early 1990s, because of the communal disturbances in India and the security fallout from the Babri Masjid demolition, Indian diplomats were asked to reach out to countries across the world to assuage concerns in various capitals about the stability of Indian society and market. The role of professional diplomats got a boost with the arrival of Inder Kumar Gujral in 1997 who was also supported by scholar-diplomats like Bhavani Sengupta. But soon, the professional diplomats of the first post-Independence decade re-emerged, as Brajesh Mishra debuted with Atal Bihari Vajpayee, and the 1998 nuclear blasts started a new era for India.

Throughout the three phases of the Nehru–Indira tenure, Rajiv Gandhi and the subsequent phase of coalition government and the 1990s till the early 2000s, the first recruits—as recorded in the *History of Services*—remained in circulation. Most of their professional careers had ended by the late 1980s or the early 1990s, but several of them like Natwar Singh, Brajesh Mishra, Romesh Bhandari, P.N. Haksar and A.P. Venkateswaran remained in circulation, often playing a pivotal role in government or in private sectors, and continued to mentor subsequent generations of journalists, diplomats, politicians and business houses. The uniqueness of these pioneering Indian diplomats from the first decade of post-colonial India lies in the fact that they did not have age restrictions. As a result, many of them like Leilamani Naidu, Girja Shankar Bajpai, Subimal Dutt and the 1898-born Kumar Pedma Sivasankara Menon (hereafter K.P.S. Menon) were on the verge of retirement by the time they were hired by the Ministry of External Affairs. At the same time, the likes of Chonira Belliappa Muthamma and Eric Gonsalves were three decades younger to the eldest members of the same service.

As a result of this age difference, the Indian diplomats of 1948 to 1958 had the unique distinction of having experienced diplomacy of the inter-war period, beginning with the Paris Peace Conference of 1919 and the Gandhian freedom struggle to the San Francisco Conference that brought in the new world order after World War II. The youngest of these pioneers came in 1958 and two foreign secretaries—Muchkund Dubey of the 1957 batch and Dixit of the 1958 IFS batch—were at the helm of affairs when the Soviet Union was dissolved.

Conceived as a special kind of a vehicle to deal with the requirements of post-colonial India, the IFS was an evolving mechanism in the initial years as it was formed as part of a consultative process, which drew on the participation of Prime Minister Nehru and several others who have been described as 'masterminds'.[39] Those formative years, however, cast a long shadow and created precedents that continue to be replicated even in the twenty-first century. The IFS has also been fiercely protective of the political leadership and have often been equated with the ideological leanings of the day, and statements made by P.N.

Haksar and his compatriots often revealed that ideological leanings were not forbidden within the service from the very beginning.

These imperfections, however, are not new to the service, which is primarily responsible for producing diplomats for the Indian republic, as some of these problems date back to the early days of the service, to the late 1940s and even before that, to colonial times. That does not mean that the contemporary IFS, which has the responsibility of promoting India's interests abroad, is similar in scale and agenda to its days of origin.

The creation of the Indian Foreign Service was the single most important administrative innovation that the Indian state had to carry out soon after Independence, for the pursuit of its foreign policy objectives. New Delhi had never before possessed a full-fledged team of diplomats with a unique Indian perspective who wanted to champion the independence of other Asian and African countries, maintain working relations with the former colonial centre—the United Kingdom—and foster a neutral approach to the contentious global politics. All these were to be pursued while conducting diplomacy to help India's economic and industrial agenda. The first annual combined competitive examination was organized by the Union Public Service Commission (UPSC) in 1947 and the first batch of direct recruits came on board in 1948.

For the IFS of the first decade post-1947, training was imparted in six phases.[40] A four-month training module was taught at Metcalfe House in Delhi, which was followed by general training at the University of Oxford and the University of Cambridge, where Indian law, history, economics and constitutional law were taught. Next came the Commonwealth Training, a two-month training exercise in London. The fourth phase of the training took place at the district level for a period of six months, during which the trainees came in direct contact with rural India and the requirements for development activities in the country. Training in the Ministry of External Affairs was next, and it lasted for five months duration and was meant to provide orientation to the young recruits with administrative insights. The sixth and the final segment of training included training for languages. This six-part 'Induction Training', which started during 1948–49, however, was meant only for the recruits who came through competitive examinations conducted by the UPSC. The *History of Services*, which recorded the career graph of the Indian diplomats of the first decade post-Independence, shows that the veterans who were recruited from the ICS and the military services and other backgrounds often hit the ground running without any further training. This probably was necessary as a specialized foreign service bureaucracy was urgently required, and those veteran former ICS officers who had some exposure to foreign or regional affairs, like Subimal Dutt, could not be subjected to some mid-career training modules as they were already established as highly reputed professionals. The six-part induction training that began in 1948 was discontinued in 1958 as the component of training in Oxford and Cambridge was found to be 'very expensive'.[41] It is this West-centric training that offered a unique flavour to the IFS recruits of the first decade after Independence. From 1959, a new training module, which focused on national affairs and the Indian foreign policy, was started.

By the early 1950s, innovations had begun at the Ministry of External Affairs. By this time, the ministry was primarily responsible for representing India on global platforms like the United Nations and helped other ministries and agencies when they had to engage the world outside. Officials were designated for different parts of the world.

The secretary-general was still the topmost bureaucrat in the diplomatic field and worked as the principal official adviser to External Affairs Minister Nehru and was responsible for the 'supervision and coordination of the ministry as a whole'.[42] The role of the secretary-general was aimed at providing cohesion to the diplomatic initiatives of India. The actual territorial responsibilities began at the level of the foreign secretary, who looked after the American, Western, Eastern and West Asian–North African (WANA) regions. That apart, the foreign secretary also dealt with the Protocol Division, which had acquired greater visibility with high-profile incoming visits during the mid-1950s. In terms of hierarchy, the secretary-general and the foreign secretary were followed by the Commonwealth secretary, who handled all the Commonwealth countries, excluding Canada, which came under the American Division. A special secretary looked after the administration of the ministry and the Indian missions and posts. The special secretary worked in close coordination with the foreign and the commonwealth secretaries. The ministry was divided into ten divisions, each of which was looked after by directors who were chosen from the ranks of joint and deputy secretaries. There was also a foreign service inspector, who was expected to visit Indian missions and advise the government on the remuneration of officials posted abroad. The designations and the areas under their command were vast and indicate the irregular nature of the early days of the IFS, and perhaps that is why attempts were on to create a semblance of order in the working of the ministry. In April 1958, an Economy Board was created to look after the continuation of temporary posts and the rental of accommodation of Indian officials abroad. Then there was the much-feared Vigilance Division that took up complaints and suggested disciplinary action against erring officials. From the tentative beginning in 1946–47, India perhaps saw the fastest growth of its diplomatic missions in the first decade and as a result, by 1958, it had 106 missions and posts abroad. Out of that total, 40 were embassies, 12 high commissions, 12 legations, 10 commissions and 14 consulates.[43] The global political map was in flux because of rapid decolonization and other political developments, and India took steps to stay in sync with the changes. For example, both Morocco and Tunisia attained independence in 1956, some months after the Bandung conference and the Nehru government upgraded the mission in Morocco from the level of a chargé d'affaires to the level of an ambassador. The ambassador to Morocco was concurrently accredited to Tunisia. That same year, India opened its embassy in Chile, which also was meant to connect with Colombia. Diplomatic relations were established with Spain, and a resident chargé d'affaires was sent to Madrid.

In 1958, riding the wave of Arab nationalism, Nasserite Egypt merged with Syria and created the United Arab Republic (UAR). It's not easy to determine which one out of the two was a greater representative of Arab nationalism, but India tilted towards Cairo and not the other great Arab city, Damascus. Resultantly, India abolished its embassy in Damascus and replaced it with a Consulate General. The UAR, an experiment in Arab nationalism, survived till 1961, when Syria left the union with Egypt. On 5 November 1961, India recognized the Syrian Arab Republic, which meant the Indian Consulate General had to be upgraded to the level of Embassy in Damascus. With establishing new missions and posts came the requirement for building physical infrastructure in capitals across the world.

Prime Minister Nehru was firmly in control of Indian foreign policy as he also held the position of the external affairs minister. He was supported by a deputy foreign minister.[44]

India of the first decade after Independence was far from being the country that it became in the twenty-first century. Its territory was still riddled with colonial enclaves, and the country had neither food self-sufficiency nor industrial capability. The span of the first recruits can be assessed by the fact that they witnessed the birth of India as well as the liberation of the last colonial enclaves and outposts like Goa, and they also stood witness when the Soviet Union was dissolved, and India broke the nuclear status quo of the world in the twenty-first century. The people who were hired went on to be present for all the historic moments of the first seventy-five years of India's history, such as the Bandung conference, the 1971 war, India's diplomacy with China, Indo-Pakistan negotiations and the nuclear diplomacy. That apart, the IFS also boasted of dramatic figures such as Harivansh Rai Bachchan, Abid Hasan Safrani and Mirza Rashid Ali Baig, who began life as a military man and became the private secretary of Mohammed Ali Jinnah before parting ways over the issue of Pakistan only to become the towering protocol chief whose legacy resonates in the South Block even now.

From the beginning, the IFS had to deal with the pressure of the ICS, which was now part of the IAS, and the IFS was deeply aware that the IAS was planning to devour it and the only person who did not allow that was Nehru himself.[45] The ICS-infused IAS felt the IFS was not necessary and wanted to disband it. A section of the bureaucracy felt strongly that the IFS was the creation of a Prime Minister who wanted to have his special tools while operating. As soon as Nehru passed away, the IAS, led by the secretary in the PMO, proposed that the IFS should be disbanded and its tasks in the Indian missions be taken over by the IAS and other central services. To deal with this challenge, the IFS came up with a committee under former civil servant Narayanan Raghavan Pillai.

Fortunately for the IFS, that phase did not last long. Soon, Indira Gandhi became Prime Minister and once again turned to the IFS, or rather the veteran ICS officers within the IFS, to deal with the diplomatic requirements of India. The IFS survived and prospered as Indira gave special assignments to P.N. Haksar, one of the first IFS officers who joined the service along with pioneers like M.R.A. Baig and Subimal Dutt. Why the remnants of the ICS, now part of the IAS, hated the IFS to the extent that they wanted its demise cannot be explained simply in terms of inter-service rivalry. The ICS was the elite of the colonial times and pretty much lorded over the subcontinent as representatives of a state that was opposed by the people. They did manage to continue in the new dispensation after 1947 but found their previous status eaten away by the manner in which the Nehru administration functioned by bringing in political nominees and people with non-administrative backgrounds into the affairs of the state. The IFS was one of the elements at the core of the new establishment, along with others like the R&AW (formed two decades later), and in the new avatar as IAS, members of the ICS fought hard to dislodge the new entrants from the charmed circle. What, perhaps, was very much unlike the ICS was the fact that the IFS were representative of the diversity of the Indian society, and nowhere was this element more in display than the IFS B.

Among the myriad lot of IFS B, there were a vast number of stenographers who brought with them language skills that were mostly acquired, because many of the new recruits were migrants who came from distant parts of the British Empire in South, Southeast and even West Asia which had fractured in the late 1940s to become multiple countries. There was even a foreigner who came from the other side of the planet and worked in the MEA till retirement and is remembered even now for being a foremost scholar of India's diaspora—I.J. Bahadur Singh.[46]

The current generation of diplomats, including External Affairs Minister Dr. S. Jaishankar and his team, are more visible as they, unlike the first recruits, work against the backdrop of social media, which can be used as a tool of public diplomacy. They are far removed in terms of perks and privileges from the ones who formed the first generation of diplomats—those who came in the first decade after India attained independence. Indian diplomats are prolific writers as their job demands them to be political reporters. Many have used that skill to write professionally while in service. The list of such writers is unnecessary to get into here, but the idea fuelling these pages is to revisit the first decade after Independence, when the first generation of Indian diplomats were inducted. Some of them, like Natwar Singh, were prolific writers, but most were not. A few like Chandra Shekhar Jha and Rajeshwar Dayal wrote after retirement. But overall, most of the first recruits like Dileep Kamtekar or Karunakara Menon Kannampilly did not leave behind written accounts of their lives and event-rich careers. For the sake of clarity and to recreate the early years of the diplomatic service, a few of those—like Natwar Singh—who had written about their own experiences as independent India's first-generation diplomats have been accommodated in this book.

But the main focus of this submission is on the diplomats who did not write about themselves because they viewed their responsibilities more as a task for the Government of India or as a subjective experience that could not be dealt with autobiographically. Needless to say, their inability or disinclination did not take anything away from the difficulties that those early Indian diplomats had to face at work or the epoch-making world events they witnessed. Most of the literature that has come out on the IFS has devoted a great deal of attention to Girja Shankar Bajpai, Krishna Menon, Subimal Dutt and Jawaharlal Nehru himself. Given the towering presence of these individuals, it is not possible to avoid them while writing about the generation of diplomats who joined in the first decade post-Independence.

This monograph thus intends to provide a perspective that is removed from the usual writing of diplomatic history which often presents the foreign policy establishment of India as a top-down structure. Such an approach neglects the representative nature of the Indian diplomatic human resource of the first decade after Independence. Modern India came to have a formal cadre of diplomats only after Independence. Diplomacy and diplomats have obviously existed in South Asia for millennia, but the specific kind of diplomats who serve the current Indian state came into being after India attained political independence.

This book, therefore, presents the complex and socially representative quilt that the IFS became at its inception. If the Indian diplomats in the first Nehru years appeared to represent the entire social structure of India and therefore looked like an attractive and vibrant collection, that was also because of the suggestions that Prime Minister Nehru received from several officials, including K.P.S. Menon (Senior) in the formative period of the service. K.P.S. Menon was serving as the agent general of India for China and was accredited to the Kuomintang government of Chiang Kai-shek at Nanking and Chungking. Prime Minister Nehru summoned him to Delhi, and he was nominated to the post of the foreign secretary. Early writers on India's foreign service have described Menon and Girja Shankar Bajpai, alongside Nehru and Sardar Patel, as being instrumental in the setting up of the Indian Foreign Service cadre.[47] There were divergences of opinion about the composition of the new diplomatic service, and two groups emerged. One group was under the newly appointed Indian high commissioner to the UK, Krishna Menon, and another under K.P.S. Menon and Bajpai. At one point Krishna Menon insisted that the IFS should draw more cadre from Indians who came with experience of having lived in the west. K.P.S. Menon and Girja Shankar Bajpai resisted that suggestion and insisted that the majority of candidates in the Indian Foreign Service should be from India and that selection should be done primarily by the External Affairs Ministry.[48] It is, therefore, to the credit of K.P.S. Menon (Senior) and Bajpai that the early years of the Nehruvian South Block strikes one as highly representative, consisting of poets, administrators, radio operators, soldiers, ex-rebels, princes and stenographers. Given the rush of the many historic developments that were unfolding in Delhi during 1947–50, the creation of the IFS probably got several unintentional inputs, but the vision of social, religious and economic diversity that it came to acquire is due to Menon and Nehru, who prevailed over the elitists and the apparatchiks of the Congress that wanted to secure this domain as some sort of a reward for their traditional social roots and past actions. A few—like Mohammed Yunus—did manage to serve in the IFS primarily because of evident political links to the top leadership. Despite being hated by some of his colleagues, Yunus executed crucial assignments, especially during the Emergency in 1975–76, when he served as the PM's envoy for the Arab and the Islamic countries.

The agenda that the diplomats were expected to implement was not very complex. Nehru himself enunciated that often in his speeches. He did so most emphatically in 1956. That year, two crises erupted, giving the world the opportunity to understand why a third approach away from the ones followed by the western and the Soviet blocs was necessary. In Hungary, Soviet tanks were sent in to suppress the aspirations of the Hungarian people, and in

Egypt, nationalization of the Suez Canal triggered an aggressive military campaign by the triumvirate of Israel–France and the UK. Both the blocs appeared deeply flawed. 'The Soviet Union forgets about Hungary; puts a cover on it and talks about Egypt and Anglo-French aggression only. The other countries forget about Egypt and talk about Hungary only,' said Nehru in a speech in the Parliament that year.[49]

At the height of the Suez war, Egypt came under attack from the UK–France–Israel alliance. Speaking in the Parliament, Nehru said that India is 'favourably' positioned to deliberate on these conflicts not because of being 'more clever or virtuous' but because Indians 'are not swept away' by the pro- and anti-communist formulations. Nehru emphasized on the need to see the problems in a 'clear perspective'. Just last year, Egyptian leader Gamal Abdel Nasser had attended the landmark conference at the picturesque Indonesian town of Bandung. It was necessary to keep Nasser in good humour to ensure Pakistan's campaign for Kashmir would not receive a warm welcome in powerful Arab capitals like Cairo and Damascus. Realism was necessary in diplomacy and economic planning as India was not in a position to antagonize the industrially advanced western European nations that were part of the American bloc. India's economic requirements often depended on support from industrially developed countries of both the blocs, which exerted pressure on India to align with them. There were strong emotions in both Hungary and Egypt, but India, the Nehru government decided, was going to maintain a policy of equidistance.

> We may have our convictions, but we are at least devoid of the tremendous passions of some of the protagonists of the cold war, this side or that side ... We have adopted a policy of non-alignment: it is there; that is what we call it; we do not

call it neutrality; neutrality is a completely wrong word in this connection. That does not mean that we have not got views of our own on various problems.[50]

The officials who formed the growing team of Indian diplomats in the first decade after Independence were expected to have a perspective of their own. Nehru's recruits were trained to have an innovative approach to problems that afflicted the world. They were meant to advance the Indian position in a world where taking an independent position was increasingly difficult. Indian diplomats were expected to have an opinion that would serve the Indian position. The agenda was clear: In the age of global warfare and nuclear weapons, India would safeguard its interest but would also try its best to defend what is believed to be in the collective interest.

And what was the newly formed Indian Foreign Service expected to achieve? Was it expected to serve shrewd goals of diplomacy to make India a great power? Or was it aimed at creating a global power out of the newly born post-colonial democracy? According to the remarks of Nehru himself, the goal was to serve the people of India in their hour of distress. On visiting Malaya in 1946, Nehru received a tremendous welcome from Indians who had just witnessed the brutalities of World War II in Southeast Asia. They greeted him with thunderous cries of 'Jai Hind'. There were thousands of Indians facing uncertain future, yet they were not short of enthusiasm despite knowing that the Government of India was not expected to deliver immediate help. Nehru was deeply moved, noted P.R.S. Mani in his dispatches. 'What can I do to meet the challenge that they offer me? I doubt my capacity—not only mine but also everybody's—in the face of such vast affection,'[51] Nehru said, thinking of the solutions that India could offer to the countries of Southeast Asia which still had thousands of Indian military men and the detenus of the Indian National Army of Subhas Chandra Bose who had fought during the war and now wanted to return home.[52] The primary goal of the Indian diplomats under Nehru was to rise to the occasion to help India's own citizens, and the first generation of the IFS repeatedly had to play that role to help Indians return home from Malayan prisons, from xenophobic rule in Burma, from the clutches of Idi Amin of Uganda, or from the Gulf in 1990–91—all episodes when the 'first recruits' delivered. The weakest Indian was to be first priority for the Indian diplomats.

2

A FRIENDSHIP AND A CATALOGUE

'YOU ARE NOT TELLING HIM anything. Your lips are sealed,' said Mrs Heminder Kumari Singh in an accusatory tone.

Dressed in a white kurta–pajama, K. Natwar Singh, her husband, responded with an all-knowing smile. Mrs Singh took off her sunglasses and wiped the sweat from her forehead as she breathed in the cool air that was circulating inside the house that the two had built with the thought of spending a post-retirement life in it. She appreciated the journalist who had come braving the summer heat to see Natwar Singh and wanted him not to be disappointed with the stories he heard.

'He has visited you so many times, but I never see you tell him any of your exciting stories. Tell him what you saw in your career,' Mrs Singh prodded him further. Her husband was not moved by her insistence. As a sort of protest, Mrs Singh sat down and turned her sympathetic tone towards the visitor who had been coaxing Natwar to share stories and said, 'You know he has not written his best stories. He simply will not write them because he has taken a vow not to spill the secrets. *You* should get *those* stories out from him.'¹

An hour ago, I had travelled to Natwar Singh's farmhouse on the outskirts of Delhi. It was my second visit in a week to the place where Singh had come to stay, taking a break from his Jor Bagh residence near the heart of activities of the Indian state where he spent most of his time over the past half century. It was in the summer of 2011 that he introduced me to his personal library, which had been nurtured with care over the decades when he travelled the world, worked with Indian prime ministers and wrote books.

My first meeting with Natwar Singh was anxiety-filled. It was during the end of 2005, and I had been tracking one of the first big crises that had erupted in the UPA government. A damaging revelation had come a few months earlier, pointing at Natwar Singh for being one of the beneficiaries in the oil-for-food scandal. Much had changed in India's diplomacy in the previous decade when the Congress was out of power. Beginning with the Jaswant Singh–Strobe Talbott negotiation of July 1998, which was accompanied by NSA Brajesh Mishra's dialogue with US Secretary of State Madeleine Albright, India and the US had taken steps that set India up in an orbit where its relationship with the US was expected to be closer than its ties with other powers. India had not given up non-alignment, but it was certainly closer to the sole superpower in the international system. The days of non-alignment, which catapulted the careers of the first diplomats of India, were now in the past. Singh was planning to play according to the new rule book of Indian diplomacy. But the scandal gave an opportunity to his opponents within the government. Within days, it became clear that the government would not step in to defend him. The TV media, with frenzied coverage, did the rest of the job.

Singh was travelling at the time when the crisis was exploding. The media gathered around his house, which was located next to the official residence of Prime Minister Dr Manmohan Singh at the 7, Race Course Road. A narrow passage, in fact, provided a short-cut to the house of the PM. His bungalow on Teen Murti Lane boasted of equally formidable neighbours. A little down the path was the house of Jaswant Singh, the former external affairs minister, and at another corner was the residence of former Jammu and Kashmir chief minister, Farooq Abdullah. I tried to get a detailed interview with Natwar Singh but could barely manage a brief one. For that particular week, the assignment was done, and I moved on to the next weekly story.

But within a short while I returned to his house at Teen Murti Lane, in an attempt to find answers to several unanswered questions. But Singh had resigned by then and did not want to indulge in mudslinging. He would not talk politics. His lips were truly sealed. The only thing that he loved speaking of was books. How are you spending your time after the recent upheaval? 'Oh, I am reading Barbara Tuchman,' he said in response. Unsatisfied with introducing me to the historian he proceeded to spell T-U-C-H-M-A-N. 'You must read her book.' I dropped in a few times between the time Singh resigned from the post of the external affairs minister in the Manmohan Singh government and the following months when I got to know him well.

Then suddenly, everything was gone from 19, Teen Murti Lane. Within days of him stepping down from office, the government machinery turned against the man they had held in high esteem as a minister just days earlier. The treatment was ruthless; the Congress leaders deserted Natwar Singh. As a reporter for *The Week* magazine, I, along with many other journalists, waited at the doorstep of Natwar Singh's residence and witnessed the power play that can only be experienced in the Indian capital. The stream of influential visitors slowly dried up; his security detail was reduced and after some time the staff quarters were dismantled and taken away by the public works department. The humiliation was wholly unnecessary and exposed the ruthless side of Indian politics. The flowerpots were gone and so was the fleet of Tata Sumo vehicles. The only person who stayed on was Johnson, Natwar Singh's faithful secretary. There was an overwhelming amount of gossip against Singh in the corridors of power, which stretched from the Ministry of External Affairs to 24, Akbar Road, headquarters of the Congress party, and the newspaper offices.

The attitude to Singh, by a strange twist of fate, had become reminiscent of the difficulties that several of his foreign service colleagues had to endure at the hands of the political leadership, starting with A.P. Venkateswaran ahead of his infamous public sacking. Foreign Secretary Shailendra Kumar Singh also faced a turbulent period when the Rajiv Gandhi government lost majority and was replaced by the government of Prime Minister Vishwanath Pratap Singh. The first major problem that a serving foreign secretary faced because of political transition can be traced to the tenure of Jagat Singh Mehta who was accused by Janata Party leader Madhu Limaye of being pro-US.[2]

According to journalist Inder Malhotra, the treatment meted out to Shailendra Kumar Singh was part of a 'devious operation'; he blamed the then PM and external affairs minister, Inder Kumar Gujral, for the way the foreign secretary had to leave before his two-year term ended.[3] The next foreign secretary, Muchkund Dubey, one of Nehru's direct recruits who came to office in April 1990, had to endure a similarly politically volatile phase as the V.P. Singh government was replaced by the Chandrashekhar government before the Congress returned to power under P.V. Narasimha

Rao. During the 1990s, Singh remained in news because of his well-publicized disagreements with Prime Minister Rao, which prompted him to join hands with other dissidents and form the All India Indira Congress (Tiwari) in 1996. It was, therefore, not very surprising when with the oil-for-food scandal, Singh had to confront the biggest challenge of his political career. Singh hit back in his characteristic irreverent style. The R.S. Pathak committee, which was constituted to investigate the oil-for-food scam, blamed him. The findings of the committee were strangely leaked to a TV channel before they were presented to the government.

After his departure from the government residence, our meetings dwindled, though our phone conversations remained on track. Finally, we reconnected in 2011 when Natwar Singh showed me his library. That was also the time when Singh was writing his autobiography and, therefore, chose to be near his library in the farmhouse. Once ready, *One Life is Not Enough* was released in a hall exploding with Singh's friends, including his former boss, former PM Dr Manmohan Singh. The past had been left behind and Singh never betrayed any bitterness. Natwar Singh's anecdotes were mostly about his interactions with Vladimir Putin, Condoleeza Rice, Jawaharlal Nehru, Indira Gandhi, Mikhail Gorbachev and King Zahir Shah of Afghanistan, who was part of Rajiv Gandhi government's initiative to have a broad-based government in Kabul after the withdrawal of the Soviet Union. His biography and the celebrations came long years after the golden age of the 'first recruits' when non-alignment was the leading principle in Indian foreign policy.

Natwar Singh has been a survivor throughout his life and career. He belonged to an era when the old order of India surrendered and melted into the new emerging bureaucracy. He belonged to the generation when the fortune of India's royal families was

A FRIENDSHIP AND A CATALOGUE

crumbling, prompting them to look for opportunities in the government and in politics. With the political storm unfolding around, Singh had witnessed the full spectrum of statecraft from the Nehru era to twenty-first century India post-Mandal and post-Babri. The training of a lifetime had served him well, but the rules of the game of throne had become more ruthless over time.

The new India that unfolded around him in the twenty-first century was vastly different from the India that he saw in the South Block till the early 1980s. Singh withdrew into his books and at-home meetings with visitors.

In February 2020, Natwar Singh called, 'I am turning ninety this year and we have a party at Taj Mansingh. You must come.' Singh's ninetieth birthday marked his reconciliation with his past. Former PM Manmohan Singh came and so did many others, cutting across political lines. A few days after this, he called again saying that one of the oldest surviving former Indian diplomats had turned 100. 'He is V.M.M. Nair. With him at hundred, there are just four of us, Eric Gonsalves, Nair, M.K. Rasgotra and yours truly, who are above ninety. Don't you think we deserve to be in the newspaper?'[4] Singh, Rasgotra and Gonsalves joined the IFS through competitive examinations, while Nair was taken on board the small foreign affairs team of British India in 1944 as he was an ICS officer.

As Natwar Singh began to recollect the life of V.M.M. Nair, he meticulously mentioned the details from Nair's life. 'Let me check my directory,' he said, recollecting details. The more he read the details, the more it became apparent that the directory that he was holding was a unique document. It was well known that the Ministry of External Affairs published a directory of officers annually. Some of these documents are available online and some others are in-house in nature. But the one that Natwar Singh was reading out from was unique, as it had records of V.M.M. Nair, one of the last few Raj-era ICS officials and one of the first few diplomats that India recruited. That is how Natwar Singh introduced me to the *History of Services*, the 'Restricted—For Official Use Only' directory, published for the first time in 1959.

Singh joined the Indian Foreign Service on 14 April 1953. He was twenty-two years old at that time. He trained in India till September 1953 and then went to Cambridge for training, as mandated for the direct recruits, during 1953–54. From 1954 to 1956, he was in India undergoing district training. During this time, he had his first brush with the high and the mighty that the foreign service exposed its recruits to as a routine. He served as the liaison officer to the Chinese cultural delegation, crown Prince of Cambodia, President Gamal Abdel Nasser of Egypt and Dr Mohammad Hatta of Indonesia. His next assignment was as the third secretary till 1958 in the Indian Embassy in Beijing. After that he returned to the South Block as an undersecretary, beginning with the summer of 1958. It is till 1958 that the career of Natwar Singh finds mention in the *History of Services*, which he held in his hands while speaking to me over the phone. Parallel to the formation of various wings of the state in the 1950s, the Nehru government had the task of forming the bureaucracy to the requirement of the new post-colonial state. Natwar Singh's 'directory' shows the innovations and the new approach that the Nehruvian state had towards forming the bureaucracy for foreign service.

The *History of Services* included the services of those like K.P.S. Menon, who served as the first foreign secretary of India from 1948 to 1952, Leilamani Naidu, the first Hajj in-charge of the Ministry of External Affairs, Subimal Dutt, who was foreign secretary at the time of publication of the *History of Services*, future Foreign

Secretary Jyotindra Nath Dixit, who joined just months before the directory was published, and Brajesh Mishra, the future national security advisor and top decision maker when India exploded nuclear bombs in the desert of Pokhran in 1998.

That was certainly not all. The list had the names of mavericks like Syed Shahabuddin, who became synonymous with the controversial Shah Bano case of 1986, Jayantanuja Bandyopadhyaya, the author of classics on Indian foreign policy which are still being read in Indian educational institutions, the Haksars, the Nehrus of Allahabad, and even the father of the future megastar of Bollywood, Harivansh Rai Bachchan, who was recruited as an officer on special duty for Hindi in December 1955. Before that, Bachchan had had two stints—as a lecturer of English in Allahabad University and as a producer in All India Radio. Hindi was not the only language that Bachchan had mastery over. The directory says 'r.w.s', which means reads, writes, speaks well, indicating what he reported as his proficiency level in Urdu, an important qualification for diplomats who had to engage Pakistan after the exodus of the masters of Urdu from government departments in 1947.

Most importantly, the directory is in fact the first compilation of the women and men who constituted the establishment figures in a country that was born a rebel, with its leaders, including Nehru himself, known to be firebrands. They spent a lifetime dismantling the colonial state that ruled them during their youth. So, the attempt to build a foreign policy organ consisting of professional diplomats, which also worked as a national security structure, at times was a novel venture. India was not just fighting her own battle for freedom from the British Empire but was also amplifying the voice of the people of all those countries that were oppressed. Max Weber had described the bureaucracy as a power elite that rests on expertise, access to information and secrecy. Apart from official secrets, the bureaucracy is also made by safeguarding the secrets of its own origins and its constituents. It is here that the *History of Services* comes across as a document of lasting importance because it recorded the detailed bio data of all the recruits of the Indian Foreign Service in its first decade, and by doing so it lays bare the personal and professional details of a generation of public officials who would go on to form the power elite of independent India. It also contrasts sharply with the Weberian definition of bureaucracy as it shows that the Nehruvian state did not have a formal structure or any clinical quest for formal structure while creating the foreign service cadre. That the cadre was created from existing groups of officials and through competitive examinations as well as from a pool of gifted individuals, like poets, writers and radio presenters, shows that the state worked according to its commitment to progressive ideas.

Many of the recruits mentioned in the directory chose to write down their stories themselves. Like Natwar Singh, Dixit, Subimal Dutt, Romesh Bhandari and Ambady Krishnan Damodaran would write and leave some of their accounts for readers, but the majority chose to stay silent, like S.J. Wilfred, Abid H. Safrani and Cyril John Stracey, who had once participated in the Indian National Army of Netaji Subhas Chandra Bose. Bhandari, however, wrote of his political experience as the governor of Uttar Pradesh, he was employed several years after his retirement, but did not leave any writing about many of his adventures in the Gulf region.

In these pages lie the story of a twenty-three-year-old teacher of English literature in University College, Trivandrum. Leaving the college after a year, he joined *The Hindu*'s editorial department in Madras in 1944; a year later, he came to Mumbai and joined *The Times of India*. Four years later, on 19 April 1949, he was posted as attaché in the Ministry of External Affairs and subsequently served as second secretary in the Indian Embassy of Rangoon from July 1949 to November 1950. Between 1950 and 1958, he would serve in Indian missions in Tokyo, London and the South Block, becoming the deputy secretary in the Ministry of External Affairs. Forty-eight years after he became one of the first recruits for Indian diplomacy, Kocheril Raman Narayanan would be sworn in as the President of India, in 1997.

The directory is also a history of Delhi, the capital of new India. For with the IFS, young people from distant corners of India came to the new city. It was here that post-colonial India was designed. New Delhi greeted Narayanan, Damodaran, Bhandari, Safrani and Chonira Belliappa Muthamma—the first female direct recruit who joined through the competitive examination—into the IFS.

The city once known for its medieval glory was now trying to define itself as the dynamic centre for a modern republic geared to address challenges. The new recruits did not just come from distant corners of India; they also came from the erstwhile Indian territories of Burma, East and West Pakistan and former princely states that boasted of their own administration, villages and other big cities. They spoke not just English, as was preferred earlier, but many other languages, as the government offices began to represent the complex pluralistic nature of the Indian people. It was also a moment that marked a break from the humongous Indian Empire of the British Crown which boasted of languages as diverse as Pashtu, Dari, Sindhi, Assamese, Canarese and Malayalam, and the new Indian republic, born on the basis of a Partition, the event that deprived the new state of several communities and languages that were part of its previous existence as the core of the Asian Empire of the British Crown.

Later, during the time of Indira Gandhi, the Indian Foreign Service would go on to create a cadre that would focus on having formally trained official interpreters. But among the first wave of officials who became part of the IFS in 1948–58, there were many who came with their own provincial mother tongues and languages learned during their days spent as part of the colonial empire. The 'foreign languages' they spoke were in fact languages spoken in the areas that were till recently part of British India but were not part of post-colonial India. So, there was Bhavandas Mangharam—appointed in January 1953 as assistant high commissioner in East Pakistan's Rajshahi—who came from Hyderabad in Sindh, spoke Urdu, Hindi and Persian and had complete command over Sindhi; Lalla Chunni Lall[5] joined as an attaché in the Deputy Indian High Commission in Lahore in April 1948, spoke Burmese, Persian, Hindi and Urdu and spanned the entire area from Yangon to Tehran in his language skills. Bhavandas and Chunni Lall, both belonging to the Grade I, Branch B of the IFS, were part of the population that was displaced because of recent Partition and imperial reorganization. Both were part of refugee settlement, evacuee's census and employment coordination departments, and the jobs that they secured in the foreign service used their language skills while providing them with suitable employment in the new India. Indeed, for a foreign service that did not have an independent existence in the early 1940s, the languages spoken by the IFS A and B branches in the late 1940s were truly diverse—including Pashtu, German, French, Persian, Russian, Bahsa Indonesian, Urdu, Bengali, Tamil, Japanese and Malaya—covering the neighbourhood of India as well as distant shores of the world.

In giving more freedom to communicate in local Indian languages within the corridors of power in the Indian capital, the new Indian republic provided a big break from the imperial past when English was the preeminent official language, but the new state was also poorer in terms of languages and communities as it simply lost them because of Partition and administrative reorganization. The first generation of IFS reflected the new state's desire to bank on past skills to build its future of neighbourhood diplomacy because the provinces of the past were the neighbours of new India. The state was ambitious and wanted to launch a million dreams and called the people to join in, and in response they came from all parts of the country. In doing that, the new IFS was also part of an attempt to preserve the old imperial India in some acceptable manner.

The North and the South Blocks were the grandest structures in the town even as new neighbourhoods were coming up in different parts of the city for the large number of displaced people of 1947. Scooters, buses, horse carriages and bicycles were the chosen mode of transport and officials lived frugally in small accommodations. Janpath had emerged as a hub of activities. Coffee shops hosted visitors who argued over the state of the world and the country. The first diplomats of India were expected to spend their lives moving from place to place. They often had to improvise on the spot and deliver in uncharted territories. They were going to be the Bedouins among the bureaucrats. But they could create continuity of function and build relations if they remembered the work and the people who mattered. The *History of Services* was the tool that would help recollecting many lives that mattered. Natwar Singh understood the importance of this slim volume and saved a copy in his library immediately.

Branch B was divided into Grades I, II and III and K.P.S. Menon (Jr), undersecretary in the department of Foreign Service Personnel, in the Preface to the directory mentions that recruitment to Branch

B of the service was 'nearing completion' in 1958.[6] It was felt that recruitment of Branch B officials had given the Ministry of External Affairs a more complete appearance and, therefore, the necessity was felt to compile a list of all officials from serving diplomats to stenographers. Prior to this, the structure of the Ministry of External Affairs found space in the annual reports of the ministry.

In all, a decade after the creation of the IFS, there were around 187 Branch A officials of the Indian Foreign Service who find mention in the first 45 pages of the *History of Services*. They are followed by 49 officials of Grade I, 55 officers of Grade II and 110 officials of Grade III of the IFS Branch B. So, starting with barely a handful of Indian Civil Service officials who had limited international exposure, a decade after 1947, India's diplomatic brigade consisted of as many as 401 officials drawn from the erstwhile ICS, the Indian Political Service, public services of the princely states, defence, refugee department, Intelligence Bureau, academia, All India Radio and the newly recruited Indian Foreign Service youngsters.

In short, the government of Jawaharlal Nehru pulled at existing human resources within the colonial administration of India in launching a brand-new service while also recruiting young officers who were trained at home and abroad in India's diplomatic requirements. Apart from language and profession, they came from diverse social backgrounds. Natwar Singh hailed from the erstwhile princely state of Bharatpur but he himself was never a ruler in his ancestral land, and in addition, he was in fact a direct recruit into the IFS. But there was at least one recruit—Pradyumma Sinhji of Kotda Sangani—who actually was a ruler. He ruled Kotda Sangani between December 1940 and March 1948. Pradyumma Sinhji became a member of Saurashtra Presidium in 1948, and on

21 February 1949, he was appointed in the Junior Scale of the IFS on probation. In the new India of the 1950s, former teachers, journalists, administrative officers and military and intelligence officers had come together along with young inductees to form the first recruits of the Indian diplomatic force.

The diplomatic service was much more than just world travel and dealing with global issues to help the budding Indian political economy. There were lives, careers and ambitions that collided, and sometimes with not so pleasant outcomes. Like every other service, there was the gossip that was entertaining and harmful in equal measure. The former ICS members who formed the bulk of the senior ranks in the IFS-A naturally formed a group among themselves. Within them, there were groups that were never officially recognized, but it was understood that such groups existed and were decisive in ensuring the advancement of careers. It was considered a matter of privilege if a former ICS officer liked and promoted a direct recruit.

Most of the names that find mention in these pages appeared first in the *History of Services* of 1958, but there were several senior members in the service who were considered close to Prime Minister Nehru and were used for the topmost or politically sensitive assignments. Among them were Vijaya Lakshmi Pandit, Girja Shankar Bajpai, B.K. Nehru and a few others. While Vijaya Lakshmi Pandit carried out assignments on the diplomatic high table, Bajpai was chosen by Nehru as the secretary-general.

The post of the secretary-general, therefore, was a rather Nehruvian innovation according to academic Surinder K. Bhutani, brother of Sudarshan K. Bhutani who was inducted into the IFS in 1955 as a young direct recruit. Surinder K. Bhutani did not join the IFS but joined Jawaharlal Nehru University in the early 1970s, and thanks to the presence of his brother in the foreign service, he would get to meet many of the early stalwarts who would share much of the gossip with him. According to one such early tale, choosing a candidate for the post of secretary-general was a decision taken by the Prime Minister.[7] The Ministry of Defence had a defence secretary as its most powerful official, but the most powerful bureaucrat of the Ministry of External Affairs during the first decade after Independence was the secretary-general. Similarly, there is no definitive answer for why the ministry was not named the Ministry of Foreign Affairs, like many other countries had named their equivalent ministries. In 1947, the ministry in charge of foreign affairs was known as the Ministry of External Affairs and Commonwealth Relations, but it was found to be a 'relic of past dualism', as during the colonial period, commonwealth relations and external affairs were dealt through two separate departments of the Government of India. On 1 January 1948, a decision was taken to end that dualism and call the department the Ministry of External Affairs.[8] For a number of years, the post of the secretary-general was maintained, and it continued till Ratan Nehru, ICS, 1925 occupied the post in 1960–63. Ratan Nehru was the last secretary-general, and the post of foreign secretary thereafter became the topmost position of the ministry.

Girja Shankar Bajpai, Subimal Dutt, K.P.S. Menon and Ratan Nehru—all were from the ICS and had joined the service in the 1910s–20s. Being a part of the exclusive domain that required them to travel to world capitals, foreign service officials were also the subject of much jealousy. Initially, the foreign service officials had the authority to bring back the vehicles that they purchased abroad without any difficulty, as the vehicles were duty free. 'As a result, the front of the South Block used to have several foreign brand cars at a time when these vehicles could be afforded only by very few,' said Bhutani. But rivalry among groups had begun to show, and according to one account, there were a great deal of internal negotiations to get the biggest postings. Surviving stories recount that Triloki Nath Kaul who began his career in 1937 as a Joint Magistrate and Kewal Singh (ICS, 1938) were known to have admirers and followers who formed a close coterie of professional colleagues within the MEA.[9]

Despite the tales of rivalry, there were also examples of upward mobility for the officials who were absorbed into the IFS or were recruited as young officers. Two such examples were of Santosham John Wilfred or S.J. Wilfred and Sambasiva Krishnamurthi.

Krishnamurthi began his career as an assistant[10] in the Finance Department of India in February 1941. Wilfred began as a clerk.[11] Both of them ultimately became ambassadors, with Wilfred becoming the Indian high commissioner to British Guyana in the 1960s, within twenty years of joining the IFS.

Marriages and love affairs also formed an important part of the gossip about the diplomats. The recruitment of Chonira Belliappa Muthamma, or C.B. Muthamma on 28 September 1949 was a landmark for the IFS as it marked the service officially becoming open to young women candidates.[12] But women diplomats were not allowed to marry during their service. Sociologist Patricia Uberoi, who knew two of the early female IFS officers—Mira Sinha Bhattacharjea and Muthamma—traces this inherent bias within the early Indian diplomats to the years of World War II, when single women were much in demand for professions such as nursing and in the post and telegraph departments where late night shifts were part of the job and war efforts as those were considered low-paying assignments for the domestic workforce.[13] This arrangement was naturally advantageous to men. A married woman could not remain in hospital nursing the war injured, and married women would not get to work late in telegraph offices.

She had noticed this practice in her childhood in Australia, where her mother had to endure similar discrimination. She later was surprised to find that the decision to marry was the reason that Sinha Bhattacharjea had to leave her job at the Indian Foreign Service.

But by the time of Muthamma's arrival in South Block, Leilamani Naidu, daughter of Sarojini Naidu, had already become a career diplomat. Naidu was the head of the English Department in Osmania University College for Women during 1941–47, and after a brief tenure as the head of the Philosophy Department in Nizam's College in Hyderabad, she was appointed in the Senior Scale of the IFS on 11 September 1948. Naidu was a firebrand activist of the freedom movement during the 1930s and the '40s; she quickly rose in importance and was inducted as an adviser for the Indian Delegation to UN General Assembly's Paris Session in September 1948.

Love stories were not rare among the first recruits. One of the major ones of that time involved Sumal Sinha, the brilliant expert of Chinese, whose proficiency in the language and culture of China was so highly valued that he was lifted from the post of professor in the department of English literature and history in Szochuan (currently known as Sichuan) University and appointed directly as the third secretary in the Indian Embassy in Nanking in the month that India became independent. There are many legends of the scholar-cum-diplomat who began his career as a professor of History in Jessore College in 1943.[14] One surviving tale is that he was known to be intolerant of shoddy notes and demanded perfection from his colleagues. Those who failed to rise to his expectation often had to face his verbal volleys. Sinha's tenure happened at a time when China was caught in an internal conflict between the nationalists (Kuomintang) and the communists and India's policy towards Beijing was in a state of flux. By 1947,

India had, for nearly a decade, a diplomatic mission in Lhasa that continued to serve as a direct link between India and Tibet. All that, however, changed on 1 April 1950, when India became the first non-aligned country to establish diplomatic relation with the People's Republic of China.[15] Sinha was posted as the officer on special duty in the Indian Mission in Lhasa in September 1950—just four months after India established diplomatic relations with China. (It would be during Sinha's tenure that the landmark decision to withdraw Indian diplomatic representation from Tibet would be taken.) On 15 September 1952, the Ministry of External Affairs announced the decision to end the Mission in Lhasa.[16] After this period, the Mission would be designated a consulate general and accredited to Beijing. Sumal Sinha, thus, became the last head of the Indian Mission in Lhasa before it was downgraded to a consulate general by the Nehru administration and allowed to be accredited to Beijing. His tenure in Lhasa lasted for three more months and ended in December 1952. In June 1958, he returned to the Indian Embassy in Beijing as a first secretary.[17]

It was here that his stint coincided with that of Mira Ishardas Malik, one of the earliest female recruits into the IFS-A who had joined through the competitive examination on 1 May 1954. Mira Malik later on became one of the foremost scholars of Chinese studies and was one of the founding members of the China Study Group. On being recruited into the IFS, she opted for Chinese as her 'compulsory foreign language'.[18] She was posted as a third secretary in the Indian Embassy in Beijing in May 1957. During the first decade of the Indian Foreign Service, only a few candidates would be recruited every year. In 1954, four candidates were recruited into the IFS and all four chose difficult languages like Russian, Persian, Japanese and Chinese. Beijing was also a difficult posting and by choosing Chinese, Malik had taken up a challenging assignment. The fresh recruits were interviewed by Nehru before they went abroad.[19] Malik was an admirer of Nehru and had met him once before briefly while inviting him for the convocation ceremony for her college. However, the meeting during the interview left Malik questioning Nehru as she felt that behind the modern outlook, there still was a traditional core in him. Nehru wasn't particularly warm towards her and asked her why she wished to take up such a challenging posting; he suggested that the one in London would have been a better option for a female. He also felt that she would not last long as she would marry, which would then require her to leave the service. Malik protested strongly and described the rule that stopped female recruits from marrying as 'stupid', leaving Nehru startled. He relented but asked, '*Stick leke toh nahin ayegi teri maa* to say, "Why are you sending her to China? Why can't you send her to a civilized place like London?"' Malik responded, 'I took my own decision.'[20]

In Beijing, she worked under Indian ambassador R.K. Nehru and witnessed the difficult days of the Chinese economy. Apart from R.K. Nehru, K. Natwar Singh and Sudarshan Bhutani were her other colleagues.

Mira Malik met Sumal Sinha, who was a decade older than her, during this time, and love blossomed between them, posing the first big challenge to the outdated 'no marriage' principle that female diplomats were subjected to. Malik chose her love, married Sumal Sinha and resigned from the IFS, and thus she became the first woman to resign from the foreign service on marital grounds.

In May 2021, I wrote a newspaper article on the 'first recruits'.[21] One of the several individuals mentioned in the brief article was Mira Ishardas Malik. A few days later, one of the readers responded angrily saying that Mira Malik was actually Mira

Sinha Bhattacharjea. He was not wrong. After all, thanks to her marriages to Sumal Sinha and subsequently to senior editor Ajit Bhattacharjea, Mira Ishardas Malik acquired two eastern Indian surnames. In the *History of Services*, however, Punjabi is recorded as her mother tongue. Sinha Bhattacharjea, unfortunately, passed away in 2009, but she is still remembered by her colleagues at the Institute of Chinese Studies, which she set up with academics and policy makers. As an expert on Chinese affairs, Mira Sinha Bhattacharjea became the favoured TV commentator around the time of the thermonuclear tests that India conducted in Pokhran in 1998. She would often make herself available in TV studios, especially when Atal Bihari Vajpayee wrote his famous letter to US President Bill Clinton, explaining India's strategic environment with a clear hint towards the threat posed by China.

On 9 November 1978, the vehicle carrying the Indian ambassador to Lebanon came under a volley of bullets, which were fired from the machine guns of fighters stationed nearby. The windscreen of the car and the headlights were smashed in the attack. The car that was flying the Indian flag was hit also from the top and bullets entered the vehicle from one side of the roof. Miraculously, the driver acted quickly and drove to a narrow part of the street where the bullets could not target the vehicle. The spokesperson of the Indian Embassy in Lebanon condemned the attack and said it was a miracle that the personal assistant and the Indian ambassador survived the volley of bullets. The Indian ambassador's residence was located in the mainly Christian part of Beirut, and he was returning home from the Indian Embassy in west Beirut. At a certain point, firing began from Achrafieh district in east Beirut.

Once the pride of the modern Arab world, Beirut was divided into Muslim west Beirut and Christian east Beirut, and diplomats often faced the wrath of the fighters.

The ambassador who survived to tell the tale was none other than Sumal Sinha, who went on to serve in multiple exciting assignments during his career. Among many credits, he also represented India at the Independence celebration of Papua New Guinea in September 1975.[22] The lack of choices for female recruits as compared to their male counterparts was never starker than the careers of Mira Ishardas Malik and Sumal Sinha. However, in diplomat Sumal Sinha, academia lost a brilliant scholar, and in Mira Malik, academia gained a scholar, who made long-term contributions to Chinese studies. With her contacts in the establishment of 1960s and the 1970s, Mira Malik provided support to Chinese studies in India at a time when anything to do with China was frowned upon in the post-1962 India. Later, when pursuing Chinese studies in post-1962 India, Mira Malik was harassed by the intelligence officials for being in touch with the Chinese. But she did not give up her lifelong pursuit of understanding and writing about China, which she had picked up in her student days.

One July morning in 2021, Natwar Singh called. 'Now, listen. Do you have a pen and paper with you?' he began.

Proximity breeds contempt, but in the case of Natwar Singh, proximity failed to breed contempt and instead bred interest. This is evident in the notes that Natwar Singh often took during his years as a diplomat. Many of his notes went on to become books on a later date. This habit partially explains Natwar Singh's legendary capacity to recollect events going back to his earliest days in government service and even his education in the 1940s. He personally believes that his mental alertness and the ability to memorize details is a skill that he developed over the decades as that was the only way to stay ahead of the competition. 'We did not have all these gadgets that are available these days for doing official work. So, we had to depend on our own memory,' he said in a conversation with this author.[23]

Foreign service also brought him in proximity to political power and literary friendships. His friendships included those with fiction writers like R.K. Laxman and E.M. Forster, but he himself always authored non-fiction, and he never revealed official or state secrets through his published writings.

A year after the publication of the first directory of the IFS in 1959, Natwar Singh was posted as an undersecretary at the Ministry of External Affairs located in South Block. Jawaharlal Nehru was at the peak of his power. An unfortunate incident took place in India's embassy in Paris during this time.

An IFS probationer was sent there to learn French when he was involved in an unsavoury incident. Natwar Singh has not revealed his name but said that the young probationer was involved in an incident of theft. He was caught red-handed, and in the process, he ended up setting fire to the papers which, in turn, triggered a fire alarm in the embassy. An unethical act by a young recruit almost brought the entire mission to its lowest point. The matter naturally reached the headquarters, and Govind Ballabh Pant, the home minister, recommended immediate dismissal of the official.

Natwar Singh felt the punishment was excessive and would cast a shadow on the young man's future, preventing him from getting a job elsewhere. He consulted Sarvepalli Gopal, the erudite son of Vice President Sarvepalli Radhakrishnan, and asked him to approach Nehru through his father. Finally, the matter was worked out and Nehru called the probationer. He didn't dismiss Pandit Pant's decision; just changed the mode of executing it. 'You have let me down,' Jawaharlal Nehru told the officer. The young officer's future in the IFS ended, but he could seek service elsewhere and Nehru allowed him to resign.[24] It was one illustration of how Nehru himself took interest in the evolution of the Indian Foreign Service and, wherever required, intervened to correct the course.

The biggest test for the first-generation Indian diplomats came in 1975, with the declaration of the national Emergency by the Indira Gandhi government on 25 June 1975. Natwar Singh was the deputy high commissioner of India in London at that time. The British press and supporters of India were shocked by the brutalities that followed the declaration of Emergency. *New Statesman*, the weekly that was read by Jawaharlal Nehru and Sarvepalli Radhakrishnan, dropped the deputy high commissioner from their list of regular book reviewers. The leftist intelligentsia, which had supported India's Independence and had friends like Jayaprakash Narayan, turned against the Indira Gandhi government. The problem facing Natwar Singh at the time of Emergency is something that IFS officers have traditionally faced from the beginning. The unofficial mandate of the first wave of official Indian diplomats was to reach out to the world, convince them about India's neutrality in Cold War bloc politics and play a role in ensuring India's developmental goals by helping in technology transfer and maintaining good relations between the political leaders. But over time, and especially with the advent of Indira Gandhi, the diplomats were also expected to 'defend' India's increasingly anti-democratic practices. The Emergency provided such a moment to Singh and his contemporaries. As IFS officers, it was their duty to support the decision to impose Emergency, but as Singh would find out, the authority of a government can't silence critics.

In October 2020, this author was travelling in Harjeet Singh's cab on the outskirts of Delhi when Harjeet, a lively Punjabi from Jalandhar, informed that 'thousands of farmers are coming'. Just days earlier the government of Narendra Modi had passed three controversial farm laws. The warning from Harjeet came true within days when on 25 October 2020, the farmers descended on the borders of Delhi and surrounded the city from all sides. What began as a temporary show of strength drew worldwide attention as a remarkable farmers' protest took shape. The protest continued for months, as the government resorted to strong arm tactics and a brutal crackdown. Throughout the winter of 2020–2021, the farmers suffered, and many perished in the extreme cold and rain, but they continued the protest. The stalemate continued as daily stories of face-offs between the police and the farmers continued to pour in. It was in this backdrop that Singh received a call from the Prime Minister's Office. Singh did not mention what was discussed with Prime Minister Narendra Modi. But the effect of that meeting was soon visible in Punjab, which was headed for elections in February 2022. Soon, Congress Chief Minister Amarinder Singh, Natwar Singh's brother-in-law, entered into confrontation with his own party and set up a new political party. Towards the end, it appeared that the government managed to avoid a political rout in Punjab and scored a victory of sorts by ensuring the defeat of the Congress, which apparently was helping the farmers. In the backdrop of this fast-moving political drama in Punjab, Modi withdrew the farm laws. The end result—farmers won, Congress lost, the embarrassed government was spared electoral humiliation in Punjab and electoral victory went to the non-Congress Opposition, the Aam Aadmi Party.

When I asked Natwar Singh about what role he played in ensuring this outcome, he gave one of those enigmatic smiles that Mrs Singh had cautioned me about. Natwar Singh had retired from diplomacy and negotiation, but he retained his old habit of negotiating nevertheless, playing a role in solving difficult problems confronting New Delhi even in the twenty-first century. Mrs Singh was correct. Her husband has not revealed all the secrets that he has collected over a lifetime.

3

'EVERYONE'S TRYING TO MAKE SENSE'

INDIA WAS THE JEWEL IN the crown, the biggest and the most important territorial possession of the British Empire. A free India, therefore, had to have a matching diplomatic footprint. That, however, was yet to become a reality. The Indian Foreign Service was formally conceived through a decision of the cabinet of the interim government on 9 October 1946. Prime Minister Jawaharlal Nehru's first concern was to ensure sound relations with the Big Powers within his policy of non-alignment and that was germane in his comments and speeches in the mid-1940s. Despite Nehru's aspiration, India did not host many foreign missions at the time of Independence. This was going to change. 'Almost from the morrow of India's independence,'[1] the Soviet Union opened its diplomatic mission in Travancore House on Curzon Road.[2] The establishment of the Soviet mission was an unambiguous statement of India's free diplomatic choices. The US was already present in town as President Roosevelt's personal representative was stationed in Delhi during the World War II years. Soon after

Independence, Howard Donovan, who had earlier served as the consul-general of the US in Bombay, became the American chargé d'affaires in Delhi.

K.P.S. Menon, the first diplomat to be listed in the *History of Services*, was sent as Nehru's first ambassador to Kuomintang China, where he served till April 1948.[3] Menon had first met Nehru in 1931, when the future Prime Minister visited Sri Lanka along with wife Kamala and daughter Indira. Menon was then the agent of the Government of India to Ceylon (Sri Lanka). Fifteen years later, he undertook an overland trip to China and wrote a book called *Delhi–Chungking*.[4] He requested Nehru to write an introduction for the book, and he agreed. During World War II, India, despite being under a colonial administration, established a 'diplomatic or semi-diplomatic relation' with China and sent Menon as an agent-general to Chungking. After the end of the war, the post was upgraded to the level of an ambassador. Menon was then chosen for that post. Menon thus had the unique opportunity to have presented his credentials to President Chiang Kai-shek when he reached China as the Indian agent general. Menon's ambassadorship to China lasted till April 1948, and the biggest event of that year was the assassination of Mahatma Gandhi on 30 January 1948. A problem now arose from the fact that K.P.S. Menon had gone to Korea just before that. The assassination was global news and Indian diplomats had to shoulder the responsibility of observing it in an appropriate manner. Menon's colleagues reached out to his wife Saraswati Menon, who gave leadership to the embassy at this juncture, and organized a multi-faith prayer service, which continued for several days till Menon returned and took charge of the embassy.[5]

In the backdrop of rapid political developments, Asian, African and Latin American capitals often threw up complex diplomatic choices. China would throw up similar challenges soon when its nationalist government was overthrown by the communist movement in 1949. Chandra Shekhar Jha, a former ICS officer who had joined as the first few diplomats in the Ministry of External Affairs, was the joint secretary in charge of Far Eastern Affairs in the MEA in 1949.

The responsibility for this wave of diplomats can be assessed by the fact that it was Jha, who in consultation with India's Ambassador to Beijing K.M. Panikkar, recommended the recognition of PRC by the Nehru government.[6] India's relations with China began to formalize with the end of the Chinese civil war in 1949. On 30 December 1949, the Government of India thus recognized PRC, and on 20 May 1950, the ambassador of India presented his credentials in Beijing. The first ambassador of the People's Republic of China presented his credentials in New Delhi on 20 September 1950.[7] The person who had put together the team consisting of the likes of Jha and Subimal Dutt was Secretary-General Girja Shankar Bajpai.

'He was short. But his personality oozed authority.' That is what Maharajakrishna Rasgotra or M.K. Rasgotra said when remembering the man who was given the task to 'set up' the Indian Foreign Service.[8] The diminutive Girja Shankar Bajpai was the agent-general of India at Washington DC during World War II.

'Bajpai was the *first* officer that Prime Minister Nehru hired to set up the External Affairs Ministry,' said Rasgotra. How Nehru came to like Bajpai so much remains unknown, but it is believed that the Bajpais, like the Nehrus, hailed from Allahabad and that common roots, and the fame of Bajpai as an official, made an impression on Nehru early on. Bajpai was a complicated Indian with a complex career which criss-crossed the political and diplomatic currents of the inter-war period between 1919 and

1939 and 1939 to 1945. In October 1941, with the war raging in the background, the British Indian government sent him to Washington DC as the agent general of India. The need of the hour from the UK's point of view was to ensure cohesion of the Indian nationalist struggle with the Allied war efforts. The role of Bajpai, therefore, was crucial. Author Harold A. Gould said the British administration of India saw Girja Shankar Bajpai as 'safe' because he was not known for being an anti-colonial sympathizer within the administration. Gould said, Bajpai was a 'patriot in his own way.'[9] Bajpai's patriotism, Gould says, was based on the fact that there could be many shades of patriotism in a multicultural society like India where for 200 years, the colonial powers manipulated the minds of the people. 'He definitely espoused some kind of political autonomy for India, more or less in the form of "dominion status",' said Gould. [10] Despite that, it should be noted that Bajpai was not in favour of any forceful attempt to wrest India's freedom from the British rulers, and on occasions, helped in the deportation and imprisonment of Indian cultural activists and poets from the United States during his tenure as agent general. In his own writing, Bajpai had not agreed with Nehru and Gandhi about the tactics to be adopted during World War II, as he took the Japanese threat to India's security seriously. For Bajpai, Mahatma Gandhi's suggestion to confront the Japanese aggression with non-violence, reflected 'a lack of realism' and revealed a 'covert sympathy with the Japanese'.[11] That Bajpai was taken on board by Nehru, despite such disagreements, to curate the Indian Foreign Service from scratch is a sign of the pragmatism that came to characterize the post-Independence administrative thinking within the new power elite, who were willing to share and learn from each other despite serious past differences.

As Subimal Dutt, one of the first teammates of Bajpai in the IFS, has written, Bajpai's differences with Nehru, however, did not go away and often would surface in crucial policy matters where Bajpai would graciously withdraw, giving space to the elder Nehru. Young Maharajakrishna Rasgotra, who joined the IFS first batch in 1949, worked at a time when Bajpai was on the drive to configure the officials of the Indian Foreign Service.

Rasgotra was a tutor in Government College, Lahore, during 1944–46, and from there, he made three quick shifts that brought him to Government College, Ludhiana, in 1948. Soon thereafter he appeared in the competitive test in the second half of 1948 conducted by the Government of India. The year 1948 was an important one for the central government services; that year, the examination for recruitment into the services was held twice. Rasgotra appeared in the examination, but the results were not declared for several months. Finally, on 27 September 1949, a letter reached him asking him to join as soon as possible. 'I rushed to Delhi, and within two days, I was on a plane to London,' said Rasgotra recollecting the routine that he and other early recruits, including Chonira Belliappa Muthamma, the first female direct recruit of the IFS, had to undergo. The double examination in a year, the long pauses in between the examination and the results and the rushed journey to London illustrate the informal condition that existed in South Block. India had achieved independence, but there was little clarity on what the official organs were going to be like. While there was a desire and a broad vision to build a service consisting of professional diplomats, there was no sign of that on the ground as there was a rush against time to get the necessary officials recruited to deal with the fast-moving requirements that India was faced with in multiple locations across the world.

'Everything didn't have a structure. People were trying to get things in order,' said Rasgotra. Behind all these moves were a few people who were using the wisdom that they had gathered in the previous decades while working with the British administration. Bajpai was one of them.

There were a few people who determined the future course for the young officers—apart from Nehru and Bajpai, Krishna Menon, the Indian high commissioner in London, was the other. Menon was able to exercise his influence on the recruits because of being placed in London, which was important for 'commonwealth training'. Faced with the requirement of state building, the fiery anti-colonials of the Quit India Movement of 1942 had gradually turned pragmatic. The former colonial master was now a partner in training a new generation of officials of the state. Rasgotra said the Nehru government felt, 'where else could we go' but to London to learn how the modern state could be run. 'The system was inherited from the British and there was a feeling that in order to run the system, it was necessary to return to London and recharge the understanding,' recollected Rasgotra about the experience that the first batch of the IFS gained.

Prime Minister Nehru had instructed G.S. Bajpai that he should remember to recruit his officials in such a way that they would represent Indian society and its composition.[12] Therefore, he hired the officials of the Indian Civil Service as 'they knew how to run the state'.[13] Bajpai, who was an ICS officer also, was instrumental in deciding to send the Indian officials to Oxford and Cambridge to study world history, diplomatic history, European history and economics. Learning European history did not help Indian diplomats much, and it would take years of troubleshooting before they could replace what they had learnt in the British universities, where they were sent in the first year of their education. Rasgotra was sent to London and then to Sorbonne where he learnt French. 'It would be years before we could develop our own diplomatic diction,' said Rasgotra, remembering that the courses as such did not help much but it was an opportunity to travel and get to meet people like Krishna Menon, who was among the chief architects of Indian Foreign Service. These interactions between the new recruits and the seniors like Menon gradually shaped the unique Indian point of view, which favoured decolonization, non-alignment, economic development and greater representation of post-colonial societies on global platforms.

He met Menon in London during his training, and Menon used to take active interest in the course that the official recruits were taking. In the year of their recruitment, Rasgotra witnessed that the MEA required staff as urgently as possible, as Indian missions had to run as per the rules that were expected from professionally run diplomatic setups. He found soon that Krishna Menon expected all the young recruits undergoing training to drop into the High Commission from time to time, contribute to the working of the mission and learn the business of diplomacy and consular work. So, between the two semesters of work, he worked at the High Commission and struck up a rapport with Menon. Over the years many things would be said about Krishna Menon, especially about his leftist leanings and his habit of delivering long speeches in diplomatic gatherings. Menon's language skills impressed young Rasgotra who had studied English literature in Lahore. Menon visited Washington DC in the 1950s when Rasgotra was the third secretary in the Indian Embassy there. 'Menon's English was impeccable,' said Rasgotra, recollecting an exchange that Menon had with a British official where he used an unusual expression that appeared unclear to his counterpart.

'Sir, I spent several years learning the language; you learnt it on the streets,' said Menon while clarifying the meaning of that expression. In the early years, Rasgotra was also witness to the unique position of secretary-general of the Ministry of External Affairs. This post was given to Girja Shankar Bajpai as a special gesture by the Prime Minister. The PM and Bajpai were of differing political orientations, but the two enjoyed a personal rapport of such an order that both tolerated each other's opinions comfortably while Nehru's opinions would ultimately make it to the level of official policy. This difference and harmony would remain a feature of the MEA during the subsequent decades, when various issues like policy regarding Israel in the 1990s and reorientation of India towards the United States would be discussed in the aftermath of the 1998 nuclear testing. This tradition of internal debate and differences had its first episode in the differences between Bajpai and Nehru over issues like India's policy towards China in the early years of the republic as well as the Indian policy towards the communist bloc.[14]

There were obvious concerns about how the post of secretary-general would shape up as the MEA also had the post of foreign secretary, which came to be occupied by Subimal Dutt later. The importance of Girja Shankar Bajpai in those years was mainly due to the fact that he was expected to carry special assignments on behalf of Prime Minister Nehru in the domain of foreign affairs. This is why the post was created for the man. 'In effect, as secretary-general, Girja Shankar Bajpai was the principal official adviser of Pandit Nehru on foreign and strategic affairs. He was given special tasks and would look after special files,' said Rasgotra. Decades later, a similar controversy would break out when Brajesh Mishra was appointed the first national security advisor of India in 1998.[15] The position of NSA became institutionalized thereafter when Jyotindra Nath Dixit of the 1958 batch got appointed as Mishra's successor during the United Progressive Alliance (UPA) government in 2004. For a brief period during that time in his formal role as the national security advisor of the Manmohan Singh government, Dixit's role had reportedly clashed with the role of the foreign secretary. The point to note is that prior to that, the issue of conflict between the foreign secretary of the Ministry of External Affairs and the NSA's office did not arise during the tenure of Brajesh Mishra, a direct recruit from 1951. Rasgotra believes that the difference between Brajesh Mishra and other foreign secretaries of the Vajpayee government did not arise as Prime Minister Vajpayee had a great equation with Mishra.[16] In hindsight, one sees that the NSA vs foreign secretary issues may vaguely appear similar to the problem of secretary-general vs foreign secretary, but in essence, there was no doubt that the first secretary-general was a special person as he set up the Foreign Service in coordination with Prime Minister Nehru, Sardar Vallabhbhai Patel and others.

Bajpai wielded the greatest influence in the selection committee, which included six senior ICS officers. Apart from Bajpai as the chairman, the other ICS officers were R.N. Banerjee, H.M. Patel, S.A. Venkataraman, V.K.R. Menon and R.L. Gupta. Two officers from the audits and accounts service, N. Sundaresan and P.C. Bhattacharya were also included.[17] The recruitment drive began in the backdrop of the departure of the British officers, retirement of a generation of ICS officers and departure of a sizable chunk of officials for the newly created Pakistan. These conditions created a paralyzing paucity of officers. Recruitment began in 1946–47.

The post of secretary-general would be the first reason for internal skirmishes in the MEA, which as Rasgotra had witnessed, did not have a formal structure to begin with. With the gradual emergence of the IFS cadre by the early 1950s, the post of the secretary-general had to be passed on to the other aspirants and the original mind behind the service, Bajpai, was given the plum posting of governor of Bombay Presidency. The post next went to N.R. Pillai, who then passed it to M.J. Desai, and finally it went to Ratan Nehru. It was during this time that the post created friction within the officers, as many thought that it lacked the necessary gravitas it had during Bajpai's tenure, and often clashed with the role of the foreign secretary, which was then assumed by Bajpai's protégé—Subimal Dutt. The structure of the MEA worked in an informal way, and it was most obvious in the way the social network unfolded within the MEA. It is said that Nehru brought Bajpai to the topmost bureaucratic post in the South Block, and Bajpai in turn brought Subimal Dutt to the MEA. Dutt, therefore, perhaps felt that he was the real inheritor of Bajpai's mantle.

The diminutive Bajpai was a towering figure within the establishment, and there was intense competition among all the men and women for his attention. In the initial years, there was a movement to create the formal structure of the MEA but, on the other hand, there were a few informal players who had to be dealt with. M.O. Mathai came on top of the list. 'He was the personal secretary to the Prime Minister and handled all his documents,' he said, recollecting the power that this former stenographer had come to acquire. It is not known what might have helped Mathai land the job of secretary to the Prime Minister, but his autobiography shows that Mathai was a meticulous and neat writer and an effective communicator. Prime Minister Nehru probably found good use of such a skill in his early days in office. Mathai was economic with praise and generous with criticism verging on slander, and on occasion, character assassination. He guarded access to Nehru and disapproved of anyone trying to get close to the PM.

Girja Shankar Bajpai with his constant proximity to Nehru was specially chosen by Mathai for criticism. Mathai did not appreciate Bajpai's privileged background and especially his rapid professional rise during the British Raj. Bajpai's strength in the bureaucracy came from the fact that he became a member of the viceroy's executive council 'rather early in his career'. Bajpai, according to Mathai, was fond of fine suits tailored by well-known brands and got a dress stitched in the US, which failed to produce the necessary effect for his diminutive appearance.

During Nehru's first visit to the US during the Harry Truman presidency, the American President sent his personal aircraft named *Sacred Cow* to London to welcome the Indian leadership. As Bajpai and Mathai followed Nehru, an American air force captain asked Bajpai if he spoke English! According to Mathai, Bajpai seethed for two days over the incident and repeatedly told him that he spoke at least six languages (English, French, Persian, Sanskrit, Urdu and Hindi).

These recollections were chronicled only by Mathai but are generally dismissed by others. Mathai, however, hinted, perhaps with a touch a bitterness, that Bajpai had managed to maintain his colonial-era high bureaucratic stature after Independence, thereby having the 'best of both worlds'.[18] Incidentally, it was Bajpai who had interviewed Mathai before appointing him to the post of the personal private secretary to the Prime Minister in August 1947. Nehru, Mathai wrote, did not 'want to be surrounded by officials completely'.[19] India's freedom did not create antipathy towards the western powers, particularly the United Kingdom, and India's freedom struggle did not create much backlash against the Indian bureaucracy, which in many instances was responsible for the harsh crackdown on Indian revolutionaries. By adopting both a pro-Commonwealth line and by inducting the ICS into the evolving administrative and foreign affairs structure, the Nehru era showed that India preferred continuity over disruption. 'It was the only option,' said Rasgotra, explaining how India remained in the orbit of the Anglo-Saxon community even after Independence. He said that the continuity had its benefits in the form of support for trade, science and tech cooperation, all of which were necessary for the growing economy of India.

Irrespective of Mathai's acidic description, Bajpai, the co-author of the Indian Foreign Service along with Prime Minister Nehru, was held in considerable esteem by his contemporaries. This was on display when the Kashmir issue debuted on the floor of the UN Security Council on 1 January 1948. On that date, the Government of India drew attention to Articles 34 and 35 of the Charter of the United Nations stating:

> [A]ny Member may bring any situation, whose continuance is likely to endanger the maintenance of international peace and security, to the attention of the Security Council. [...]
>
> Such a situation now exists between India and Pakistan, owing to the aid which invaders, consisting of nationals of Pakistan and of tribesmen ... are drawing from Pakistan for operations against Jammu and Kashmir, a State which has acceded to the Dominion of India and is part of India. The Government of India request the Security Council to call upon Pakistan to put an end immediately to the giving of such assistance which is an act of aggression against India. If Pakistan does not do so, the Government of India may be compelled, in self defence, to enter Pakistan territory, in order to take military action against the invaders. The matter is therefore one of extreme urgency and calls for immediate action.[20]

The conversation on the matter began on 15 January and was held between the Indian delegation led by N. Gopalaswami Ayyangar and the Pakistani foreign minister Sir Zafrullah Khan. They came to the conclusion that a three-member commission should be set up to look into the Kashmir issue. The agreement over forming the United Nations Commission for India and Pakistan was reached on 20 January 1948, and the members of the Commission included Czechoslovakian diplomat Josef Korbel. The UN delegation came to Delhi and stayed at the Cecil Hotel, which was known to be one of the few elegant hotels in town and catered largely to the European guests. The delegation arrived in the summer of 1948 and was stunned by the severity of the north Indian summer. Korbel wrote admiringly about Bajpai.

> On July 13, Sir Girja Shankar Bajpai, Secretary-General of the Ministry for External Affairs, was invited to present the Kashmir case before the Commission. Sir Girja, a small man with a shy smile, perfect manners, and ivory-cut hands, with the English of Shakespeare and himself the quintessence of ancient Indian culture and Oxford schooling, was a great diplomat of the English school. He had served in the British India government and during the war had represented India in Washington.[21]

By 1958, Bajpai would be out of the MEA and would have passed away after a stint as the governor of Bombay. His name, therefore, did not find mention in the directory of that time—the *History of Services*—which names other pioneers who worked with him.

That the diplomatic brigade would have the comingling of multiple traditions and expertise was perhaps foretold at its inception, and it was most visible in the two schools that existed during 1947–52. Bajpai and his protégé Subimal Dutt represented the Indian Civil Service school and K.P.S. Menon 'rather embodied the traditions of the Political Service (IPS) coined by officers like Olaf Caroe or Hugh Weightman.'[22] These three officials would have been described as the 'troika'.

In 1948, the Indian Foreign Service had started recruiting young officers to drive the foreign affairs of the new Indian state. But, in fact, the real requirement was for individuals who had a fair understanding of both sides of history—before and after 1947—especially in central Europe. It was this requirement that might have prompted Nehru to hire one of the most mysterious characters to have ever become an Indian diplomat. A.C.N. or Nanu Nambiar was considered multi-talented. For many readers in India, he was a journalist who wrote for *The Hindu* from European capitals, but for some, he was a character who operated from the margins of world politics, and some believed that he was a player in the world of intelligence. Among the many achievements of Nanu Nambiar was his role as a deputy of Subhas Chandra Bose. He had played an active role in setting up the network of the pro-Axis 'Free India Centre' (Azad Hind Office) in Germany in 1942. An accomplice of Sarojini Naidu's revolutionary brother Chatto, who was killed in Stalin's purge in the Soviet Union, Nambiar had been Nehru's private ear in the heart of Europe for many years. Starting with 1927 when Nehru along with father Motilal, wife Kamala and sister Krishna visited Brussels and Berlin on the way to Moscow, where the Soviet rulers had invited them to participate in the celebrations marking a decade of communist rule. After nearly two and half decades in Europe, Nambiar arrived in Delhi after India attained independence. Nambiar's biographer Vappala Balachandran has written that while visiting India, he expected to be a foreign correspondent for the *Hindustan Standard*. But Prime Minister Nehru had a different plan for Nambiar. Nambiar was someone he could trust, and in the midst of the changes that were underway, he required trusted representatives in distant locations of the world who could relay important developments to him. Nambiar fitted the bill, and Nehru dismissed his chances of returning to a career in journalism and asked him instead to become a member of India's foreign service, just like several others who were active in the national movement and now were serving in diplomatic positions. 'You will not (go back to Europe); go and see K.P.S. Menon,' said Nehru.[23] Menon was the foreign secretary at this crucial moment, and Nambiar was appointed as the counsellor in Berne, Switzerland. It was in these tumultuous set of circumstances that a one-time journalist and a deputy of Netaji Subhas Chandra Bose in Europe, who had a strong reputation of being a gatherer of information of all kinds, was appointed a counsellor in the Indian Embassy in Switzerland. The name of Nanu Nambiar did not appear in the *History of Services*, as it included only those who were still in service at the time of its publication.

Nambiar did not have a long career in Indian diplomacy but can be viewed as an interesting experiment, which can be explained purely as an outcome of Nehru's plans of pursuing foreign affairs. Europe was exceedingly difficult in 1947. The Allied powers had emerged victorious, but continental Europe was still in the early stages of recovery, and the ruins left by the air raids were still lying around in the great cities of Germany, France, Belgium and Italy. Germany, divided between the Allied powers and the Soviet Union, was in a delicate situation that had to be handled with a lot of caution. Someone with a deep understanding of the political situation of the continent could have delivered political assessments on the ground correctly to the Indian leadership. Nambiar took the post of counsellor in Berne in the second half of 1948 where he began working under Dhirubhai Desai, son of Bhulabhai Desai.

The early years of the Indian Foreign Service appear to have several characters with mysterious pasts and the addition of Nambiar added to that mix. As it is expected, an informal gathering can often fall short of a strict adherence to professional values and Nambiar probably was no exception to that. He soon began to have difficulty with the private secretary of the ambassador—Soli Batliwala. There were reports that Batliwala exerted influence over the wife of the ambassador, Madhuri Desai.[24] Soon, media reports began to emerge back in India about the power equation in the mission. A scandal of sorts broke out which Nehru did not approve of. Balachandran did not mention it in his writing, but the Prime Minister had probably learnt his lesson and appointed Nambiar as the high commissioner to Sri Lanka. Nanu Nambiar loved India, but he loved Europe a bit more, and there was no way that he would have left the comforts of Berne to become the envoy of India in warm Colombo. Nambiar declined the offer and left for Geneva, resuming work as a journalist. After two years, Nehru offered him the post of the Indian ambassador to Sweden. He liked this posting, but after a year in Stockholm, he was sent as India's first ambassador to West Germany. This posting was not without its irony, for Nambiar with his chequered career had been arrested twice in Germany in the past. He was arrested first by Hitler's police in 1933 for his alleged role in the burning of the Reichstag. Then, in 1942, he was brought to Berlin by Netaji Subhas Chandra Bose, and, in 1943, he was asked to assume charge of the Indian freedom struggle in Berlin when Netaji left for Japan. But after World War II, he was arrested again—this time by the victorious Allied powers.

4

THE OUTSIDER BECOMES AN INSIDER

THE CAREER OF AN IFS TOPPER

*A**AI* HAD A PERSONAL RELATIONSHIP with her in-house deities. They were her friends and confidantes. She worshipped them daily and prayed to them for her family's well-being. On special days, she would offer a generous puja, with fruits and sweets, and then place her demand. Usually, the demands were fulfilled probably because of her own hard work. But 1952 was a special year. Her son was a young man now, and he had appeared for the competitive examination for the Indian Foreign Service. The chances of her son Dileep Shankarrao Kamtekar, who had a law degree from Bombay University by the time he turned twenty-four, clearing the test with flying colours were rather high, and *Aai* felt confident about her son's ability. But as the examination rolled on and weeks of tension engulfed the house, she decided to give an extra push to her deities. She took them all out from the prayer room and placed them in a basin full of water. It was a threat that they would be consigned to the tub for as long as it took Dileep Kamtekar to clear his examination. Perhaps partly because of his own abilities and partly because of the extreme step that his *Aai* took to coerce the gods, Dileep Shankarrao Kamtekar cleared the test and became eligible for the Indian Foreign Service. His mother was satisfied, and the deities were taken out of water and placed back in the prayer room. The house was decorated, and the gods were rewarded with fresh clothes, sweets and fruits.[1]

The Kamtekars were a well-known Marathi family who had worked for the Gaekwads of Baroda for years. His father Shankarrao Anandrao Kamtekar served as a judge under Gaekwad rule. The family was touched by the winds of transition blowing over India as well as the aspiration of the clan to see their son make it to the larger body of officials who would be active at a national level. For that, the preparation had begun much earlier and the Kamtekars, whose mother tongue was Marathi, made their son Dileep Kamtekar speak in English at home. The tacit understanding was that his fluency in the language would help him clear his examination and pave the path for his selection in a central government service. The young boy, however, was not told that he would have to be a diplomat; the family simply expected him to be able to clear the test for the Indian Administrative Service, the successor of the Indian Civil Service, the topmost service of the colonial administration. The English training at home was, therefore, aimed at the Indian Administrative Service, the topmost service of the immediate post-Independence years.

Kamtekar went to Baroda College and subsequently had a law degree from Bombay University, where the future top cop Julio Ribeiro was among his batch mates. For a while at this time, he toyed with the idea of joining politics, but his father had made up his mind back when the young man was a little child. Kamtekar Junior's sudden change of mind was overcome by parental opposition. Kamtekar's son, the historian Professor Indivar Kamtekar in JNU, said that his grandfather had argued that joining politics would require substantial financial resources, for which the family was not prepared. So, with this background of discussion at home, Dileep Kamtekar appeared in the civil service examination of September–October 1951. The results of the test appeared on 28 January 1952, and he secured the second rank.[2] The first fifteen on the merit list secured the top ranks in both the IAS and IFS exams, but not all the candidates could be considered for the IFS, as the number of provisional seats in the foreign service was just six—though finally just five made it to the IFS.[3]

Apart from Dileep Shankarrao Kamtekar, Jagdish Chand Ajmani, K.S. Bajpai, Thomas Abraham and A.P. Venkateswaran were the others in that list of IFS recruits. All the five candidates recruited that year went on to be distinguished in the service during the next four decades, with all of them going on to lead major Indian missions across the world, and A.P. Venkateswaran became the foreign secretary during 1986–87.

Indivar Kamtekar recounted that during the interview for the IFS, his father found that barring him, most of the candidates had links with the bureaucratic or political elite of the time. Venkateswaran's father A.S. Panchapakesa Ayyar was an ICS officer, K.S. Bajpai's father Girja Shankar Bajpai was one of the founders of the IFS along with Prime Minister Nehru and his elder brother Uma Shankar had joined the IFS in 1948 and Jagdish Chand Ajmani's brother Khub Chand was also an ICS officer who was absorbed into the IFS. The interviewers had found that Kamtekar was a regular reader of *The Economist* and was very well informed of international developments and specifically marked him for the IFS.

The Independence of 1947 reached its desired goal five years later in 1952, as it was in that year that the first elected government was formed under the leadership of Jawaharlal Nehru. Dileep Shankarrao Kamtekar joined the IFS on 2 April 1952. It was a watershed point in the history of India and also for boosting India's bureaucracy.

The foreign service, which the Nehru–Bajpai duo had been nurturing since Independence, was now on course, and fresh young recruits were being hired every year as a matter of routine. And so, the service that had begun with a collection of the old traditional elite was fast changing. K.P.S. Menon's argument to create a representative diplomatic brigade proceeded parallel to the evolution of the democratic process, beginning with the 1952 election. The ICS and the princes still dominated the ranks that were created in the previous years, but new and aspiring citizens of the country were knocking on the door, too. Kamtekar did not have a foreign degree, nor did he come from a highly privileged background. His childhood was spent under British rule, but his youth was shaped by the enthusiasm of independent India. The first sign of the changing contours of the bureaucracy would soon greet Kamtekar, and it appeared in the interview for the IFS that was held in Delhi. As all the shortlisted candidates waited for the interview board, they introduced themselves to each other, and it turned out that all the candidates barring him knew each other already. They were not strangers to each other as they belonged to the same class of people who had an early exposure to governance during the decades spent under the colonial rule. Kamtekar was the only one who was an exception. Legend has it that during the interview, one of the interviewers mentioned to him that they were happy to find an 'outsider' like him in the interview, as otherwise it would appear as if a cosy circle of individuals were giving the top-rung government service to their children alone. Kamtekar stood first in his batch of five IFS officers inducted that year.

In the early 1950s, hope and creativity erupted in India, and it was a good time to be a young government officer. India was facing many challenges, but a new generation of government officials were getting ready. Soon after his induction, Kamtekar was hurled into the training process for the IFS. The six-phase training of the IFS covering institutions at home and abroad was aimed at 'polishing' the officers who were from different parts of India and diverse social backgrounds, away from the traditional ruling classes. Kamtekar, like other officers, was sent to the University of Cambridge, as the Government of India had an arrangement with the university to train officers through a year-long exposure to its international environment. Kamtekar was one of the handful who received the unique mix of national and international training in diplomacy during the first decade after 1947.

Kamtekar's daughter, Rachana Kamtekar, who teaches philosophy at the Cornell University, recollected that her father went to Cambridge with the expectation of reading the classics but was quickly disappointed by his professors, who were clear they were not going to teach him anything of that sort, as the year-long stint would only suffice to just provide him the set academic module for the professional life of a diplomat—and not of an academic. After the basic training in Cambridge, Kamtekar trained for German as that was his 'compulsory foreign language'.[4] Along with learning the language, the period gave Kamtekar the opportunity to live in the post-war Germany. Berlin was a divided city, and the wounds of the devastating war that Hitler's actions had triggered were visible everywhere. The dire economic condition was most visible in the lives of the average Germans. During his days of language training, Kamtekar lived as a paying guest with a German family for whom the presence of the Indian guest was of significant financial importance. The host offered him a cup of coffee and bread on the first day at the breakfast table. The breakfast summed up the condition of the war-ravaged and divided Germany in the 1950s. Kamtekar had travelled the previous day and was obviously exhausted. On seeing the spartan breakfast, he said, 'What! No eggs?'[5]

Responding to the young Indian officer's demand, the German family produced a boiled egg and offered it announcing, 'An egg for the Indian prince!'[6] Kamtekar's breakfast in Germany changed from that moment onwards, and the princely egg remained on the menu as long as he stayed with the German family. He, however, made a lifelong friendship with Germany, where he would return to serve his last posting in a fateful moment in the history of India and his personal journey.

After the two-year training in the UK and West Germany during 1952–54, Kamtekar spent a year undergoing departmental training in the Ministry of External Affairs in Delhi. It was an important exposure to the new bureaucracy, its intricacies and internal conflicts. Already, the young officers of his generation were waking up to the fact that for all the talk of the anti-colonial attitude of Nehruvian India, the government was also deeply entrenched in the old ways of conducting business. Indivar Kamtekar, therefore, believes that the Indian state that came to replace the colonial state of the British Raj in fact indulged in the business of 'concealment of continuity'.[7] This argument finds resonance in the work that Sir Humphrey Trevelyan (later Lord Trevelyan) did as part of the interim government under the leadership of Jawaharlal Nehru. An officer of the Indian Civil Service, Trevelyan was a joint secretary in the ministry during 1946–47, and it was he who drafted the rules for training and recruitment in the Indian Foreign Service at that time. K.P.S. Menon had acknowledged him for laying the ground for the establishment of the foreign service in India. A reflection of that was visible in the way the officers were sent to Cambridge to be educated and polished as part of their diplomatic training. He would also have two shocking experiences when two important postings—Singapore and Paris—were denied to him, as two other officers with better political connections were ultimately chosen for the posts. It was during this time that Kamtekar had the opportunity to work with Foreign Secretary Subimal Dutt, and Dutt confided in Kamtekar his opinions about the emerging foreign service workforce. Dutt was a stickler for discipline and merit and often did not approve of the political interference that the Indian Foreign Service was subjected to under the Nehru government, wherein Prime Minister Nehru was the face of Indian diplomacy and was responsible for bringing in a number of officials whose induction into the service was not entirely transparent. He reportedly described some of these officials as 'trash', as they did not clear the competitive examination, and maintained that the former ICS officers and the directly recruited IFS officers alone made the mark as they were hired through the competitive selection process. In candid moments, Subimal Dutt thus introduced Kamtekar to the pros and cons of the IFS.

Kamtekar's first posting was to Berne. Soon thereafter, came another important assignment.

On 1 September 1957 began Kamtekar's first big promotion, which catapulted him right in the middle of the biggest political crisis that had erupted in the Arab world. The region had been hurled into a ring of public unrest, beginning with the crisis in Lebanon where political opposition against President Camille Chamoun quickly turned into a near-sectarian conflict that prompted US President Eisenhower to send American troops to

Lebanon for the first time in July 1958. There was criticism against President Chamoun for not favouring the unity of diverse Arab countries under the flag of Arab nationalism, for which Egypt and Syria had emerged as major regional players. As the American troops were getting ready for a regional intervention, anger swept the Arab streets, and the impact was felt in Iraq—a major oil producer by then—most severely.

Baghdad had become the seat of the Hashemite dynasty, which had the blessing of the United Kingdom, just like the other wing of the Hashemite kingdom that was led by King Hussein in Jordan. The Hashemites originally were in Hejaz in Saudi Arabia but were displaced after a war with the house of Saud and came to govern Baghdad and Jordan (with the additional right over the third holiest place in Islam), allegedly with generous help from the British imperial power. The Arab world had been a matter of debate among the Prime Minister and the MEA officials from the beginning of the Indian Foreign Service. This debate was necessitated by the emergence of Israel on 14 May 1948. India was weighed down by multiple considerations in its policy towards Israel in the beginning of the Indian Foreign Service. On the one hand, as a secular state, it agreed to recognize Israel but did not establish diplomatic relations with the country, which was allowed to maintain a consulate in Bombay. The argument in favour of this policy was that the Arab states had to be kept away from Pakistan, which had emerged as a regional challenger soon after its birth on 14 August 1947. The policy had to be crafted in such a way that the West, which was close to Israel, would not be antagonized and the Arab states would not be alienated either. That, however, did not mean that there would not be occasional disturbances in both the axis that India maintained on the West-Israel and the Arab-Soviet lines. And these disturbances required quick handling.

Iraq, therefore, was an important destination that Kamtekar was exposed to early in his career when Rangiah Subra Mani or R.S. Mani, a former ICS officer, was the Indian ambassador to Baghdad. Mani was seconded to the IFS permanently on 1 November 1954.[8] At the time of Kamtekar's posting to Baghdad, a communication that R.S. Mani exchanged with Foreign Secretary Subimal Dutt explains the balancing act that the South Block had to pull through. In the letter to Mani, Dutt had written that the time was not 'ripe' for India to open full diplomatic relations with Israel, mainly because it wanted to ensure the Arab states would support India at the diplomatic level as India too had played a role—a chaotic one but one that was helpful—in bringing an end to the Suez Canal crisis of 1956. India maintained a cautious position and intervened whenever either of the two sides went overboard, like when the Israeli consul wanted to distribute publicity materials to the locals in Bombay or when the Arab League wanted to open a branch office in India.

The ruling elite of Iraq consisted of King Faisal II, Prince Abdallah and Prime Minister Nuri al-Said. The troika had carried out large-scale development projects but was deeply unpopular and perceived as puppets of the British government. On 14 July 1958, the rule of King Faisal, Prince Abdallah and PM Nuri al-Said came to an end when a group of military officers known as the Free Officers under the leadership of the charismatic Brigadier Abd al-Karim Qasim overthrew the monarchy. The public outrage against the king boiled over and all three rulers were executed by the military. The Free Officers of Brigadier Qasim were inspired by Arab nationalism and wanted to undo the setbacks to Arab pride that had taken place during the previous few years, beginning from when Israel was set up as a homeland for the Jewish people.

The Indian mission in Baghdad was important for multiple reasons. First of all, during the previous decades, the country had emerged as a major exporter of petroleum, and India required to cultivate good relations with Iraq. Khub Chand, a former ICS cadre (1935)[9] who opted for the Indian Foreign Service in 1948,[10] had signed a peace and friendship treaty on behalf of India with the Government of Iraq in 1952. The underlying message was that the two countries would maintain friendly ties to ensure smooth commercial transactions that would be beneficial for the development of both sides. The location was important, and Khub Chand apart, Baghdad also became the base of Muhammad Yunus, who had debuted in the Indian Foreign Service as the first Indian envoy to Jakarta during October 1947–June 1949.[11] So it was in this mission that Kamtekar arrived as the political disturbance erupted. The Iraqis welcomed him with open arms, and Kamtekar quickly made friends among Baghdad's new power elite, but New Delhi instructed him to maintain friendships with all sections of the Iraqi political class, and so he reached out to the Opposition. This brought him under the radar of the law enforcement authorities. At that time, no one knew that the rulers of 1958 were not installed forever and that bitter internal fights would break out soon. Years later, it was here that Kamtekar would witness the chilling effects of a carnage. The ruthless nature of Iraqi politics was made alive for him on a mid-summer day after the birth of his eldest son in 1959. Once, when milk ran out at home, the couple went around Baghdad driving their car in the intense heat. After some time, a few Iraqi police officers approached them to inquire about the matter. 'Next time, please tell us to fetch you the milk. That'd be better than driving around in this heat,' said the police officers, making it clear that the Indian officer was under the active surveillance of Iraqi police.

Over the next three and half decades, Kamtekar went on to serve first in junior positions and then as India's ambassador to Poland, Mexico, Australia, Malawi, Mauritius and Switzerland. The countries that he went to more than once were Iraq and Germany.

The 1950s were also a decade of love, and Kamtekar fell in love with a Punjabi Sikh. Kamtekar's future wife was born in Lahore and came to India against the backdrop of communal riots. She and her mother went to stay at Kurseong, which is one of the towns in India that attracted a large number of refugees. The family of an Indian diplomat during the 1950s and the '60s could travel to India at government expense. So, the Kamtekars would visit Delhi and Baroda every alternate year. Every summer, the family would pack up and fly Air India, as that was the only airline the diplomats were allowed to use while flying to visit family in India. His children recollected, the government's financial support in travelling back home was very helpful as Kamtekar, like other Indian diplomats, saved very little money; sustaining a family in a single-income household would prove to be tough.

Thanks to the policy of non-alignment and Nehru's presence, India's voice mattered at the global level. India played its role in the Suez Crisis, in the Korean war and other notable flashpoints. But the first recruits, mostly young men and a few women, carried a secret. They, however, could not keep the secret hidden, as it was most visible when it came to travel and tourism.

The government gave a first-class allowance to the Indian diplomats only for the last leg of their journey to the station of service. That meant the officers and their families would travel economy class for the early part of their travel and would be upgraded only on any connecting flight to their destination so that they could exit the aircraft through the front looking like important figures.[12] Whether this arrangement was indeed devised for helping the public image of diplomats from one of the biggest third world countries or planned to save necessary foreign currency is not known, but over time, diplomats and their families perhaps came to feel that it was more like a public relations exercise to provide the host country with the image that the diplomats were from a well-to-do economy, which India at that time was not. Travelling was, however, the least of the problems; the real challenge was in setting up missions in places that did not have any Indian diplomatic footprint during the first fifty years of the twentieth century. It is true that with the advent of the post-colonial government, India lost a few missions, like the ones in Kashgar and Lhasa, but there were dozens more that came up in places like Africa and Southeast Asia, where India's diasporic and economic requirements were urgent.

One such posting came Kamtekar's way in Malawi in the mid-1960s. Malawi, formerly known as British Central Africa or Nyasaland, attained independence in 1964, and India decided to establish a mission in the stunningly beautiful country. The country was located along the elongated Lake Malawi, and its beauty came from the play of sun and cloud in the backdrop of the enormous lake. Kamtekar arrived in Malawi without any local staff base, with wife and young son Indivar and the responsibility of setting up the High Commission and other infrastructure.[13] Once in the country, he discovered that the Indian people had reached places in the world much before the Indian state and that the Indian community in these locations could be a great support structure for Indian diplomats there. He, therefore, reached out to the local Indian community, seeking help to set up the mission. The local Gujarati and other communities enthusiastically responded to his call and within a short while helped build the premises of the High Commission, residences for staff and other required infrastructure. Till now, Kamtekar's model of working in Africa with the help of the local Indian community remains the tested model of conducting diplomatic affairs in most of Africa, where the local Indians are closely linked to the embassy and often help each other, keeping the momentum of bilateral relations going despite the uncertainties that are known to be endemic in Africa. The mission in Malawi was shut in 1993 due to administrative reasons for nineteen years and was reopened in 2012. A popular name till this day in Malawi happens to be India. A lot of men in the country are named India.

Decolonization meant the birth of new countries, and by supporting decolonization, India ensured that every newly independent country would be ready to establish relations with India. Mauritius was a special territory for India from the beginning. Indian workers were brought to Mauritius to work on sugar plantations from 1820s. After the abolition of slavery, indentured labourers were brought to the island from India, and in all, nearly half a million Indian indentured labourers were reportedly brought to the territory over the next few decades till the early twentieth century.[14] The painful narratives surrounding the transport of indentured labourers from colonial India to other parts of the British colonial empire added to the melancholy of foreign rule in an India that forced dispossessed Indians to leave home for distant parts of the world. Following Independence, Indian leadership therefore took an active stance regarding the countries that had acquired Indian populations in this manner. Mauritius, being the closest of the locations that received Indian indentured labourers, received priority as Nehru became the Prime Minister.

Soon after India's Independence, diplomatic relations were established with Mauritius, where the Indian representative was called 'commissioner'. With the non-aligned movement as part of Indian foreign policy, it was necessary for India to get newly decolonized countries on its side to add to its voice on international platforms, and Mauritius, with its unique attachment to India, was well-suited to be a new regional friend. It would also be the important outreach into the islands of the Indian Ocean that India wanted.

In all, there were eight commissioners of India in Mauritius. Three of the first-generation professional diplomats were sent to Mauritius to serve as India's commissioners. J.N. Dhamija, a former member of the Royal Naval Volunteer Reserve, served during 1958–60, and P.R.S. Mani, who had served as Nehru's expert on the Southeast Asian region during his visit to Malaya in March 1946, was sent to Mauritius as the commissioner. The third and the last IFS to serve as commissioner was Avtar Singh, who had started his career in the Indian Army in 1942, experienced military action in Myanmar and was awarded military honours for bravery during World War II. Avtar Singh was sent as commissioner in 1967 and became the first Indian high commissioner to the island nation when Mauritius gained independence on 12 March 1968. Dileep Kamtekar was the second high commissioner of India to the newly independent Mauritius, and he arrived in 1969 with his young family.

The Independence of Mauritius revived the spirit of independence in India, once again at a difficult political juncture in the career of Indira Gandhi, and she visited the country that she called 'chhota Bharat' or Little India in 1970, a year before the epic events unfolded all across India. Kamtekar's tenure in Mauritius, however, was disrupted by a bout of asthma, and he came to Delhi to recover.

The posting was greatly welcomed by his family who were happy to return to the hostel at Kasturba Gandhi Marg. The stay soon turned more eventful than it could have been in the Indian Ocean region as developments in East Pakistan began to roll with remarkable speed. The thirteen-day long war came with blackouts in Delhi and the family lived in the hostel and followed the rules that required them to keep lights switched off during air raid sirens. The IFS was twenty-four years old when the war in East Pakistan exploded. The IFS officers' quarters in Delhi became the place where war, youth and family matters predominated. Calls of duty and education tugged at bonds of love and young kids left home for boarding school education. The Indian diplomats spent most of their time away from home but the culture that the children of the first-generation officers experienced was equally unique. India was in the era of licence-permit raj and outside products were not allowed in bulk, so children of the officials created their own culture, which used to explode during summer breaks in Delhi.

Things began to change when the Government of India began the allowance for the education of diplomats' children in the 1970s. So, every year, the families would travel to Delhi and stay at the hostel for the officers of the Ministry of External Affairs on Kasturba Gandhi Marg which would be transformed into a summer camp. Here, in this multi-storeyed building, officers of the IFS would thus converge with their families for a couple of months. The vacation of the families would be longer than the officers', and they would spend around two months there. The hostel would take the shape of a warm summer camp as families from different parts converged there carrying stories and items from far corners of the world. The children who grew up in these hostels, like the children of the Kamtekar family, would naturally go on to form lifelong friendships with each other as they felt more at home in the Indian surroundings. Raising families in different locations, often within racially charged environments, had their own impact on the children of Indian diplomats in those early years, as they would often be subjected to racial discrimination but could not do much about it. Kamtekar's daughter Rachana would, however, notice that the children of American diplomats were treated with some kind of deference by school authorities in places like Iraq and Poland; the cultural markers would signify the special place for the children of diplomats of developed countries. The children of western countries would also often display that cultural difference via their choice of stationery or even food items like burgers and Coca Cola which, naturally, would not be the first thing that children of Indian diplomats would prefer.

The wives and the children of Indian diplomats during those early years also ended up participating in the business and the process of hospitality that the Indian diplomats had to indulge in as a part of their daily work. Kamtekar, for example, would consult his family, and every member would enthusiastically participate in the process of laying down the cutlery and planning the 'protocol' for the special dinners that would require certain important guests to be seated in a particular order to ensure incident-free hospitality. This aspect of the diplomat's life would be looked after by the 'representational allowance'. The hospitality of an Indian diplomat was always the talk of the town because of the variety of Indian cuisine and drinks that they offered to the guests, and this was more

THE OUTSIDER BECOMES AN INSIDER

so in eastern Europe, where the austerity measures were pretty severe. The Kamtekars were witness to some of these austerity measures during their stay in Poland, where Dileep Kamtekar was posted from the spring of 1974 to 1977. Poland was under communist rule since the end of World War II, and in 1970, the government dealt with major riots over inflation and food prices and a new leadership came up. In the 1970s the situation had not improved much, as the Kamtekars would find. There was a scarcity of food and basic items in the Polish market, and some regular items like liquor and meat were easily available only in special shops for diplomats.

On top of that there was all round surveillance of foreign diplomats and their family members, and the bugging of residences with listening devices and cameras was part of normal life. Kamtekar's daughter Rachana recollected that the family had to go on with their daily work disregarding the listening devices and cameras placed in the house. 'Once a camera fell from the ceiling into the bowl of soup of a guest,' said Rachana Kamtekar, remembering a hilarious incident that she witnessed. 'All important conversations had to be held outside.'[15] The surveillance was a small price to bear for the Indian ambassador's family considering the importance that Poland had acquired in the Indian technology and defence markets. During his stay, Kamtekar would visit the shipyards in Gdańsk and other coastal cities to interact with Polish ship builders who built a number of ships for India during the 1960s and the '70s. The ambassador's wife would have to launch the ships which, as a rule, could be launched only by a lady. The Polish officials would insist on a launch by breaking a bottle of champagne, and the Kamtekars would politely insist on following the Indian convention of breaking open a coconut on the hull of ships to mark an auspicious beginning. The stint in Poland was significant as it coincided with major world events like the 'oil shock' of 1973, which had forced India to tweak ties with the Arab world, and the focus of India's friendship within the Arab world shifted slightly from Egypt to the Gulf region, which was the centre of global energy politics and required India to intensify friendship with cash-rich countries like Iraq, Saudi Arabia, UAE, etc. Kamtekar was sent to Baghdad, his second posting within two decades in the beautiful and historic city.

Iraq was flush with money, and there was a spurt in purchasing power, which gave India an export market nearer home. Export of Indian merchandise to Iraq soared during the mid-1970s while Iraq also gave India large contracts for constructing infrastructure networks and buildings. This also meant that Indian labourers were being sent to Iraq, and the embassy had to look after their well-being. Kamtekar travelled across different parts of Iraq like Nineveh, Mosul, during his stationing in Baghdad to ensure the safety and security of Indian labourers. In one particular case, as recollected by his daughter Rachana Kamtekar, an Indian labourer was imprisoned after he used abusive words for President Saddam Hussein. Kamtekar rushed to the prison where he was kept and got the man out after some difficulty but found, to his horror, that the labourer had been tortured during his brief stay in the prison. The labourer's fingernails had been taken out as punishment. While Iraq prospered during the Saddam Hussein years in the 1970s, such tales of the brutality of the regime abounded. His second stint in Iraq during this time was particularly difficult as he found that all his friends and political contacts of the 1950s had been eliminated by Saddam Hussein in his bid to ensure that no challengers that could morph into a threat in the future were left.

THE OUTSIDER BECOMES AN INSIDER 113

For the family of diplomats like the Kamtekars, a special role was designated for the bag, the Diplomatic Bag. The Diplomatic Bag was a special item in the life of the MEA, its diplomats and the family members of the diplomats.

The primary function of the Diplomatic Bag or the Bag was to carry communication from the South Block to the missions. The bulk of the documents in it would consist of classified official papers that pertained to diplomatic and administrative matters. The rest of it would be from family members.

Because of the official secrecy surrounding the bag, the Government of India ensured that the bag would be delivered as far as possible by Air India and would then be collected by the resident diplomats. Diplomatic bags carried in Air India aircrafts would thus end up in the diplomatic missions of London, Frankfurt and other destinations in Europe and North America and East Asia. After that, a specially designated officer from the Indian missions in nearby countries would visit the nodal mission to pick up the bag. The Diplomatic Bag was the source of official communication as well as personal letters. Families scattered across the world would be united by the mails carried in these diplomatic bags, whose main purpose was to move the official and personal information of the Indian diplomats in a secure manner. For this particular purpose, the Ministry of External Affairs served as a post office.

From India's neighbourhood to the other part of the world in Mexico, Kamtekar had served continuously for around three and half decades; yet, the history of his event-filled career is rarely discussed. There is no explanation why Kamtekar did not write his memoirs like a few others of his generation. One explanation for the lack of his personal history is that Kamtekar was deeply rule-bound in his conduct and was thus prevented from writing his accounts by the shadow of the Official Secrets Act (OSA). Kamtekar's post-retirement phase was also plagued by his growing eyesight problem. Daughter Rachana Kamtekar says that they probably contributed to his inability to leave his accounts in his own words. An episode where his personal account would have helped in clearing the air was his last posting in West Germany, where he served as the Indian ambassador.[16] It was then that the DW submarine scandal broke out. Though his name was not associated with the scandal, he did protest to a newspaper when he felt the reporter had dragged his name in unnecessarily. In the history of India's first-generation diplomats, Dileep Kamtekar will be remembered as someone who set up Indian missions in places where they did not exist before. His career shows what a typical Indian diplomat's career should have looked like in the twentieth century.

5

RAJ

THE ENVOY FOR 'LITTLE NATIONS'

IN THE FIRST HALF OF 1936, as Europe received the first whiff of the rise of Nazi Germany, French aviator M. Chantereine undertook an epic cross-continental air journey. He planned to fly to the French possessions in India. He had attempted similar journeys in 1930 and 1932, flying from Djibouti to Dakar—both French outposts—and had made a name as an adventurer who flew his light aircraft to distant lands owned by France. Accompanied by his two friends, the aviator arrived in Karachi on 20 April.[1] It was a difficult adventure at the dawn of civil aviation when passenger aviation was taking mini steps towards achieving a worldwide footprint. More importantly, it was an attempt to connect France with all the foreign possessions that it had gathered during the past three centuries. The flyer and his team travelled to Karachi and wanted to fly back to Afghanistan and Iran but only after they had flown all the way to Pondicherry. On their way to India, they flew to Damascus, another French outpost that was part of the French mandate Paris got after World War I. Chantereine wanted to establish a connecting link between the French possessions in India and the commercially viable routes of Air France. This would also improve the postal union between France and the French possessions in India, it was said. The idea was to connect Paris with French possessions in India and further increase ties to French Indochina.[2]

French Indochina at that time had an area of 2,85,000 square miles and a population of 21.6 million, which was governed by a governor-general. The French possessions in India consisted of five separate locations—Pondicherry, Karaikal, Chandernagore, Mahe and Yanam. These covered an area of 196 square miles with a total population of 1,86,410 as per the census of 1931. Out of all the locations, Pondicherry was of supreme importance as the governor of all the French possessions in India resided there.

In 1936, the French air route to the eastern hemisphere was operated by Air France. It started from Marseille in the European section and traversed through Naples, Corfu, Athens, Beirut, Damascus, Baghdad, Bushehr, Jask and Karachi. After reaching Karachi, the service proceeded via Jodhpur, Allahabad and Calcutta without touching Delhi, as it was serviced by a local operator. From Calcutta, the air route would proceed to Akyab[3] or Sittwe, and Yangon and Bangkok, from where the route divided into two, heading to Hanoi and Saigon. In the summertime, this entire route from Paris to Saigon or Hanoi would take a week. Air connectivity and a more efficient postal union were of great importance for France mainly for financial reasons. Apart from Chandernagore (now Chandannagar), the other four French possessions were on the coast and had port facilities that had imports in excess of 96 million francs in the calculation of 1931 and exports of over 173 million francs.[4] In all, 271 vessels visited these four ports during that period. It was felt that if all the four ports that were contiguous to the Madras Presidency could be connected to the main 'arterial aerial highway',[5] it could have boosted chances of a regular French air service in India. The new ideas about the commercial viability of the French possessions were linked with the currents of freedom that were flowing in India and other parts of Asia. With the 1935 Government of India Act and the upcoming election of 1937, the future of the British Empire in India was becoming increasingly clear, but such clarity was wholly missing regarding the French possessions though they were of commercial importance to France, and with the advent of air travel, could play an important role in connecting bigger French colonies in Southeast Asia with Paris. Over the next decade, as France dealt with the brunt of the Nazi war machine, its possessions in India did not figure prominently in the national agenda.

India became independent in 1947, but it did not possess all the defining elements necessary for the formation of a state. It had citizenship and public support and a claim to sovereignty as well as law enforcement agencies, but it did not have territorial coherence because of a number of reasons, including the presence of enclaves belonging to France and Portugal. The situation, however, began to change with India attaining independence, which brought along euphoric public opinion that favoured complete decolonization of India and the establishment of the rule of the new republic across the length and breadth of the sovereign territory of India. With the end of World War II and the beginning of post-war reconstruction in France, Paris returned to Asia for one last time. However, Paris felt that the question of colonies in India and the independence of British India were two separate issues. Sources in the Foreign Ministry of France said, months before India became free, that the two issues—freedom for India and status of French Indian possessions—are 'absolutely independent'[6] of each other.

In reality, the fate of the French territories in India were connected to France's vast possessions in Southeast Asia as much as with the future of the Indian sovereignty. It did not take long for trouble to begin, primarily because of the prevailing strong anti-colonial public sentiment that surrounded these small enclaves as protests targeting the French territories in India intensified. Over the past three centuries, the French and Portuguese colonies were entrenched in India through political and commercial dialogue, and during World War II, the French colonies were better integrated with the rest of British India because of joint war efforts. In March 1949, India began to discuss the fate of the customs union that gave the French territories access to the larger Indian market. Under the Customs Agreement signed during the war, India collected the customs duties and paid Rs 6.5 lakhs to the French settlements. With the end of the customs union, this subsidy would end, and all articles exported and imported into the French territories would have to pay duties as per the tariff rules of the Government of India. Dissolving the customs union would effectively end the free movement of goods between the French possessions and the rest of India. The dissolution would make the continuation of French presence in these territories absolutely untenable as it would adversely affect the lives of the people in these territories. For example, French India did not produce any cotton and was entirely dependent on nearby metropolitan centres for textiles. Supply of raw cotton, coal and food grains from other parts of India would also be subject to similar restrictions. From April 1949, as per the available information, India was on track to regard the French territories as 'foreign country' and a customs cordon would be formed around them because of the ending of the customs union.[7]

The war had left France vastly weakened, and its might after World War II was partly because of the trans-Atlantic alliance she entered. Reorganization of the sovereign territory had already exposed India to international pressure as Kashmir, Hyderabad and other major princely states were incorporated into the emerging India, but an open quarrel with France over its territories was not going to serve anyone's interest. India maintained amicable relations with France while firmly following a mix of local economic and political actions to gently coerce the French into leaving India. France was, however, a great colonial power of the nineteenth century but it was also a power that was humiliated by Nazi Germany during the war. After the war, the western alliance endured and helped France regain its global position of power. One of the ways for regaining French glory was by re-establishing dialogue between France and its vast colonial possessions in French Indochina, which consisted of modern Cambodia, Laos and Vietnam. While France aimed to become a bigger player in Asia, its ambition was handicapped by domestic problems as the Fourth Republic was not yet politically stable. French presence in Asia at this time received great help from the United States, which sent hundreds of millions of dollars in military and economic support to France for its Southeast Asian possessions. Taking on France, therefore, was also risky as it could antagonize the United States. It was in this set of circumstances that India took the initiative to overthrow the last colonial 'pimples' from the Indian map.

By refusing to extend the customs union, India in fact prepared to impose an economic blockade around the five territories that could not survive without free commercial interaction with the nearby Indian cities and production centres. Mirza Rashid Ali Baig, former sheriff of Bombay and one of the first recruits into the Indian Foreign Service, went on to leave his mark in the last

European enclaves in India. Baig was posted as the consul general in French Establishments and Portuguese Possessions in India in Pondicherry during this crucial period of 1947–49 when most of the quiet moves were made to extract the French Establishments from the control of Paris. The government of France, in a statement in the National Assembly of France on 8 June 1948, announced that the future of these Establishments would be decided by the people of French India. This policy was interpreted by India as a subtle attempt to prolong French influence in South Asia. However, it was unlikely to be easy as the people of these enclaves were divided along pro- and anti-merger lines, and expectedly, a group wanted the French presence to continue as the locals did not really have any rancour towards French rule. While India expressed its position by dissolving the customs union, the prevailing public opinion was expressed by the Congress party, which played an aggressive card on the ground by mobilizing public sentiment in favour of liberation of the European enclaves.

On 1 May 1949 Joseph Stalin stood like every year at the Red Square in Moscow and reviewed the military might of the Soviet Union that defeated the Axis powers in World War II. Stalin, despite the criticism of intolerance of critics, was at the peak of his power, and under his command, the Soviet Union was on track to end the nuclear monopoly of the United States within the next four months. The biggest war in human history changed the map of Europe and unleashed a cascading effect that changed the political map of the world and triggered a confrontation between the Soviet and the western bloc. Stalin was shaping the world with his thoughts and orders. On that day, the Order of the Day said, 'While engaged in the building of Communism, the Soviet people must never forget the danger of a new war which the ruling circles of the United States of America want to unleash.' The western capitals had formed the North Atlantic Pact, and Stalin described it as a 'threat to peace' and asked the Soviet armed forces to stand on guard for the next big war. The grand parade took place with the display of Soviet fire power, and Stalin's son Major General Vassily Stalin led the fly-past over the square which included a roaring fighter aircraft in the sky. Stalin, dressed smartly, smiled and waved at the cheering crowd and raised his arm to a salute.[8]

In the diplomatic stand, a little distance away, stood the Indian chargé d'affaires Rajeshwar Dayal and his charismatic wife Sushila Srivastava. The Indian ambassador, Vijaya Lakshmi Pandit, had been transferred to the United States as the ambassador to that country, and the young Indian diplomat was left in charge of handling the embassy.

Dayal had joined the Indian Civil Service in 1933, becoming magistrate and collector in the United Provinces. He served as the home secretary of UP during 1946–48 at the peak of the communally charged period when India was born. In 1948, the Indian Embassy in Moscow had emerged as a major posting and a number two to the ambassador, Vijaya Lakshmi Pandit, was required. The choice was made and A.D. Pandit, a well-known government servant, was selected. Unfortunately, Ambassador Pandit did not find A.D. Pandit suitable. She felt that she would have to spend the 'rest of her time in Moscow explaining what relation Mr Pandit was to Mrs Pandit!'[9] It was then that Rajeshwar Dayal was asked to join the foreign service, leaving his parent cadre, the ICS, in which he was one of the eleven candidates inducted in 1931.[10] Dayal sought his younger brother Harishwar Dayal's opinion. Following his elder brother's footsteps, Harishwar Dayal had cleared the ICS examination in September 1937 and was inducted into the Indian Political Service (IPS). In March 1944, he joined the Ministry of External Affairs as undersecretary. Harishwar Dayal was a polyglot and knew French, Russian and Tibetan. Among Indian languages, he was fluent in Hindi, Bengali, Oriya, Marathi and Gujarati. It was with the counsel of his talented younger brother that Rajeshwar Dayal responded to the news that the Government of India had selected him as the number two in the Indian Embassy in Moscow. Harishwar Dayal had told his elder brother that the foreign service held a great deal of new opportunities, but he warned him to stay away from the challenging responsibilities of getting into the United Nations and Pakistan-related assignments. As luck would have it, the United Nations and Pakistan would consume a great deal of Rajeshwar Dayal's nearly two decades' long service in the Indian Foreign Service.

From Moscow, Rajeshwar Dayal was summoned to handle a pressing crisis in India's east, where the large-scale displacement of population from East Bengal had created a difficult humanitarian situation demanding urgent solutions from New Delhi. So, in 1950, Dayal was rushed from Moscow to Assam, where his responsibility included giving shape to the Nehru–Liaquat Ali pact, which firmed up the exchange of populations that took place during and in the immediate aftermath of the partition of British India. India had gained Independence, but it was not going to cover itself in a quilt of isolation, and instead, it was to provide an international voice and leadership for many countries that were seeking a voice for themselves. The United Nations that India had founded along with other important nations of the world in 1945, for a post-World War II world, required India's attention; it had emerged as a platform where India could place its opinion on issues that mattered to its people. The biggest problem was that the United Nations that was born on the basis of a grand and idealistic Charter had begun to slip down the path soon after being born. The world had been through a major disaster that ended with the atomic bombing of Hiroshima and Nagasaki, but new and more dangerous wars and controversies were still raging in Korea, Southeast Asia and unjust imperialistic games were afoot in Asia, Africa and Latin America. To contest such developments, and to bolster its requirements, India had to utilize the platform provided by the United Nations, and Rajeshwar Dayal's mandate at the UN included that. He arrived at the New York headquarters of the UN as the alternate representative of India to the Security Council with the rank of a minister in 1950 and was promoted to Permanent Representative of India to the UN in January 1952. This was the post that he would hold till September 1954.[11]

In 2011, at the peak of the Arab Spring, I visited Tunisia. My destination was Libya, and it was impossible to land there as air connectivity had come to an end. In Libya, the strongman Muammar Gaddafi was murdered brutally by fighters from Misrata who chased him along the coastline and finally tracked and cornered him in Sirte, where Gaddafi met his bloody end. The managing editor of *The Week*, Philip Mathew, in a weekly meeting, laid down an ambitious plan for covering the exceptional violence that the Arab Spring had heralded in north Africa and asked me to write a report on the developments in Libya and Tunisia. The assignment gave me an opportunity to visit the old currents of history in Tunisia and Libya. In Tripoli, one part of the population maintained cautious silence while another part celebrated. In a feat of euphoria, they dedicated two roads of the once beautiful Libyan capital after UK Prime Minister David Cameron and French President Nicolas Sarkozy. Above the capital, French and Italian aircrafts under the aegis of the North Atlantic Treaty Organization carried out security sorties, establishing western control over the oil and gas facilities that continued to operate even as the Libyan government fell. The black Apaches and fighter jets reminded one of a link that stretched back in time all the way to the great wars of the twentieth century. In 2011, a lone Tunisian man who had gone to buy bread, in anguish because of his inability to buy the bread, which had become unaffordable due to high inflation, drenched himself in fuel and struck a match, setting himself on fire. That incident triggered a fire that made my travel to North Africa possible.

On 18 January 1952, the French rulers of Tunisia had struck up a similar fire by arresting nationalist leader Habib Bourguiba. Bourguiba, leader of the Neo-Destour party (New Liberal Constitutional Party) was a legendary figure among the Tunisians and his arrest by the French triggered a revolution that was to lead to a number of events unfolding in that region during the rest of the decade. Journalist Andrew Roth described the arrest of Bourguiba as a 'calculated risk' that the French had taken. Roth had witnessed the massive demonstrations that had broken out after the arrest which proved that Bourguiba was no lightweight and that he enjoyed the support of all sections of the Tunisian society. Prior to his arrest, Bourguiba had managed to travel to Egypt and the United States and had met a wide spectrum of leaders from the developing world. The arrest of Habib Bourguiba was therefore an incendiary moment for Tunisia, with the potential to trigger widespread disturbances in the region. India naturally wanted a discussion on the situation urgently in the UN Security Council (UNSC). But the UNSC was not yet disposed towards discussing issues related to anti-colonial struggles, as most of these struggles would target UNSC members like the UK and France—two of the biggest colonial powers. The lack of interest in allowing discussion on the anti-colonial movements raging in the Arab and African world revealed that the world had not changed much despite the highly ambitious Charter of the United Nations.

It was left to Rajeshwar Dayal to remind the UN that it was created to discuss issues that were relevant to the member countries and the humanity at large. Under an order from Prime Minister Jawaharlal Nehru, Dayal informed the UN that India had been holding discussion with the countries of the Arab-African bloc to raise the matter. He wrote to the Afro-Asian nations, reminding that this decision denying voice to the 'little nations' marks 'a trend that threatens to become a habit' of denying the rights mentioned in the UN Charter whenever Big Power interests are involved and 'so throwing the UN back into the chaos of June 1945' at San Francisco.[12]

It was not an easy situation. France had emerged out of World War II, ravaged by Nazi occupation, and it had built its immediate post-World War II policy in Tunisia based on the history of North Africa during the war. During the war, Bourguiba was imprisoned by the French, but the Germans had set him free, and he had rejected Italian attempts to court him. In the early 1950s Bourguiba campaigned for freedom in London and reached out to India and Indonesia, seeking support. His political focus had impressed Prime Minister Nehru.[13] There was no doubt, however, about Bourguiba's nationalist credentials, as by the early 1950s, he had established his credentials as a nationalist with years of exile and struggle against France. Yet, France was adamant that the matters related to Tunisia and Morocco were part of its domestic agenda and could not be discussed at the global level. The French policy on Tunisia was centred on 'Trust France', a declaration that representatives of the French government made to gather support from the Tunisian and Moroccan Arab population. 'France is a country of loyalty. We have a constitution. We shall keep to our undertakings,' said the French Minister of Pensions M. Emmanuel Temple, reassuring the Tunisians.[14] What began for the French in Tunisia was also playing out in Southeast Asia, especially in Indochina, where the French would face their moment of reckoning during the same time. The fate of colonial France was linked with the future US power, and the United States was caught between its responsibilities in Korea, Vietnam and its international image as the saviour of the world. There were obvious similarities between the French position on Tunisia in the early 1950s and the Dutch policy on Indonesia in the immediate aftermath of World War II. India opposed both policies.

Tunisia was not the only place that was going through a phase of turmoil in the early 1950s. Nationalism was on the rise, and Egypt too was caught in the eye of the storm.

On 4 April 1949, ten European countries and two North American countries—Canada and the United States—came together to form the collective security organization named the North Atlantic Treaty Organization (NATO). The formation of the NATO was a move that tacitly acknowledged the failure of the United Nations and the promise of collective security enshrined in its Charter. It was understood that the United Nations was deeply divided among the western bloc and the Soviet bloc that received the quick support of the Asian and African countries. The European and the North American powers formed their own grouping as a deterrent for any possible military move from the Soviet side. The formation of collective security organizations outside the ambit of the UN and deep divisions within the UN were fast eroding the international order that was born after World War II. At the same time, inside the UN, the older colonial powers, the UK and France, were determined to hold on to whatever colonial possessions they were left with. It was the last phase of colonialism and the two were determined to try their best to prevent the dissolution of the last colonial vestiges in Asia and Africa. It was then that the first wave of Arab Spring happened in Tunisia, a prominent French colonial outpost that the French had regained after the defeat of the Axis powers.

As the late colonial powers refused to leave their privileges, the decolonized countries responded by extending support to the Asian-African bloc of nations. Jawaharlal Nehru's foreign policy at this time chose to extend support to the victims of colonial exploitation—be it in Africa or Latin America. Rajeshwar Dayal had his task cut out for this duration, and he steered the Indian response at the United Nations, which was barely seven years old at that time. The Indian position was aimed at utilizing the American position on Tunisia, as it played against the American dependence of Asian support for the problems it faced in Asia. The French reacted angrily and questioned the legitimacy of the UN in holding discussions on the actions of the French government. The French considered themselves to be above scrutiny, but India sided with the so-called Afro-Asian bloc and the issue was kept alive at the UN General Assembly throughout 1952 as the Tunisian crisis became a test for the survival of the United Nations. Finally, after a prolonged stalemate, the United States supported a full-fledged discussion on Tunisia in the UN General Assembly. The United States did not want to antagonize France; nor did it desire to fuel misunderstanding with the emerging post-colonial bloc at the UN. Finally, however, the US chose to go with the Afro-Asian powers.[15] It was a moment of triumph for the Afro-Asian bloc at the UN. Decades later, the UN Security Council and the General Assembly discussed almost all issues irrespective of opposition from the permanent five members in the UN structure. Over the decades, the inherent weaknesses of the United Nations have persisted but in 1952, for once, the United Nations was able to deliver on the Tunisian question. The result of this diplomatic win would be visible soon when Tunisia became free in 1956. From Tunisia in North Africa, Dayal's next assignment would take him to the heart of Africa, to Congo.

'The African jungle can be a ruthless enemy and so we fought it ruthlessly.'
—*Congo Harvest: Wealth of the World* (1950)

Deep in the African forests of Congo grew gigantic palm trees. For thousands of years, the palm trees grew as part of the natural forest, which gave timber and food to the people. But the people had known for centuries the unique properties hidden in the palm fruits. From time immemorial, the people of the Congo had climbed these trees to bring down the palm. They would deseed the palm, boil the seeds and painstakingly pound the softened seeds and the fibre with a pestle and mortar. Afterwards, the large seeds now reduced to a juicy fibre would be squeezed through bamboo mats and primitive sieves. The final product would be drops of nutritious oil that would accumulate in wooden vats. It was this pure, naturally derived oil that would be used by the Congolese to cook their food and nourish their skin. This palm oil was the magical item that was used to nurture health and beauty and support the food cycle of the Congo's ancient people. The life of the Congolese people, divided among their tribes, customs and ancient beliefs, had continued on the banks of the magnificent and bountiful Congo, the river that gave the region its name. But in the nineteenth century, the fate of Congo finally began to change with the arrival of the Belgian colonizers. The world got to know about the ancient custom and the oil of the Congolese people, and the beauty market of the world beckoned the enterprising businessmen of Europe. In 1911, when most of South Asia was under the control of the British Raj and provided a ready market for the consumer products of Europe, an Englishman, William Lever, got a grant of nearly 2 million acres of land in the Congo for setting up an industry that would bring beauty products and creams created out of the Congo's palm oil. So, the vast expanse of Congolese forests was cleared and burnt for the first time in its history. The ancient historic forests were cleared and replaced with carefully laid palm trees that yielded palm fruits for a vast industrial network of oil and beauty products that were carried out through a newly laid train network and shipped to colonies and large markets like India, the crown in the jewel of the Raj.

Ambassador Rajeshwar Dayal and his wife Sushila Srivastava[16] had just settled into the aircraft in Brazzaville when he heard the heavy sound of military boots. The aircraft, full of passengers, was waiting for the plane heading to Paris to take off but an aggressive military commander with a group of security personnel entered the aircraft. Dayal saw the military men say a few words to the cabin attendants, who then hurried to the seat where he was sitting and broke the news that the Congolese military men wanted to question him. The leader of the team almost immediately came to the seat where the Indian couple sat and said that they suspected that a rebel leader of Congo was being smuggled in the aircraft by the Indian diplomat. An argument, which was peppered by intimidation and disagreement, ensued and finally, after some persuasion, the raiding team was convinced that Dayal was not smuggling any Congolese leader out of the country in the aircraft to Europe.

Congo was far from anything Rajeshwar Dayal had handled in his career as a civil servant and a foreign service officer. But conflict and turmoil were something that he had handled from the first day in the civil service, because he joined the service at a time when India was exploding with political turmoil and divisive politics. Conflict, therefore, was nothing new to Dayal. Dayal had started his career during the declining years of the British Raj, and like many of that era, his house reflected the fissured public sentiments of the time. Educated in Nainital, Dayal had a common link with Nehru as he went to study in Allahabad, Nehru's hometown. However, the real radical element of his life was his wife Sushila Srivastava, daughter of the powerful Sir J.P. Srivastava, the member of the wartime cabinet of the viceroy. With his 'Churchillian'[17] belly, cigar and whiskey glass, Sir JP was a favourite of the satirists and cartoonists, as he represented the comprador colonial elite of India. Sir JP's children rebelled against his political beliefs, and Sushila Srivastava, who returned from Cambridge in 1939, was part of the left-wing movement. In Cambridge, she fell in love with a scholar who hailed from a prominent Shia family of Mysore—Agha Hilaly.[18]

The Srivastavas, originally hailing from Kanpur, were known for their secular lifestyle, but they did not inter-marry with the Muslims of north India. So, the Sushila Srivastava-Agha Hilaly love was crushed, and she was married to fellow Kayasth civil servant Rajeshwar Dayal.[19] As the son-in-law of the powerful and influential Sir JP, Dayal was destined to have a bright career in the colonial set up. In the 1930s, Sir JP purchased *The Pioneer* and launched the Landowners' Party, which contested the 1937 election against the Congress but lost. Dayal's future father-in-law was rewarded for his strong loyalty to the king and the British Empire and was made the civil defence member of the viceroy's Executive Council. Rajeshwar Dayal belonged to a privileged section of Indian society which was navigating the crosscurrents of nationalist movement and a declining colonial administration, which was inexorably moving towards its exit from India. The Sir J.P. Srivastava Group gained fame during the 1920s and the 1930s because of the favourable treatment from the British government, which allowed the sugar and textile mills under his control to make enormous profit. But with the relentless march of the nationalist struggle, it became clear by the early and mid-1940s that freedom for India was inevitable. With the rise of the free Indian state, a new business class arose that displaced the likes of Sir JP. By the time of his death in 1954, Sir JP's industrial prominence had been replaced by the growing fame of his son-in-law and his daughter.

After his handling of the Tunisian issue at the United Nations, Dayal was transferred to Yugoslavia. The additional importance of Yugoslavia was because of the strong ties between Prime Minister Nehru and Yugoslav leader Marshal Tito. Rajeshwar Dayal had married Sushila Srivastava in 1948 and exactly a decade had passed when they were in Yugoslavia. It was then that big developments began to rock the Paris of the Orient, Beirut, the capital of Lebanon.

During India's Independence struggle, the leaders built close relations with the Arab nationalist leaders. The port of Suez was the favourite, and ships carrying Indian leaders, famous all over the world for their struggle against the mighty British Empire, would stop at the port, so the Indian leaders could interact with the Arab leaders. But soon after 1947, dramatic events began to take place in most of the Asian and African landmass—which included the historic Palestine where the first Jewish state, Israel, was born on 14 May 1948. The drumbeats of war which began playing with the birth of Israel led to two wars in quick succession within a span of eight years between 1948 and 1956. The second war, which was fought between Israel–UK–France and Egypt, gave India the first opportunity to get involved in the post-colonial conflicts of the region where the two Cold War blocs, riding on powerful ideologies like Zionism and Arab nationalism, nearly collided. The war broke out over Gamal Abdel Nasser's decision to nationalize the Suez Canal soon after the US and the UK withdrew their support for his dam project at Aswan. Spurned by the west, Nasser opened a new front by taking over the Suez Canal, the maritime artery that connects the Indian Ocean with the Mediterranean and the Atlantic Ocean. The war that broke out brought the UN on to the scene and the first UN Emergency Force (UNEF) was formed to safeguard the Gaza Strip, which was in Egyptian control. The UNEF, which came to stabilize the situation, included a good number of Indian soldiers as well. India was, therefore, gaining diplomatic leverage in the region even as the region remained in ferment.

The introduction of the Arab world's biggest crisis in the 1950s, however, followed a different trajectory, which was absolutely new for post-colonial India. Krishna Menon, Nehru's ambassador to the United States, had become a prominent figure mainly because of the fact that he was considered close to the Indian Prime Minister and partly also because the US was increasingly left without friends in Asia. The Soviet Union was a tough adversary and so was 'Red' China, which was holding American soldiers captive since the war in Korea a few years earlier. In fact, Krishna Menon went as far as requesting President Eisenhower to establish relations with the People's Republic of China, which was a staunch adversary of the US at the time. Left without any other friends, President Eisenhower had little option but to engage deeply with India, which followed neutrality in international affairs. With Egypt, UK, France and Israel caught in the Suez Crisis of 1956, Nehru arrived in Washington DC to discuss the war. The discussion with Prime Minister Nehru left no doubt in the mind of his host that India felt Nasser was the best option in a volatile region, and that removing him would open the floodgates of extremism and his successors would be far more radical than Nasser, which could be a long-term setback to the diplomatic goals of the United States. Nasser had already surprised the West with his moves and invited the Soviet engineers and technicians to operate the Suez Canal after the Anglo-French engineers were withdrawn. The increased Soviet presence around the Suez Canal could become even greater in case Nasser was forcibly removed for posing an immediate threat to global commerce. India's concern was to ensure safe passage for ships that could bring supplies and technology from Europe to its ports, but the Americans viewed the situation with worry, scanning the region for zones that could provide greater opportunity to the Soviets who were looking to expand influence, taking advantage of the power vacuum because of the decline of Anglo-French presence in the region. Weeks after Nehru visited Washington DC, President Eisenhower, in a special address, presented the Eisenhower Doctrine, which allowed any of the West Asian and North African countries facing possibilities of Soviet/communist takeover to seek assistance from the United States. The announcement escalated the situation. A year after President Eisenhower declared that the United States would intervene in the Arab world to prevent 'communist aggression', beginning a phase that was to last well into the twenty-first century, Egypt and Syria joined to form what was known as the United Arab Republic or UAR. With domestic problems in Lebanon increasing because of the highhandedness of the pro-West Camille Chamoun government, the situation quickly escalated as the Americans felt that an Egyptian–Syrian intervention in Lebanon was imminent. Chamoun, who had already extended his support to the Eisenhower doctrine, now urged the US to intervene militarily to contain the uprising against his government. The problem soon turned Gordian, and none of the primary actors—US, UAR, Lebanese leaders—were in a position to find a solution. As a result, the United Nations formed a crisis resolution team consisting of Ecuadorian diplomat Galo Plaza, Rajeshwar Dayal and Norway's Odd Bull. From 1952 to 1954, Dayal had served as India's PR or the Permanent Representative at the United Nations in New York, and during these crucial years he made an impression in the nascent UN bureaucracy, which felt that he could be of great help in difficult circumstances. His first tenure as the PR of India at the UN began at the fag end of the tenure of the first secretary-general of the UN—Trygve Lie—and continued with occasional interruptions of domestic Indian duties till the end of the tenure of the next secretary-general—Dag Hammarskjöld.

The Lebanese population constituted of the Maronite Christians, the Shiites, Sunnis, the Druze and other ancient groups—everyone belonged to some kind of a minority grouping or the other. There was intense rivalry among these groups in Lebanon, which had seen a change in power with the fall of the Government of Bishara Al Khoury and the advent of President Camille Chamoun. In Camille Chamoun, staunch anti-Soviet, Eisenhower had the ally he needed to counter Nasser. In the summer of 1958, when Chamoun sought a re-election, which was not allowed by the Lebanese constitution, the crisis turned into a street fight and several Lebanese protestors died in police firing. The crisis was complex—a government suffering from low public legitimacy sought foreign military assistance to quell a rebellion at home saying that a foreign power, the United Arab Republic, was assisting the rebels. The United Nations under Secretary-General Dag Hammarsköjld acted quickly on 11 June 1958 and formed the United Nations Observation Group in Lebanon (UNOGIL). The speed with which the United Nations, which was just over a decade old, acted in this case was to become a precedent for other crises that followed. Rajeshwar Dayal had left his station in Belgrade and gone to New Delhi for a vacation in June when the Lebanese crisis broke out. He received urgent summons from Hammersköjld, who wanted him to serve as part of three 'experienced and impartial personalities'.[20] Hammarsköjld's assignment for Dayal was to last six weeks, or through the summer months, and Dayal accepted the task, but what was supposed to be for a few weeks lasted six months.

For this complex and sensitive political mission, which involved the two Cold War blocs and regional political players like Egypt and Syria, Hammarsköjld chose Rajeshwar Dayal and Norwegian Major General Odd Bull under the chairmanship of Ecuadorian politician Gallo Plaza Lasso. Because of their immediate intervention, the Lebanese crisis could not escalate, but it gave an indication of the problems that lay ahead of Lebanon, Syria and the region—problems that would blow up two decades later with the beginning of the Lebanese civil war in 1975. But in 1958, because of the intervention from the UN and the fatigue of the immediate past conflict of 1956, the situation did not escalate further, and Lebanon's fragile social-political fabric received some temporary relief. For Rajeshwar Dayal, that international peace-making exposure was the beginning of a long innings in the business of peace. The Lebanese assignment by the 'three experienced and impartial personalities' was to give two more decades of peace for

Lebanon, which would not know peace for decades once the civil war broke out in the mid-1970s.

The presence of Indian soldiers in the UN mission in Gaza after the war of 1956 and the presence of Dayal in the Lebanese crisis of 1958 was a clear sign from the Nehru government that India would support the UN system's peace-making attempts. India had attained independence just a decade earlier and worldwide, there was a current of decolonization, but the world was also divided into Cold War blocs that made both decolonization as well as development for the newly independent countries difficult. The presence and investment in the multilateral platform of the United Nations was, therefore, vital to place India's opinion in cases that mattered to Indians. The strategy was to ensure that technology and assistance from the west as well as logistical support from the friendly countries like Egypt—which controlled access to India through its ownership of the Suez Canal and enjoyed popularity among vast sections of the Indian masses—could be ensured, as these were of great importance to the decade-old country.

Raj or Rajeshwar Dayal's career coincided with the setting of the colonial sun and the rising of the post-colonial rule, and it thus involved a large number of civil servants—both British and Indian—whose destinies would mingle with each other. Dayal belonged to one of the last few batches of Indian civil servants who would be called upon to serve the newly free India, but there were similarly talented British civil servants who had left India even as political independence was becoming a reality.

A year before Rajeshwar Dayal joined the ICS and was posted in the United Provinces, Ian Dixon Scott or Ian Scott was selected to be in the Indian Civil Service. Despite the ongoing protest against the colonial administration, the idea of serving in the Raj territory in the heart of India was still appealing for young officers of the Crown. Ian Scott prepared for his posting in India and chose Marathi as his language. Apart from the language, he was taught Indian history and Indian law. In those days, Bombay was connected to both the present-day Maharashtra, Gujarat as well as Sindh. Even though he was preparing for a posting near Bombay, where the language spoken was Marathi, ultimately, he would be posted in a far more challenging assignment. He arrived in Bombay for his service but immediately he was sent to Karachi where he had to learn Sindhi and worked as the assistant district officer for two years. He then moved 400 miles away to Sukkur, which was known for a major irrigation project built across the Sindh, where he served for a year as the assistant district officer before being ultimately transferred to the Indian Political Service and sent to the Northwest Frontier Province of the Pathans and the legendary Khan Abdul Gaffar Khan or Badshah Khan. He stayed for ten years. 'We lived in day-to-day crisis,' said Ian Scott, recounting the time that he spent in India.[21]

Scott's stint in the NWFP ended a decade later, after the end of World War II, when he was asked to proceed to Delhi for an interview with Viceroy Lord Wavell, who was presiding over a volatile confrontation between the Muslim League and the Congress, which was ruling eight provincial governments. He served as the deputy assistant secretary to Lord Wavell and then joined the staff of Lord Mountbatten as the date of transfer of power came closer. Ian Scott did not have any idea of the future that was waiting for him after the end of the British Empire, but his fate would draw him back to a project that India and Rajeshwar Dayal would be involved in.

In 1947, he was transferred to Karachi as Pakistan was born a day prior to India. Ian Scott would go on to play a role in multiple difficult scenarios soon after his departure from India, but even in the last days of his stay in South Asia, there were hints of what was to come. In Karachi, Scott and other British officials were staying on after the transfer of power. This phase was difficult particularly as the British civil servants, who till a few weeks earlier were in charge of the law-and-order scenario, were suddenly asked to stay at home and watch as the mayhem broke out. In Karachi, thousands of Hindus were asked to evacuate in trains and ships, and on one occasion the Hindu refugees, unable to evacuate because of a technical problem on their ship, were asked to spend the night in a temple. It was here that a frenzied crowd attacked them, taking advantage of the communal situation. The horror-filled screams were etched in the mind of Ian Scott, who recounted it towards the end of his life in an interview.[22]

At the end of his service in India, a new career awaited Ian Scott—just like several of his Indian contemporaries found a new career and opportunities in post-colonial India. Such friendships proved to be useful, as India wanted to engage the new world order on its own terms. Scott would not have to deal with the Indian leadership this time as he had to while serving in the office of Governor General Mountbatten in 1947. This time, he was to represent the UK as the British ambassador to Congo while Rajeshwar Dayal would represent his country and the United Nations. While the criticisms of continuing with the veteran ICS officers were well-known in the new Indian state, there were also some benefits of continuing with them as they had a social network that transcended national boundaries.

At this time, the United Nations was barely a decade old, but it was already a strong arbiter of the world divided into Cold War camps. Hammerskjöld was faced with the explosive crisis of the Congo, and he required a strong team. The crisis in Congo was partly created by an illusion. For decades, the Belgian rule had been extractive of Congo's resources, and the markets in the colonial world were flooded with products made from the naturally occurring oil and ingredients of Congo. The outside world chose to believe the appearance of the well-planned towns and the growth of infrastructure in Congo were signs that the country was progressing like other post-colonial societies. The good news came in during the Brussels Round Table Conference when independence was promised within six months. Independence, however, did not mean a change in the place of Congo in the global hierarchy where it was a crucial supplier of raw materials that determined the fates of several major industrial houses in the west. The crisis in Congo was because of many factors, but it was also because of lack of proper planning and capacity building. The Belgians were taken by the publicity of being a benevolent ruling class and the Congolese were swept away by the emotion of decolonization. The central government of Congo was unwilling to be governed by foreign forces after Independence and wanted to assert its authority. On the other hand, colonial residues survived in the Congolese army, which was mainly led by Belgian officers. The main weakness of the army was the seething discontent in its Congolese soldiers who rebelled against the Belgian officers four days after Independence. The all-round mayhem that broke out crippled life, and the administration in the 'infant state'[23] called for help from the United Nations.

6

VIDESH MANTRALAYA
THE MAN BEHIND THE TERM

THE NEHRU ERA WAS AT its peak in 1955 when Hindi gained momentum in the Ministry of External Affairs. It was felt that the language of the masses should be promoted, and the documents regarding diplomacy and foreign affairs should be made available in Hindi. For a few years, English had been the language of India's diplomatic activities. English dominated the corridors of power in the South Block. Now, Hindi, the language of news media and popular culture, had to be given a chance. But there were a few problems before Hindi could debut in the South Block.

The governance structure of new India was still under the grip of 'Raghuviri Hindi', a kind of Hindi that was being manufactured by Dr Raghuvir, a member of the Rajya Sabha in the Parliament who was among the enthusiastic supporters of Hindi in government affairs. Among his most famous contribution was the description of a train in Hindi—*lauhpath gamini*—which is recollected even in the twenty-first century as an example of a phase when the enthusiasm of a certain section of the political class was matched by the bureaucratic manhandling of Hindi's prospects. It was in this backdrop that a discussion was held in the presence of Prime Minister Nehru; it focused on deciding the Hindi names of the ministries of the Government of India. There was an overbearing tendency within the MEA to stick to literalness, without using wit and context, and that made translation a tedious job. The meeting took up the task of translating the 'External Affairs Ministry', and a group of linguists under the leadership of Dr Siddheshwar Verma zeroed in on *par-rashtra karya mantralaya*. The translators obviously felt it was necessary to find an equivalent word for 'affairs' and despite brainstorming for many hours had come to a consensus about getting rid of a lengthy translation. The need of the hour, however, was not a translation of the 'External Affairs Ministry' label, but an expression that could sum up these three words. At the meeting, it was Harivansh Rai Bachchan, the famous poet of Hindi, who suggested 'Videsh Mantralaya' as the Hindi equivalent of the 'External Affairs Ministry'. Jawaharlal Nehru favoured Bachchan's idea, and since then that has been the term used to refer to the Ministry of External Affairs in India. As a matter of fact, Harivansh Rai also suggested 'Desh Mantralaya' as the Hindi name for the Ministry of Home Affairs but that was not favoured as it seemed to encompass all ministries of the Government of India.

That Bachchan, one of the masters of twentieth-century Hindi literature, was part of the Indian Foreign Service is long forgotten and only a trivia seeker would get to know that the author of the landmark *Madhushala* (1935) was appointed an officer on special duty at the Ministry of External Affairs in December 1955. Bachchan was an established name in the Hindi literary scene and was a widely admired academic figure in Allahabad.

As a fellow resident of Allahabad, Harivansh Rai Bachchan was known to Nehru, since the much younger poet belonged to the cultural milieu of the Ganga–Jamuni Tehzeeb, which nurtured the unique nationalism of northern and eastern India, radiating from the universities and colleges of Allahabad, Patna and Calcutta. Bachchan was deeply convinced about the place of Hindi in the emerging India of the 1940s and the '50s. In the early 1950s, Harivansh Rai Bachchan applied and got admission offers from both Cambridge and Oxford to study English teaching methodologies. He was a widely celebrated Hindi poet, and his works were read in all literary meets or *sahitya sabhas*. The 1907-born Bachchan had pursued his literary ambition in difficult circumstances but never gave up and over time, became a votary of the greater use of Hindi in the affairs of the state.

There is no doubt that the admission that Bachchan secured in both Cambridge and Oxford were in recognition of his fame as an author in a modern Indian language, which was yet to be discovered by the West. Having secured the admission, he went to Delhi and met Education Secretary Humayun Kabir, who was prompt in dismissing any possible scholarship for Bachchan. A similar near-dismissal came also from Maulana Azad, the education minister of the Nehru cabinet. Having met a series of rejections, Bachchan sought time from Prime Minister Nehru and met him in the Parliament. Nehru remembered Bachchan, the poet, and gave a patient hearing. On learning that he had failed in securing a scholarship, Nehru called his personal secretary in Parliament, B.N. Kaul, and asked him to arrange a scholarship of Rs 8,000 for Harivansh Rai Bachchan. Armed with the scholarship, Bachchan, a young father of two young boys named Amitabh and Ajitabh, left his family behind to spend fifteen months dedicated to research and writing. The connect thus forged between the poet and the first Prime Minister of India was strong.

At the Ministry of External Affairs, Bachchan was shocked at the state of the 'Hindi Section'. Everything about this section in the ministry was contradictory. The letter that reached him with the job offer was written in English and the Hindi 'Section' had just a room to itself, with a table and three chairs. The main issue, though, as Bachchan found out soon, was not the lack of physical facilities but the *use* of Hindi. He argued strongly in favour of using Hindi.

While the exposure to the MEA and diplomacy were new elements to Bachchan, the corridors of the government and the whims of new ministers in the post-1947 India and the bureaucracy were not novelties for him. He had earlier worked at All India Radio, where the minister B.V. Keskar had introduced many radical changes that drew strong responses from poets and the literary crowd of Allahabad, Patna and Delhi. In 1955, Keskar, the minister of information and broadcasting, visited Allahabad. One of his major initiatives led to the appointing of 'established writers'[1] as producers of All India Radio with the aim of exploiting their fine modern literary and language skills available for spreading radio across the country. In September that year, Bachchan was appointed as a producer of Hindi at Allahabad Radio Station on a one-year contract and a monthly salary of Rs 750. From a teacher, Bachchan thus became a producer of All India Radio. In the winter of that year, Harivansh Rai Bachchan took leave to participate in *kavi sammelans* (poet gatherings) in Benares Hindu University and at Holkar College Indore. Soon after he reached Indore, a trunk call from his wife Teji Bachchan informed him that the Ministry of External Affairs had informed her that Harivansh Rai, so far known as a teacher, a poet and a name on All India Radio, was now appointed at the Ministry of External Affairs as an 'Officer on

Special Duty (Hindi)' with a salary of Rs 1,000. This was a slight improvement for the poet from the Rs 750 that he was drawing at All India Radio. Teji Bachchan advised her husband to leave for Delhi immediately, as the next day happened to be a Tuesday, an auspicious day for fresh beginnings. On 27 December, Harivansh Rai Bachchan, whose poetry would gain worldwide fame, joined the MEA as the person in charge of promoting Hindi in India's diplomatic affairs. Promoting Hindi was not easy for Bachchan as the culture of having an official language was still new. The appointment letter described Bachchan's job as 'to help and assist in the progressive use of Hindi in the Ministry of External Affairs', and he would soon have a taste of what that job would look like.

One day, the sub-committee on non-scientific vocabulary met under the chairship of Ramdhari Singh Dinkar, whose poem would later become the rousing call against Indira Gandhi's Emergency rule. The discussion progressed somewhat like this. First came the dilemma over what should be the Hindi term for 'customs', which they decided to call *sima shulka*. Next came 'Customs House', which was named *Sima Shulka Sadan;* and finally came the quest for the Hindi equivalent of customs house officer, which was translated as *sima shulka sadan adhikari*. At this point adding a dash of humour, Dinkar said that the three Hindi phrases could be passed as a *chaupai* from Hindi poet Tulsidas.

Bachchan later recollected about the work that he was expected to do for the budget session.

It was decided, soon after his arrival at the MEA, that the annual report of the ministry, which is generally published in English, should for a change be accompanied by a Hindi translation. Nehru wanted Bachchan to lead the effort and write the translation in a 'clear and accessible style that could form a model for other ministries'.[2] Bachchan and his teammates from the tiny Hindi division completed the translation on time. This drew a great deal of appreciation from the Prime Minister.

A fortnight before the budget session, Nehru placed a dictum outside every office that read, 'I am not interested in excuses for the delay, I am only interested in work done on time.' Needless to say, there was a great deal of pressure on all departments to complete the work ahead of the deadline. Bachchan's work at the MEA was a landmark of sorts in the promotion of a post-colonial language to the status of a near national language with extensive official usage, and expectedly, there were many problems that he encountered. For example, there were many English words of a technical nature that did not have Hindi equivalents. To deal with their translation, Bachchan adopted a liberal attitude, and he borrowed extensively words from Persian, Arabic, Sanskrit and even English and other local languages.

The exposure to South Block was a shock for Bachchan. Apart from the dilapidated and neglected condition of the facilities dedicated to the Hindi Section, there was an all-round air of denigration of the language. All communication in the ministry was conducted in English, and use of Hindi was mocked at. Bachchan made his presence felt in the MEA by suggesting that only Hindi should be used in the staff room of the ministry. He was reminded of the rule of Ranjit Pandit, the late husband of Vijaya Lakshmi Pandit who had suggested that only Hindi would be permitted to be spoken in the circular room of Anand Bhavan. Bachchan felt that Pandit's initiative was effective as he made everyone who violated his principle pay a fine. Needless to say, given the all-India nature of the staff room of the MEA, Bachchan's diktat had no chance of success. Nevertheless, he became the first serious champion of Hindi in the MEA. A major part of Bachchan's responsibility in the MEA included translating the speeches of the

President and the Vice President which obviously included good segments on foreign affairs. Bachchan was grateful for the support that he received from Nehru for promotion of Hindi, but he held his own when it came to holding the integrity of Hindi in the face of other languages.

Harivansh Rai Bachchan saw that Nehru and Gandhi believed that there was a 'common form of language' between the two '"pure" extremes of Hindi and Urdu'. Nehru believed in this middle ground language between Hindi and Urdu, but Bachchan did not. He would often argue with Nehru about his dream of a 'common form of language', but neither he nor Nehru changed their respective positions.[3] Out of the decade in the MEA, Bachchan spent eight years under Nehru, and he would go on to work on a Hindi–Urdu dictionary, which Nehru commissioned two years before his death. Bachchan, the Hindi purist, did not agree with Nehru's quest and was not surprised that the dictionary, which was published after Nehru's demise in 1964 by the Central Hindi Directorate, remained unsold. The volumes, according to him were 'fodder for the ants in some godown'.[4] Bachchan's purist style was not based on some dogma. He just believed that Hindi should be 'laced' with both Sanskrit, on one hand, and Persian, Arabic and Turkish, on the other, but 'laden' with neither. This interesting attitude would go on to create the easy official Hindi that continues to be in use in the Ministry of External Affairs.

Soon Bachchan came up with the idea of teaching Hindi to the non-Hindi speakers in the MEA, and for this he created a curriculum. The first person who was drawn to the experiment was a Tamil-speaker, which brought some satisfaction to Bachchan. However, soon, an official Hindi training module was set up, and professional teachers were recruited, bringing Bachchan's own experiment of teaching Hindi to non-Hindi speakers within the ministry to an early end. In the meanwhile, Bachchan tutored several fresh IFS recruits—including K. Natwar Singh—in Hindi.[5] Undaunted, he also experimented with annotating files in Hindi and drew a strong negative response. When he sent Hindi notes to English files, the response was: 'Kindly translate into English'. The note was not a sign that the recipient officer was unfamiliar with Hindi, rather that this sort of initiative was not welcome to the serving bureaucrats. Perhaps they felt that the poet was clearly out of rhythm in his initiatives. Bachchan soon came to the understanding that the entire Hindi department of the MEA itself was a 'cunning diplomatic subterfuge'.[6] Bachchan reached the conclusion that for Hindi to prosper in the corridors of power, the desire to have 'Hindi sections' should be eliminated, and officers should be forced to carry on business in Hindi with whatever understanding of the language they could muster. By this time, obviously, the entire ministry had learnt of the initiatives of Bachchan, and a call came from Foreign Secretary Subimal Dutt who urged him politely to go slow. 'A more outspoken and less seasoned officer than Subimal Dutt might have put it more plainly: "Do what you're told to do, and keep your suggestions to yourself.",' Bachchan wrote.[7]

This was by far the most adventurous part of his stint in the MEA.

After settling into the MEA, Bachchan had taken an assistant translator, Ajit Shankar Chaudhuri, who later became known as Ajit Kumar in the Hindi literary world. It was here that Bachchan had his first brush with the famous Nehru temper. Bachchan's autobiography has a recollection of the difficulties that he and his family of four faced during the early months of his stay in Delhi and how Nehru had personally intervened to ensure the Bachchans got a decent accommodation, but when he found that the famous poet was getting carried away by his literary temperament instead of the administrative and pragmatic requirements of his job, Nehru did not hesitate from raising his voice. As per the established convention, the President of India had to address a joint session of both the Houses of the Parliament, where members of the Lok Sabha and the Rajya Sabha had to be present. As per practice, the President of India would deliver a speech in English, which would be followed by the Vice President reading a translation of the same speech in Hindi. On this particular occasion, President Sarvepalli Radhakrishnan thus had to deliver the speech in English and a translated version was to be delivered by the Vice President. On the scheduled date, the English speech by the President reached Harivansh Rai Bachchan, and he produced a first-rate Hindi translation of the text and sent the draft to the PM, who would naturally take a look before passing it on.

Unexpectedly, a call came in for Bachchan from the PM. Nehru wanted to see him in his study in Teen Murti Bhavan. He had the copy of Bachchan's translated speech before him. He said he had done a 'good job', but the complexity of his literary Hindi had made the text 'obscure'.[8]

Then came the sign that Nehru had run out of patience. There was no doubt that Bachchan was a legendary poet who was forced to work as a translator for the Ministry of External Affairs, a job that probably did not suit his public stature. But he was a special translator chosen by Prime Minister Nehru himself. So here was the perfect clash of egos of two men held in high esteem in their respective domains of governance and literature. Nehru pointed out that the high-quality Hindi of the translation would have suited any other person but in this particular case, the speech was to be delivered by Vice President Zakir Husain.

'Do you realize who is to read this speech? Dr Zakir Husain—and he won't even be able to pronounce some of the words you have used,' Nehru said. Bachchan had enough by this time, and he said, 'Panditji, language cannot be changed to suit the convenience of some individual's pronunciation; why don't you have the speech translated into Urdu?' Nehru exploded.

'*There is enough trouble in this country*. Even if we get it translated into Urdu, we'd have to call it Hindi—and what's the difference between the two, anyway?'[9] Bachchan, in his honest endeavours, had forgotten the realities of India and was about to get the Vice President of India into a difficult situation. The Vice President stumbling over difficult Hindi words while reading a speech in the Parliament would not have gone down well before the media and the critics of the Nehru government. And Nehru was also right to some extent in his own way because the speech could not possibly have been translated into Urdu, as the Indian Constitution only allowed for the use of Hindi speeches in such sessions, and a Hindi speech with many Urdu words, therefore, would have to be called a 'speech in Hindi' and not an Urdu speech. The clash was won by Nehru, who regained his composure quickly and charmingly asked Bachchan to go back and produce a text that Dr Zakir Husain would not find difficult to read. Bachchan obliged.

The spat, however, highlighted Bachchan and Nehru's differences as far as language was concerned. Nehru believed that there was a middle path for Hindi and Urdu, where both the languages could borrow from each other and thrive, but Bachchan disagreed with that thought. He felt there existed a pure Hindi, which could have a separate identity away from Urdu. Hindi could have the influence of Urdu, Farsi and Arabic, but it could not be tied into a creole form by mixing it with other languages. Bachchan was fired by the zeal to create a new language for a new India, and he did not hesitate to cross swords with the Prime Minister, who in his case was also his employer.

In 1957, Guru Dutt's *Pyaasa* hit theatres across India. The hauntingly beautiful film carried a political message. For the first time, Indian cinema was being used to express disappointment with national politics. The spirit of independence, which pervaded India and its Bandung days of 1955, was now a thing of the past, and there was cynicism in the air as reflected in *Pyaasa*'s song, '*Yeh duniya agar mil bhi jaaye toh kya hai* (What's the use of this world even if we make it ours)'. The protagonist was shown capturing the feelings of the era by singing the words of poet Sahir Ludhianvi, saying, '*Yeh mehlo, yeh takhto, yeh taajo ki duniya, yeh insaan ke dushman samaajo ki duniya ... yeh duniya agar mil bhi jaaye toh kya hai?* (These thrones, these palaces are of a world that is the enemy of mankind. So, what is the use of this world?)' The young of the generation had been disappointed. The refugee influx from the west and the east were shaking India to the core, its economy was struggling to stand on its toes and corruption at high places was no longer rare. That year, the Prime Minister's son-in-law, Feroze Gandhi, had brought to light the Mundhra scandal. Freedom, for which millions sacrificed their lives, and wealth were not safe anymore, and the disillusionment had started with the Nehruvian age. '*Jala do ise, phunk daalo yeh duniya* (Burn down this world),' sang Guru Dutt. That growing disillusionment with Nehruvian domestic politics indicated a shift in political culture, national security and subsequently the foreign affairs of India.

It was in this context that an elaborate plot was discovered in India. It was reported that revolutionary Ranbir Singh Sehgal had met Abdul Qayum Khan, the Pakistani Muslim League leader, and the two plotted the murder of the Prime Minister and Home Minister Govind Ballabh Pant in May of 1957. It came to light that Khan had promised help to Sehgal; if Sehgal and his friends could assassinate Nehru, then Khan and his supporters in the Pakistani intelligence services promised to send them sufficient money and weapons in assistance to bring in a revolution in India.[10] The entire case was laid bare by one Jarnail Singh, a co-conspirator who had turned approver and helped the government in dealing with the investigation.

The Ranbir Singh Sehgal case revealed that India's security was fragile and could be disturbed by myriad elements both internal and external. The case tried in the court of Sardar Pritam Singh Pattar, the additional sessions judge in Ambala, showed that external elements with the help of revolutionaries in India could easily ignite a serious law and order problem. The Indian state had become independent, but its share of security threats had also increased many times. The case was widely reported and all the five accused—Ranbir Singh Sehgal, Hira Dass, Harbhajan Dass, Pritam Dass and Suchittar Singh—pleaded not guilty to the charge. Jarnail Singh revealed that the Pakistani government's senior police officials, Nazir Ahmed Rizvi, Ghulam Hussain Butt and Agha Mohammed Ali, had given Sehgal modern weapons and ammunition with the aim of unleashing a gun and bomb attack targeting Prime Minister Nehru when he was being driven towards Manali. Assassination was no stranger to South Asian politics. During the anti-British struggle, many British officials were targeted and killed or wounded by Indian revolutionaries. This found a new beginning with the murder of Mahatma Gandhi on 30 January 1948. In Pakistan, Liaquat Ali Khan, the first Prime Minister of Pakistan, was murdered on 16 October 1951. The post-Independence period was expected to be an age of milk and honey, but events proved that India had a long road ahead before achieving the ideals for which the nationalist leaders suffered long years of hardship and many jail terms.

Among the incidents that indicated the changing times and emerging problems at hand was the murder of Ajai Kumar Mitra. Mitra had started his career in the Imperial Tobacco Company of India, where he worked till September 1949 and became a direct recruit in the Indian Foreign Service, which he joined on 27 September 1949. His recruitment made him a contemporary of Rasgotra, Muthamma and Deva Rao Baglodi, the other direct IFS recruits of that year. He knew Bengali, Hindi, Urdu, French and Spanish, and also spoke Portuguese as an optional language. With a command over several European languages, it was natural that Mitra would be drawn to Europe. In December 1961, Mitra was posted in the Indian Embassy in Vienna. On 7 December 1961, Mitra reportedly received an anonymous threatening phone call. Following this, he sought police protection. A week later, he told a colleague to be with him as some visitors were expected to meet him. It was this colleague who found Mitra in a near coma on 13 December. On medical examination, it was found that Mitra had taken a large number of sleeping pills. The doctors were surprised by the number of pills that Mitra had taken. To add to the mystery, Mitra's young son had gone missing almost simultaneously. It was known that Mitra hailed from an affluent family and that they owned several sugar mills in India.

With the murder of diplomat Mitra in Vienna came the rumour that he was involved in a sensitive mission to prevent the smuggling of gold. The details of his mission were not known, but his colleagues maintained that his mission involved preventing gold smuggling. They maintained that Mitra was instrumental in the nabbing of several smugglers in India. What, however, added to the mystery was the fact that foul play was suspected in the incident, but a month later, the Austrian authorities declared that Mitra had committed suicide.

The controversy, however, refused to die down and was taken up in the Parliament by leaders like Renu Chakravartty of the left and Hari Vishnu Kamath of the Forward Bloc who said that the death appeared suspicious. Kamath alleged that just before his death, Mitra had filed a report to the Government of India that revealed that certain 'highly placed persons' were involved in a gold smuggling racket. Prime Minister Nehru assured the members of Parliament that the matter would be looked into.[11]

It was February of 1962 and the chief secretary of Tripura, B.N. Raman, had a unique problem in hand. He was told that three visitors from Dhaka had arrived in Agartala and were now demanding to meet him. The superintendent of jail in the capital of the state, which was still being governed by a Territorial Council and was under the heavy influence of the benevolent royal family, had informed him that the three were led by a distinguished politician who has been a member of Parliament in Pakistan and used to reside in Karachi but left the city once Martial Law was first announced in 1958 under General Ayub Khan. The visitors insisted on total secrecy but obviously had a political agenda. The sudden appearance, the name of the leader of the small delegation and their remarks came as a surprise to the jail superintendent of Agartala.

In the spring of 1962, the political atmosphere of South Asia was vastly different from what it was to become later in the 1960s and especially in October–November that year when the Sino-

Indian war broke out. The borders between India and Pakistan were not heated, and the border between India and East Pakistan was especially placid although the Intelligence Bureau kept a sharp eye on the developments inside East Pakistan. Linguistic disaffection had begun in East Pakistan with the Language Movement or Bhasha Andolan that took off on 21 February 1952, when thousands of people, especially students of Dhaka and other parts of East Pakistan, defied the Government of Pakistan. The movement was followed by the emergence of the demand for self-rule in the legislative assembly election of 1954 in East Pakistan. Indian authorities kept a close watch on the developments in that region, but few expected that a secret political delegation would reach Agartala—instead of Kolkata or even Cooch Behar—across the eastern frontier of East Pakistan. The obvious reason in selecting Agartala for such a rendezvous was to keep the exchanges low profile and below the radar of the East Pakistan authorities.

Raman, an Andhra Pradesh cadre IAS officer, was told that the person who was insistent on maintaining secrecy was Mujibur Rahman, one of the tallest leaders of the Awami League. Sheikh Sahib or Sheikh Mujib was yet to be known as Bangabandhu, a title that he would earn at the peak of the struggle for the liberation of Bangladesh.

Sometime after the announcement of Martial Law, Sheikh Mujib took a flight from Karachi and returned to Dhaka. He began as a staunch supporter of Pakistan, but the dream broke up with the imposition of Martial Law as participatory democracy was dealt a death blow. Mujib planned a secret and low-profile visit to India and only shared the news with his close friends Tarek Ahmed Choudhury and Malik Moazzam Hossain who owned a tea estate near the border of Tripura. Both Hossain and Choudhury were his friends since his student days in Kolkata. The plan was to travel by train from Dhaka till the train station nearest to the tea estate, and then he would reach the western border of Tripura with the help of local supporters of the Awami League. From the beginning of his political life, Sheikh Mujib was fond of students in schools, colleges and universities, and with time, these youngsters provided him with a major network of supporters, especially in East Pakistan. Several students and student leaders were roped in by him to act as supporters for the Agartala trip, but none of them knew anything about the final destination of the journey. The plan, as it was understood, was made to avoid detection by the intelligence operatives of the Government of Pakistan who used to maintain a strong presence in the railway station in Dhaka to prevent political figures from travelling out of the city. Among the democratic leaders, the military government kept a strong watch on Sheikh Mujib, and he was under strict orders not to travel out of Dhaka. Sheikh Mujib thus planned the outing from Dhaka with caution, keeping in mind the chances of being spotted.

In view of the surveillance risk at the railway station of Dhaka, the plan was for Mujib's closest supporters to board the train there and then help Mujib board the train a little distance away from the city at Tongi. Accordingly, he asked a young activist who was studying engineering, Mortuza Khan, to work with him on the journey. Mortuza reserved a compartment and boarded the train at Dhaka station; a second compartment was booked by Tarek Hossein Choudhury, who was a law student and activist for the Awami League. Soon after the train left the Dhaka station, Mortuza pulled the chain, brought the train to a halt and deboarded the train while helping Sheikh Mujib and his companion Reza Ali to board the train.

The journey of Sheikh Mujib to Agartala was a thrilling, perilous adventure unheard of in the history of politics in South

Asia till then. For decades, there was no definitive account of that journey, and though the definitive account was first printed by a publisher in Dhaka who accessed the manuscript of late journalist Anil Bhattacharya, it is not yet fully known who on the Indian side assisted Sheikh Mujib in organizing his journey. However, it is clear that Sheikh Mujib had alerted different persons in different localities and had entrusted them with responsibilities to make the journey possible. For example, neither the train's driver nor the security guards came to check on the cause of the chain-pulling despite the disruption that it caused. This smooth chain-pulling has convinced some people that Sheikh Mujib had planned it with the secret support of the cadre of his party coming from different walks of life, including employees in the railways.[12]

The wars of 1962 and 1965 were yet to erupt and the final showdown of 1971 was even further away, but there were signs all around that the era of idealism, as displayed by the Nehru government in handling questions on Tunisia, the Hungarian uprising and the Suez Canal crisis of 1956, was coming to a close. A harder and more ruthless order was emerging.

7

THE FIRST EVACUATION OF INDIANS IN A FOREIGN CRISIS

WORLD WAR II ENDED WITH the beginning of an era of fear, and no one represented that more than US Senator Joseph McCarthy. Alongside fear, there was equal amount of hope. The philosophers who had left continental Europe had established themselves in western universities. Soldiers who fought in the war now returned home and became novelists and journalists. By 1953 there were signs of fear all around, but rebellion was not far behind—James Baldwin had debuted with his stunning literature on the American scene. African Americans were asserting themselves despite rising incidents of lynching and riots.

Then, history took a definite turn on 29 August 1949. At 6 a.m. on that day, Lavrentiy Beria, chair of the special committee on the atom bomb, and scientific director of the Soviet nuclear weapons programme, Igor Kurchatov, waited in a safe location with a door open to watch their creation light up the sky. At the prefixed moment, the Soviet atomic bomb exploded atop a tower in Semipalatinsk, Kazakhstan. As the fireball rose towards the sky, drawing into its fiery mouth, dust, bricks and construction materials from houses that were built to test the power of the weapon, a terrifying shockwave spread all around the experimental site. The Soviet scientists were scared of failure because the Soviet ruler Stalin, the slayer of Nazi Germany, was unforgiving when it came to those who did not deliver what he wanted, and he wanted parity with the United States—not in firepower but in nuclear power, something that had overshadowed Soviet glory in the last phase of the war when the Soviet tanks rolled into Nazi concentration camps and liberated victims of the Holocaust. Beria knew what Stalin would ask him. The hungry red mouth now engulfing everything that his eyes could see on the horizon left no doubt that this was indeed the weapon that had reminded American physicist J. Robert Oppenheimer of the Bhagavad Gita conversation between Sri Krishna and warrior prince Arjuna. Krishna, the charioteer, had taken the form of the Lord of the universe to convince the prince to fight and said, 'I am time, the destroyer of the worlds.' As Beria looked through the door, he could see that exact same destroyer of the worlds—death itself. But it was not enough; Beria wanted to be certain, and he famously asked, 'Is it the same as the American one?' Beria's question expressed the anxiety that was felt in the Soviet bloc and the United States, where it echoed and ricocheted till it created the 'red scare'. And it was in the midst of this decade of paranoia, long before the arrival of the Indian IT industry, that the Indian diplomats stationed in New York witnessed the first sensational success story of an Indian entrepreneur.

Sajjan Singh Sarna, a Sikh from Rawalpindi, belonged to a well-regarded Sikh family. The Sarnas were known to have descended from a family of devout Sikhs who had worked between Kashmir

P.R.S. Mani (on the right) during his military years.

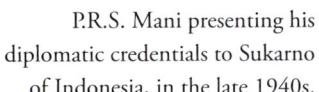

P.R.S. Mani presenting his diplomatic credentials to Sukarno of Indonesia, in the late 1940s.

In this 1958–59 photo, Chairman Mao (in the middle) is seen along with the Chinese chief of protocol. The Indians from the left: Sudarshan Kumar Bhutani (IFS, 1955), third secretary; K.M. Kannampilly (INA veteran, joined diplomatic service in 1947 but confirmed in the IFS Senior Scale in 1955), counsellor; G. Parthasarathy, ambassador of India to China; Brigadier Sharma, military attaché; Sumal Sinha (IFS, 1948), first secretary; Shankar Mishra of the Intelligence Bureau; and Mira Ishardas Malik (IFS, 1954), third secretary in the Embassy of India in Beijing.

Mira Ishardas Malik visiting a factory in China in the 1950s.

A driving licence for small vehicles issued to Mira Ishardas Malik by Chinese authorities during her stint in Beijing (from May 1957 to 1961).

Mira Ishardas Malik with Sumal Sinha. They got married but separated soon after their posting in China in the late 1950s.

Mira Ishardas Malik travelling in China.

Dileep Kamtekar (third from the right) with Indira Gandhi and Sanjay Gandhi (sixth from the right) during a 1970 Mauritius visit.

K.M. Kannampilly (standing) and M.S. Devadas during their teaching days, before WWII. This photo is probably from the late 1930s.

From left to right: Jawaharlal Nehru, M.R.A. Baig, Panchen Lama, Chou En-lai and Dalai Lama at a cultural event during Chou's visit to Delhi.

The Kannampilly family in Rangoon in 1953.

K.M. Kannampilly at work.

Kannampilly in Beijing in the late 1950s or early 1960s.

Ambassador Kannampilly and wife K. Madhavi in Jakarta in 1969. Jakarta was his last posting. (Photo courtesy: Balachandran Kannampilly)

The Kannampilly family in Kerala in 1982.

M.R.A. Baig (second from left) with Jawaharlal Nehru and Chou En-lai.

Nehru with M.R.A. Baig, wife Tara Baig, daughter Ayesha and son Zahid, in 1961.

Nehru and Baig with Vice President S. Radhakrishnan.

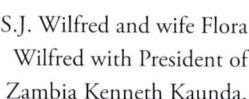

Nehru with Baig at South Block during a visit by foreign dignitaries.

S.J. Wilfred and wife Flora Wilfred with President of Zambia Kenneth Kaunda.

```
                    1, Safdarjung Road           MINISTER
                    New Delhi              INFORMATION & BROADCASTING
                                                   INDIA

                                            October 9, 1964

         My dear Flora,

                  Your nice drum arrived a long time ago but
         I cannot remember whether I have written to you
         to thank you for it.  I am living in such a rush that
         it is becoming more and more difficult to keep up
         with any personal correspondence.  Today I am specially
         busy as I leave for Europe tomorrow evening to
         attend the Executive Board of UNESCO as well as other
         work including some connected with my Ministry.

                  Mrs. Mukul Banerjee who is taking this letter
         is an old friend.  She has been incharge of Women's
         Department and the Foreign Department of our Congress
         Party for many years and is an able and enthusiastic
         person as well as extremely nice.

                  With every good wish to you and Mr. Wilfrid,

                                          Yours sincerely,

                                              Indira

         P.S. The nicest room in my new
         house is the library which is decorated
         with all the African things I brought back
         from my trip.
```

Indira Gandhi's letter to Flora Wilfred.

Wilfred with daughter Shanthy in Salisbury (Harare).

Indira Gandhi with Flora and S.J. Wilfred in British Guyana.

Chandra Shekhar Jha during his 1962–1964 posting in Canada as the Indian high commissioner.

A telegram from Israel PM David Ben-Gurion to Nehru, assuring support to India during the 1962 war.

A copy of *History of Services*.

K. Natwar Singh with a copy of *History of Services*.

and Punjab and were known to have served the faith wholeheartedly. He left for the United States in his youth and grew up to be a pioneering businessman who made a career by selling items that fascinated Americans. Americans in the 1920s viewed India as a land of exotic faith and practices on the other side of the planet and Sarna soon evolved into an importer of Indian textiles, incense and metal items. His family recounted that sometime in the early 1950s, Sajjan Singh Sarna dreamt of bells. Bells are associated with temples and places of worship in India as well as with cows that often can be seen sporting them around their necks while grazing. The sound of the metal bells of his dreams was similar to the ones that he had seen in his childhood. A sudden fascination grew inside him. In the meanwhile, after Partition, his family, which was based in Lahore, had shifted to Delhi and Moradabad. His cousins had opened a brass handicrafts unit, which was being looked after by his cousin Mahinder and his wife Harmohini. Sarna came up with the idea of bringing the bells of India to his adopted homeland. He sensed, there was a market for the bells around Christmas. The bells arrived in Sajjan Sarna's store, and he started treating them as separate individuals with names and attributes written for each of them. Each bell came in a different shape and style. Some were manufactured for Christmas and had Santa Claus etched on them, and others were inspired by ghunghru bells; many were designed to swing in the air to create a serene atmosphere.

The bells that he sold from his New York store went on to become a phenomenon and the Bells of Sarna brand became part of the Christmas season as well as daily life and train culture of the US, as the Sarna bells were used in railways. This was a success of Indian soft power manufactured by ingenious Indians who valued family ties while also displaying a desire to bridge unfamiliar terrain. The success of this typical Indian business strategy added wind to the wings of India's new-found identity. India was a newly decolonized country, and the Sarna bells announced India's arrival. One of those who witnessed the spectacular public success of this typical Indian business in New York was Eric Gonsalves, the vice consul in the very small Indian Consulate General in New York City where he served from March 1954 to August 1955.[1]

America was gripped by fear and an obsession with the Soviet Union when Rose and Eric Gonsalves arrived in New York. Indians were a new community in New York, which had a great reputation as the city of immigrants. New York was the city where they came to be saved, and it was expected to be different from their place of origin, where they had faced hardships. In the overwhelming environment of fear, New York was expected to be an island of solace. Living up to the expectation, the city turned out to be the opposite of fear, and the arrival of the Bells of Sarna showed the Gonsalves family that there is a warmer side to the United States.

Very soon they would discover this warmer side personally. Rose Gonsalves conceived her first child in New York and had a premature delivery. The young couple had no family members in New York, although they did have Jewish neighbours who were warm and supportive. Gonsalves did not have sufficient money, and so he had to take a loan. The lawyer working for the consulate stepped forward to help him secure it, and his neighbours helped at home and the hospital. The doctor in the hospital did not take his full fees and only took what the Consulate's allocation was for such cases—which was a small part of the doctor's fees. The warmth that American society displayed convinced Gonsalves that there is a warmer side to American society beyond the environment of fear. This experience would stay with him and help him later in career.

The past sits on India in layers, but Burma Bazar of contemporary Chennai has little trace of its past. Beginning with the late 1950s a series of events unfolded right in Burma and would ultimately facilitate the creation of the bazar on the other side of the Bay of Bengal.

Decolonization of the landmasses of Asia and Africa was one of the pillars of the Nehru government, but the removal of colonial control unleashed long-buried divisiveness in certain areas. Decolonization left Myanmar particularly vulnerable to this problem, as the end of British control quickly unveiled ethnic tensions targeting Indians in particular. The Burmese Republic was born on 4 January 1948 and immediately thereafter the new state began serving notice to Indian-origin government employees who had been employed there since the days of the British Empire in South Asia. Both India and Burma were new South-Southeast Asian post-colonial states with intersecting nationalities and ethnicities that dated back to the colonial political order. However, patience was not a virtue of decolonization, and Burma displayed that problem right at the beginning. Unlike the Indian political leadership, which was reconciled with diversity, the Burmese rulers were oriented towards uniformity. The new Burmese government asked the Indian employees to leave as they were considered outsiders. India maintained friendly ties with Burma while maintaining a sympathetic attitude to the Indians there. New Delhi wanted to ensure that the employees that Burma wanted to sack should be given financial compensation like salary and pension. Alternatively, Delhi was inclined towards providing employment to them in India. The second option, however, was not countered by the fact that the creation of Pakistan had unleashed a major refugee crisis that had put pressure on India's economy. The problem with Burma strangely increased with the end of decolonization, which would reach its climax by the time Gonsalves would be sent there.

He had come to Yangon, after a stint in the headquarters, where he had framed the IFS PLCA (Pay, Leave and Compensatory Allowances) Rules of 1961 that gave the service discipline and orientation over the coming years.

There were signs of trouble as Prime Minister Nehru was ageing, and political activities in the region had intensified. Gonsalves landed in Yangon to join the Indian Embassy under Ambassador Rangiah Subra Mani, a former ICS officer who had earlier served in Baghdad.

Gonsalves had just settled into the Indian Embassy when the 2 March 1962 coup took place in Myanmar, overthrowing the government of Prime Minister U. Nu, who had ruled in 1948–58 and again from 1960 till the coup that brought to power the first military ruler in General Ne Win.

The shock of the coup can be measured by the fact that New Delhi hosted U. Nu, Madam Nu and their daughter during 11–17 January 1962. The Burmese Prime Minister was accompanied by a big delegation. Next was the visit by the Armed Forces Goodwill Mission comprising the members of the Burmese Army, Navy and the Air Force for a twelve-day long sojourn starting on 23 January.

U. Nu was one of the founders of the non-aligned movement, and the arrival of the military ruler was a shocker to Prime Minister Nehru who considered U. Nu to be a close associate. He was a regular visitor to India. In March 1960, U. Nu visited India on a pilgrimage just before he went into election and visited again during 11–21 November that same year.[2]

Before that, U. Nu invited Nehru on a visit to Yangon, and the two together toured Rourkela and Bhilai, where the new steel plants were under construction. It was also during the U. Nu era that Burma passed laws that would later trigger one of the biggest problems of post-1947 India. During this period, the Burmese Parliament passed the Burma Immigration (Emergency Provisions) (Amendment) Act, 1957 and the Registration of Foreigners (Amendment) Act, 1957. According to the Burma Immigration (Emergency Provisions) (Amendment) Act, 1957, the Government of Burma could 'deport' any foreigner if they found him or her in violation of the provisions of the Act.[3] It was, of course, promised that the law would not be used to target Indians and other foreigners 'harshly or unjustly'.[4] After Independence, Burma had begun to experience crippling economic challenges and the foreigners were facing difficulties in sending remittances home. India took up the problems of the nationals residing in Burma. The legal justification for a crackdown on the 'foreigners' was ready, and the arrival of Ne Win gave Burma that opportunity. Ne Win was not a stranger to India.

India maintained a pragmatic approach, and between when U. Nu was out of power and General Ne Win was serving as the Prime Minister, the latter visited India during 8–10 October 1959, when he met Nehru.[5] India trained members of the Burmese military, as was required by Yangon. But Gonsalves recollects that out of the two—Ne Win and U. Nu—Nehru was firmly for U. Nu.

Nevertheless, after some consultation with the Indian Embassy, Nehru agreed to recognize the military rule in Yangon. Early that year, Myanmar was squeezed between two Asian giants—India and

China—but by the end of that year, India's international stature had suffered a big setback as the Chinese forces overran Tawang and reached Tezpur in Assam. The resulting loss of respect took away the sparkle that Bandung had added to the Nehru era, and Myanmar's military rulers took advantage of this altered regional scenario.

More than half century before the Rohingya crisis was to be unleashed in 2017, the first major persecution of 'foreigners' took place in Myanmar in 1963. The issue was dealt with by Gonsalves and his colleague Pascal Alan Nazareth. That year, Ne Win, unable to handle the gigantic economic problems facing Myanmar, took some drastic measures without caring for the human miseries that his steps caused.

For many decades during the nineteenth and the early twentieth centuries, Myanmar's business sector was dominated by Indians. It was easy for Indian businessmen from the north, south and west to be in Myanmar. Tamils were a prominent community in Myanmar at that time. The Indian community had vast experience of conducting business, and they dominated sectors like timber and agriculture. Nearly a million Indians resided in Burma—as Myanmar was known then.[6] Indians were no longer foreign to Myanmar and had contributed to creating a multicultural country which already had deep roots with India due to its rich Buddhist heritage. But there was a problem between the Indians and the Burmese which was witnessed by the Indian diplomats posted in Myanmar.

Washed by the mighty Irrawaddy, Chindwin and Salween rivers, Burma produced an enormous amount of rice, and the Tamil Chettiars emerged as crucial in this rice trade. They gave loans to the rice traders and would use the British administration to their advantage at times when the money was not returned.

In the process, they earned a reputation for being tough on the native Burmese. The entire Indian community was smeared by that reputation rather unfairly when the Burmese were faced with an economic downturn in the late 1950s.

However, the military rule, in search of finding a solution to the economic woes of Myanmar, zeroed in on the 'foreigners' and private entrepreneurs. The atmosphere of intolerance escalated just before the demise of Nehru in March–April 1964, when Myanmar nationalized shops.[7] Private businessmen were served notices, and the Indian settlers were asked to leave. What happened next was nothing short of a tragic spectacle. A large number of Indians who were leaving had several requirements. They wanted to travel safely and did not want to be detained by the authorities in Yangon, but they also wanted compensation, as the Myanmar government had taken over their businesses. The Burmese military ordered a strict order to strip Indians of all their jewellery. The measure went to such an extent that even women wearing wedding rings were asked to surrender the rings. Naturally, there was uproar within the local Indian community which was not a weak minority. Indians were present in all sections of the Burmese economy, and they were vocal. However, India's stock had suddenly fallen in the backdrop of the war with China and the Burmese military felt nothing could stop it from carrying on with its bizarre economic plans. There were several occasions when the might of the Indian state was stretched to the extreme and the expulsion of lakhs of Indians from Burma was truly one of the biggest crises that India had to deal with after independence alongside the Sino-Indian War of 1962 and the Liberation War of 1971. What made the Burmese crisis particularly dangerous were the vast number of people who were affected by it and the problem of transportation that existed as thousands had to be transported by ship.

Gonsalves, who is now in his mid-nineties and resides in Bengaluru, recounted how as a thirty-five-year-old chargé d'affaires he saw the rising anger among the community as well as within the embassy which was largely manned by young officers in their twenties. Diplomatically, India had suddenly become an isolated power. It was well-known that Delhi was in disarray after the humiliating defeat of November 1962 and no high-profile former ICS officer turned ambassador wanted to serve in Burma in such a hostile situation. That left the young officers to deal with the situation as best as they could. 'I am sure an officer acting on his own in a similar set of circumstances today would have the riot act read,' said Gonsalves, recollecting the measures that the Indian Embassy in Yangon took in 1963–64 to deal with the challenging situation that the Indian population of Burma had to endure because of the whimsical economic policy of the Ne Win administration.[8] Without guidance from New Delhi Gonsalves, who had the embassy under his command, came up with a solution to the crisis facing the Indian community. As the chargé d'affaires of the mission, he promised that the mission would safeguard the valuables of the Indian community.

In response, thousands of Indians queued up outside the Indian Embassy with their precious jewels and gold items. So, Pascal Alan Nazareth, a younger colleague of Gonsalves sat on a chair with pen and stickers, and each item that the Indian community brought in was carefully documented and packed away in the lockers of the embassy. There was a real fear that the families were about to be robbed of their family heirlooms by the Burmese state, which had earlier made their lives difficult. The embassy did not turn them away and instead took the items for safekeeping. This was done without consulting the Burmese authorities, who were surprised by the Indian Embassy's action, which they could not stop. Within three days, the embassy collected gold and jewellery worth more than Rs 2 crore from the Indians—a substantial amount for that time.[9] Outside, chaos reigned as many Indians were herded to the Race Course in Yangon, and a mad rush ensued to dispose of property at a distress rate as fear spread all around about impending doom. Indian diplomats also faced greater insecurity and had to live at an isolated house near the Shwedagon Pagoda, protected by the Buddhist monks who lived nearby. The Burmese intelligence kept a close watch on the visitors and the Buddhist monks acted as 'watch dogs' safeguarding Gonsalves and his colleagues. The Burmese authorities agreed to discuss the matter after the embassy had acquired the valuables that were deposited with a branch of the People's Bank in Burma.[10] The Indian Foreign Secretary Yezdezard Dinshaw Gundevia came to Yangon at this time to oversee the situation and during the discussion tried unsuccessfully to convince the Burmese government to stop the campaign. He didn't succeed, but the Burmese agreed in principle that the valuables belonged to the Indian community.

According to the oral history of Gonsalves preserved at the Indian Council of World Affairs, the Indian population in Burma at that time was around 10–15 lakhs.[11] The shape of that forced exodus can be compared only with the Rohingya crisis of 2017, which similarly consisted of more than a million Rohingya refugees being displaced from Myanmar's Rakhine province by the military junta. The Indian population expelled from Burma during the hostile period of 1962–64 was comparable in size but did not attract as much attention as the Burmese did not target Indians with the same brutality that they unleashed on other ethnic minorities like the Rohingyas and ethnic groups like the Chins and Karens. But the economic hardship was equally intense.

The Indian Embassy in Yangon had the responsibility of sending them back, and Gonsalves says that finally at least 3 lakh Indians were sent back from Burma. In view of the very large number of people stuck in the crisis, a decision was taken to transport them via ship. Soon a ship was requisitioned from the Haj service of the Government of India for the task. The ship belonging to Mogul Lines was found to be lying idle and was pushed into ferrying passengers from Burma to Calcutta. The journey over the turbulent Bay of Bengal took around three or four days. The extent of the operation can be assessed by the fact that the ship was still plying when Gonsalves returned, ending nearly three years of service in Burma in December 1964. By that time, over sea and overland, around 3 lakh Indians had been transferred back home. A good number of them were given loans in India against the receipts they had got by depositing jewellery with the Indian Embassy in Yangon. Many of them returned to Chennai, then known as Madras and with all the items that were not available in socialist India, set up the Burma Bazar of Madras, where the items that they brought along were much sought after.

Thus was born Burma Bazar, one of the oldest grey markets of India where people from all over India would come shopping for foreign consumer items before the era of liberalization dawned in the 1990s.

The sights of that time stayed with Gonsalves forever. India would go on to evacuate nationals from many countries over the subsequent decades, including from Iraq in 1990 and from many countries like Libya, Ukraine, Yemen and Sudan in the twenty-first century, but the evacuation of 1963–64 was far more difficult because of the lack of infrastructure and resources. 'Indians had to leave in ships and many left overland through difficult terrains, leaving their homes and established lives behind,' recollected

Gonsalves speaking to this author.[12] After the airlift of Indians from Kuwait during the 1990 Gulf war, the operation with Air India became known as the largest evacuation in the Indian history. Gonsalves did not maintain numbers back in 1963–64 and says that with the 3 lakh Indians relocated back, the operation from Burma was indeed the biggest refugee relocation that the Indian government had overseen till date. In the context of the subsequent similar operations, Gonsalves seems to be correct.

The action of the Ne Win government triggered a humanitarian crisis, which mingling with the bitter after taste of the defeat of the 1962 war, created a dysfunctionality that came to symbolize India. The tragedy unleashed on the Indian settlers in Burma was further amplified by the fact that throughout the early 1960s, the Nehru administration took several measures to help Burma irrespective of the hostile measures that Burma was planning against the settlers. A year before Nehru's demise, in May 1963, Burma was hit by cholera. India was one of the first countries to rush to help Burma, and the Indian Red Cross gave one lakh doses of the cholera vaccine, half of which were offered as gifts.[13] After touching the height of fame in Bandung, the Nehru era drew to a close through the military setback of 1962 and the humanitarian crisis unleashed against Indian nationals by the Ne Win government of Myanmar. Gonsalves feels that subsequent history did not give the exodus from Burma enough attention though it probably is the biggest humanitarian tragedy with few parallels in Indian history and diplomacy.[14] The biggest setback of Nehru's prime ministership was the defeat in the Sino-Indian War of 1962, but that was not the problem that Nehru was occupied with on the day of his death. On 13 May 1964, Nehru instead wrote to Ne Win urging him to 'generously accept' those Indians who wished to stay on in Burma and become a part of the Burmese society. He also argued for the safe return of those who wished to come back to their homes in India. 'If these people are to come away to India, I am sure Your Excellency will agree, they must be enabled to come home with at least part of their assets to enable them to start afresh in India.'[15] Nehru promised Ne Win that a senior Indian official would be sent to Burma to ensure smooth repatriation of those who wanted to return. Four days prior to Nehru's demise, Foreign Secretary Y.D. Gundevia thus arrived in Yangon to deal with the Burmese rulers.

In the 1950s, the power of the Ministry of External Affairs was rivalled by the Indian High Commission in London. The high commissioner of India was a special post as India–UK ties remained strong despite India attaining Independence. India's membership in the Commonwealth further made its relations with the UK special. The MEA asserted India's independence from London but that had to be done tactfully without antagonizing the established western dominance. The High Commission had a staff of 1,300, which was higher than the entire Ministry of External Affairs in Delhi. It was in this backdrop that Vijaya Lakshmi Pandit and V.K. Krishna Menon would evolve. Both of them went on to leave their marks on multiple first recruits who happened to work under them in the mission in London during the Nehru era. Gonsalves served as the private secretary to both Pandit and Menon—two entirely different personalities. One loved to live in style and the other lived frugally.

A challenging foreign posting arrived on the table of Eric Gonsalves at the Ministry of External Affairs in December 1971. He was serving as the joint secretary (South) in the MEA when the order arrived. So, leaving the post-16 December euphoria in Delhi behind, Gonsalves arrived at the Embassy of India in Washington DC, only to be met by a strained India–US relationship. At the peak of the short India–Pakistan war, which lasted for thirteen days, the US Government had sent the Seventh Fleet to the Bay of Bengal, but the show of strength came a bit late and by then the Indians had turned the tide of the war to their advantage, leading to the surrender of Pakistani forces. Both sides maintained normal diplomatic relations but there was no political warmth left. Gonsalves was posted as the minister in charge of political affairs and also handled the responsibilities of the deputy chief of mission.

Gonsalves was appointed in the Junior Scale of the Indian Foreign Service (IFS) through competitive examination on 24 May 1950. Starting with his early postings in New York and western locations like London, he had come to the understanding that there is an inherent desire in the western capitals to move on with issues, and this was especially true for the United States, which began as a supporter for independent India but was unconvinced about Nehru's non-alignment and turned outright hostile when Indira Gandhi fought the War of Liberation of 1971. Veterans like D.P. Dhar, who served as the policy planning adviser to the PM at the height of the war, and the advisers who carried out a number of undercover operations during this period played an important role in indirectly nurturing the impression of a pro-USSR tilt of India during this period. This obviously did not go down well with the US. The United States that Gonsalves thus witnessed in 1955 had evolved, and President Richard Nixon was in charge. In his previous posting, Gonsalves was sent into the immigrant capital of the world in New York, and in the spring of 1972, he was sent to the heart of American bureaucracy, statecraft and espionage—Washington DC. He soon realized that diplomacy in the American capital was often conducted in cafes.

He surveyed the restaurant scene of the American capital and would patronize the finest restaurants that were conveniently located near the embassy or centrally located in the city. It was in these cafes and restaurants that he would meet his counterparts and contacts who would prove to be useful. In view of the difference of opinion between Indira Gandhi and Richard Nixon over the Liberation War of 1971, political warmth was missing at the top level, but the formal structure of communication among officials of the two sides continued unobstructed, thanks primarily to the guest list of Ambassador L.K. Jha who continued to enjoy prominence in Washington DC.[16]

Gonsalves discovered a nice French restaurant located near the Indian Embassy and began to frequent it. Soon, it turned out that his favourite table in the restaurant was also favoured by another patron of the restaurant named Lt General Vernon A. Walters. Walters, who began as a soldier and a linguist, was known to speak several languages and was the favoured translator of multiple presidents of the United States, including Richard Nixon. From 1972 till 1976, Walters served as the deputy director of Central Intelligence—a time that coincided with landmark developments like the Watergate scandal that erupted in the summer of 1972 and the exit of the US forces from Cambodia in 1975 and the end of the Vietnam war. It is said that Walters flew 1.5 million miles in the early 1980s often, as a special or secret envoy of President Reagan. In 1972, Walters was already a legend in his profession when Gonsalves was in his early forties. The two struck a friendship that continued for many years.

After twenty-eight years in various postings across the world, Gonsalves returned to Delhi as an additional secretary in the MEA from his previous posting in Japan. Soon after his return, he got involved with the then External Affairs Minister Atal Bihari Vajpayee in building ties with China from the ruins of 1962 war. There was some progress in the ties. The harassment of Indian diplomats which began after the defeat in the Sino-Indian war of 1962 had reduced greatly. Overall, the situation remained serious, but both sides had restored diplomatic relations by 1976 and a visit by Vajpayee was thought of as appropriate. The visit, however, went down as ill-timed as it coincided with China's invasion of Vietnam.

The young officer who had joined with a BSc degree from Madras University was part of several major developments that had taken place in the previous three decades. He was part of the peace process in the Korean peninsula in the early 1950s and over the years acquired a deep understanding of how to engage the superpowers—the US and the USSR—which was further supplemented by his stint in Washington DC from 1972 to the mid-1970s.[17] Gonsalves, in short, understood that irritants and even major differences could be managed if interlocutors could maintain contact discreetly. 'Diplomacy was a restricted business,' said Gonsalves recounting his training during the Nehruvian age.[18]

In 1980, the world began to change again. Just days before New Year's Eve, the Soviet troops rolled into Afghanistan crossing from the central Asian republics of the Soviet Union, starting what would become a decade-long quagmire. The Soviet leadership in Moscow claimed that the move was part of a strategy to stabilize the leftist government of Kabul, which had been a victim of internal bickering for the past few years. But the movement of the Soviet war machine towards the south alarmed the world.

A little distance away in New Delhi, a new government came to power as Indira Gandhi was elected after an exile from power that lasted just three years. During the exile, the world had begun to show signs of disturbance. In India, a political elite that challenged the Congress leaders had come to power. In Pakistan, the military had taken charge by overthrowing Zulfikar Ali Bhutto, and in Bangladesh, a phase of instability, which had begun with the assassination of Sheikh Mujibur Rahman in 1975, continued. The Indian government, however, was different as it had established overall dominance in the region with the war of 1971, and Indira Gandhi felt disappointed that the Soviets, whom she considered friendly, had not reached out to her or taken her into confidence before sending its army to Afghanistan. She was sworn to office on 14 January but this time, Gandhi was worried that the Soviets had displayed a tendency to work on their own without consulting her. The opportunity for such a conversation with Moscow knocked on her door soon when long-serving Soviet Foreign Minister Andrey Gromyko arrived in Delhi a month after Indira Gandhi took charge in January 1980. The conversation was cold, and Gandhi conveyed that being out of power did not render her inaccessible for old friends and supporters, emphasizing that the Soviets should have informed her about their Afghan venture.

The Soviet Union had been a solid supporter of India and played an indispensable role in the war of 1971 against Pakistan, but like the proverbial camel that was tied outside the tent but became a discomfort when it entered the tent, the Soviet troops, by reaching the Khyber Pass, had come too close for comfort. That apart, Indira Gandhi no longer needed to depend on the left parties of India in her foreign policy making—unlike her earlier decade-long stint as Prime Minister. The left parties, particularly the Communist Party of India (CPI), had previously played a behind-the-scenes role in her interactions with the communist bloc, and as a result, she depended on the CPI, which nurtured the first generation of strong Moscow–Delhi activists like Benoy Roy who provided a strong ideological training for a generation of academics and political and cultural activists towards Moscow.

By the late 1970s, the winds of change were visible not just in India's neighbourhood but also within the country. Sectarian, religious and ideological differences had softened the Afghan society, and similar elements were spreading deep within other major societies in the world and most importantly inside India. India's developing economy required support for solid technology transfer from the developed parts of the world, and Indira Gandhi had already shown that India would reach out to whoever had the right and affordable technology. Without technology, India's development train would slow down with obvious ramifications for the unity and integrity of its society. In the previous three years, when Prime Minister Morarji Desai and Prime Minister Chaudhary Charan Singh presided over the Government of India, major changes took place in two of the largest and most important Muslim countries—Iran and Saudi Arabia. The developments concerning these two countries would send shockwaves across the Muslim community of the world and contribute to creating a churning.

On the one hand, the Islamic Revolution of Iran began on 7 January 1978 and finally ended with the overthrow of the rule of the old elite represented by the Shah. On 16 January 1979, Reza Shah Pehlavi left Tehran and with his departure ended the rule of the last emperor of Persia. The next government was established under the leadership of Ayatollah Khomeini who was in exile during the previous years in Europe. The establishment of the Islamic rule in Iran—a Shia-majority country—would add dynamism to the Islamic sphere where authoritarian rulers dominated. The Islamic rule of Iran was backed by an Islamist-Republican Constitution. The popular nature of the revolution sent clear messages to the monarchies across the Gulf, where various factions and secret movements had been spawning for many years. On 20 November 1979, the Great Mosque of Mecca was taken over by hundreds of militants under the command of Juhayman al-Otaybi, who claimed the dynastic house of Saud had lost legitimacy as it had come under the influence of the west. The siege lasted for two weeks when the Saudi forces, supported by French commandos, restored control of the holiest shrine of Islam and arrested Juhayman and his accomplices. By then, however, the lives of hundreds of pilgrims who had gathered at the mosque had been lost in what turned out to be the most violent incident in Mecca in the last century. Alongside these major developments, there was the civil war in Lebanon which began in 1975 and soon evolved into a communal war that was fought along religious lines and later also along sectarian—Shia vs Sunni—lines. In Pakistan, General Zia ul Haq's government executed Prime Minister Zulfikar Ali Bhutto on 4 April 1979. These developments, of course, added to political currents in South Asia.

On 13 August 1980, the Muslims of Moradabad congregated at the Eidgah of the city to celebrate the annual Eid ul Fitr festivity, which was being marked after thirty days of fasting and prayers during the month of Ramzan. People gathered there dressed in white kurtas and the air was fused with itr, a floral fragrance used by the Muslims of Uttar Pradesh on festive days. By 9 a.m., around 60,000 Muslim citizens had gathered at the Eidgah. The number of the faithful who had arrived that morning was far beyond the capacity of the Eidgah. As a result, the crowd spilled on to the road till quite a distance. In view of potential law-and-order concerns, a strong arrangement of security was put in place. Outside the Eidgah, social outfits and political parties like the Congress, BJP (which had been formed on 6 April 1980 by the merger of Bharatiya Jana Sangh and the Janata Party) and the Muslim League offered refreshments to the gathering, and the overall political and administrative machinery was supported by the police who had put up a stall where the Additional District Magistrate D.P. Singh was seated. Sixty to seventy police personnel—most carrying sticks—were present at this spot.

As the prayers began under the guidance of the local imam, a pig was seen near the entrance of the Eidgah. The instant reaction of those located near the gate of the Eidgah was to drive away the pig, as the animal is considered impure from the point of view of Islam. The crowd asked the police constables nearby, for the security purposes of the congregation, to help in driving away the pig—a request that the policemen reportedly declined. In the crowd, amidst a series of escalatory loud exchanges, somehow the impression was generated that the animal's entry into the alley was facilitated by the police. Incensed at the disruption caused by this small altercation, a larger group immediately intervened, and within minutes, a volatile confrontation erupted, with firing and stone pelting allegedly from the side of the congregation. The initial round of violence injured several police personnel, and the senior police officials, including ADM D.P. Singh, were surrounded and beaten up. It was reported in the news that D.P. Singh was dragged away by the agitated crowd and his dead body was found a little distance away after a short while. After losing senior government officials in the sudden eruption of violence, now it was the police armed with firearms who fired into the crowd, injuring and killing dozens who just a few minutes earlier were praying and exchanging greetings with their compatriots. There are several accounts of the incident, and the exact number of the dead and the wounded remain disputed. While newspapers published the next day reported that the total number of the dead was twenty-four, other accounts indicated the number was much higher than that—around 250 to 300.[19] Survivors who ran away from the spot recounted how white kurtas turned red and how white hair turned crimson as bullets crisscrossed the air and snuffed out lives. Families were destroyed forever. Two days later, Prime Minister Indira Gandhi began her speech from the ramparts of the Red Fort, marking Independence Day by paying tribute to those who were killed in the violence of Moradabad.

In a frightening way, the Moradabad riots of 1980s showed that the more India was made to change, the more it remained the same.

India in 1980 was not the country that it was in 1967 when Indira Gandhi was sworn to office for the second time, after the general election. There was a huge difference between the India of the 1960s that Indira Gandhi had inherited from her father Jawaharlal Nehru and her immediate predecessors Lal Bahadur Shastri and Gulzarilal Nanda and India in the 1980s. The internal security scenario as well as the regional and global factors were vastly different, and the dangers to the Indian state created after 1947 were getting stronger. India's neighbourhood and the strategic backyard of the Gulf, which supplied energy and foreign remittances, had a series of strongmen who sought engagement with India. Iraq's Saddam Hussein, Libya's Muammar Gaddafi and the rulers of the oil-rich United Arab Emirates were some of them who required sustained engagement. India's security architecture at home, in its neighbourhood and in the strategic backyard had undergone dramatic transformation and that apart, there were the global players who had created sufficient problems already in Afghanistan.

A new security threat emerged from the state of Punjab, which had earlier become the boon that supported the Green Revolution. Sikh militancy was no stranger to the Indian government, but this time around, the intensity of the problem was different. The Government of India moved quickly against this backdrop of a new generation of security threats and emerging choices.

It was a time of great silence and introspection for India's policy makers. More so because like a great ship, India had to be steered carefully as it quietly planned to implement a course correction. This course correction would test India's diplomacy, economy, security and its society. Within weeks of the swearing-in of Indira Gandhi as the Prime Minister came the first show of curiosity from the American side.

Indira Gandhi at this hour leaned towards the formidable L.K. Jha.

One and half decades earlier, Jha served as the secretary to Lal Bahadur Shastri, and in 1966, on being sworn in as the Prime Minister of India for the first time, Gandhi had felt Jha was conservative[20] and would not fit in to deliver as part of her secretariat. Instead, Jha had become the governor of the Reserve Bank of India during the late 1960s, when Indira Gandhi took radical steps like the nationalization of several banks. Jha subsequently became India's ambassador to the United States during 1970–73, when India fought and won the Liberation War of 1971 despite grave opposition from the Nixon administration. Indeed, she used a triumvirate of veteran administrators and diplomats—L.K. Jha, B.K. Nehru and G. Parthasarathy—and their younger colleague Eric Gonsalves. The first two had begun as part of the ICS, and G. Parthasarathy, also known as GP, started as a journalist before being drawn to Nehru's government. Despite the obvious absence of the earlier decade's trust with the Soviet Union, there was nothing much that the new government of India could do to steer India towards the United States, as the return of Indira Gandhi in Delhi in January 1980 coincided with the last leg of the presidency of Jimmy Carter in the US whose popularity had been affected by the Iran hostage crisis which began on 4 November 1979. Subsequently, sixty-six US diplomats were seized by protesters and fifty-two of them were held hostage in the US Embassy in Tehran for more than a year as the Carter administration tried multiple options but failed to bring the crisis to a conclusion because of the virulent anti-US sentiment in the post-Shah Iran. As a result of the prolonged crisis, the Carter administration went into a mode that allowed no chance of recovery. The great turnaround of India's foreign policy, therefore, had to wait for the outcome of the presidential election in the United States that would take place in November 1980. The result of the election held on 4 November 1980 was on expected lines and ended the suspense in New Delhi. Ronald Reagan, a former Hollywood actor, defeated President Jimmy Carter decisively. In this dynamic backdrop, on 19 January 1981, American diplomats and Iranian representatives met in Algiers, in a meeting mediated by the Algerian government, and reached a settlement of the Iran hostage crisis. The next day, Ronald Reagan was sworn in as the next President of the United States, and within hours, the Iranian diplomats were freed from the besieged embassy in Tehran. The news of the release of the US diplomats, as it appeared on television, indicated that finally there was a strong leader in Washington DC. For India, which was looking for a window of opportunity to engage a powerful leader of the US, the long-awaited moment had arrived.

Though the great bend in Indian foreign affairs would be pioneered by Indira Gandhi, the beginning was made on the day of her victory during the election of December 1979–January 1980.

Several world leaders made international trunk calls to Indira Gandhi as the news of the victory of her Congress party spread across the world. One of the first callers was President Jimmy Carter of the United States, whose administration had a difficult relationship with India under Prime Minister Morarji Desai. As

Indira Gandhi rushed to receive the telephone call in her 12, Willingdon Crescent residence, which was being swept by a sea of supporters, she whispered to her friend and confidante Pupul Jayakar that she suspected it was her friend British Prime Minister Margaret Thatcher who had nudged President Carter to reach out to her.[21]

The telephone call would pave the way for greater interactions between the two sides as President Carter's envoy Clark McAdams Clifford visited Delhi a few weeks after Indira Gandhi was sworn in for what turned out to be her last term in office. Clifford was part of the Washington elite, like Vernon Anthony Walters, and belonged to a coterie of Cold War-era politicians and lawyers who had been part of the US power structure of the post-World War II decades.

Indira Gandhi called for a small team to meet Clifford which included P.V. Narasimha Rao and Eric Gonsalves, then the secretary in charge of the eastern affairs at the Ministry of External Affairs.[22]

At the meeting, Indira Gandhi placed her cards on the table and explained the regional scenario to the American guest. Clark Clifford was aware of the possibilities that had opened up in South Asia because of the invasion of Afghanistan by the Soviet Union. Indians had become suspicious of the real intent of the Soviet forces; on the other hand, the Pakistanis had become indispensable to the Americans as they were necessary to deal with the Soviet forces stationed really close to Peshawar and other Cold War-era military stations inside Pakistan.

This placed the US in a position to warm up its ties with India but made Pakistan, already part of its Cold War partnership, a more attractive partner. Indira said that bolstering US–Pakistan relations would be a setback to India–Pakistan relations. The discussion between the Indian PM, Clifford, Gonsalves and Rao had to be communicated to the American side. For this crucial task, Indira Gandhi chose her cousin B.K. Nehru. An ICS, Nehru had not opted for the IFS but played several high-profile diplomatic roles for both Nehru and Gandhi.

His ability for informal engagement brought him close to a large number of western, especially American, officials, bankers and celebrities. He could thus reach out across the political divides of the Cold War and engage the western officials on difficult subjects like India's relations with the Soviet Union and the non-aligned movement, which appeared to be under the influence of anti-Israel Arab leaders like Egypt's Nasser. He served under Jawaharlal Nehru who had vowed to keep India non-aligned, but B.K. Nehru had vowed to lead the life of a professional government official and did not opt for any of the Gandhian trends like abstinence, khadi and vegetarianism. He enjoyed the simple pleasures of life while being close to those who had chosen to lead a spartan life. This attitude allowed B.K. Nehru to maintain the degree of ambiguity that he adopted even in his personal life, including his marriage to Fori, a Jewish woman of Hungarian origin who had lost members of her family to the Nazi rulers of Germany during World War II.

In a curious sort of way, B.K. Nehru had become an unofficial conduit for India–Israel relations several decades before the two countries would establish diplomatic relations in 1992.

A year after the 1962 India–China war, news went out that the Indian government under the ailing Prime Minister, Jawaharlal Nehru, had been preventing Indian citizens from visiting Israel and vice versa. The news reached US Congressman Emanuel Celler who wrote to the Indian ambassador to the US on 17 July 1963 enquiring about the obstacles that the Indian government had been allegedly placing before its citizens as well as Israeli citizens to prevent people-to-people interactions. Celler was a formidable American politician from New York who served in the House of Representatives for nearly five decades. It was obvious that the Israelis had powerful friends in the United States, and they wanted to convey to the Indian side the pressure that they could bring to bear on New Delhi if the Government of India intervened in controlling people-to-people contact. B.K. Nehru enquired with the Government of India back home and wrote back to Celler in the first week of September denying the existence of any obstacles being put up by the Indian government to stop people-to-people contact.[23]

B.K. Nehru was, therefore, experienced in the way diplomacy sometimes delivered in unwritten and unmentionable ways. The victory of Ronald Reagan in the United States in November 1980, and Delhi's restlessness about the intention of the Soviet Union—a few hundred kilometres away—in Afghanistan, provided him one more opportunity to delve into the vast social network that he had cultivated earlier in the United States.

B.K. Nehru was resting in his residence in Chandigarh and planning a trip to New York, as it was something that he had to do as a member of a committee of the United Nations. Just then came a phone call from Indira Gandhi who asked him to go to the United States and engage the Ronald Reagan administration. He had just won the election, and Indira Gandhi thought it to be a good idea. She wanted to reach out to Reagan and convey that India was not ideologically opposed to the United States. B.K. Nehru arrived in the United States soon thereafter and began to reach out to as many people as he could. He met George Woods first and was introduced to Jack McCloy, the former head of the

International Bank for Reconstruction and Development (the World Bank) and the former commissioner of post-World War II West Germany.

Jack McCloy got B.K. Nehru an appointment with William Casey and Richard Allen, who were to be designated as director of the Central Intelligence Agency and the national security advisor of the Reagan administration, respectively. It was the first such high-level back-channel discussion in the changing circumstances between a top-level Indian policy influencer and US bureaucrats. B.K. Nehru broke the ice with the Reagan administration at a time when India, after a decade of being staunchly anti-US, had come to realize that friendship in foreign affairs came with an expiry date.

The meeting between B.K. Nehru and the Casey–Allen duo served the purpose of introducing India to the upcoming security team of the newly elected President of the United States. The Reagan era began on an optimistic note with the immediate release of the captive American diplomats in Iran.

After the return of Indira Gandhi, two back-channel visits—by Clark Clifford and B.K. Nehru—activated the political exchange between the US and India, which had been nearly frozen especially for Gandhi. There was no formal declaration, but there was an unofficial ban on a visit by Indira Gandhi to the US. During this period, Eric Gonsalves visited Washington DC repeatedly as part of his responsibilities in the Ministry of External Affairs. Sometime after the visit by B.K. Nehru, Gonsalves received a message that his friend from his Washington days, Vernon Anthony Walters, had been appointed as the special presidential envoy.

The dialogue started by Gonsalves in the cafes of Washington DC with Vernon Walters had stretched over the next decade and, over time, included several figures in the Reagan administration. It ultimately led to the breakthrough dialogue between Gandhi and Reagan in October 1981 in Cancun on the side-lines of the North-South Summit. This led to the 1982 state visit by Indira Gandhi to Washington DC. India entered a new chapter of relations with the Soviet Union as the US reignited its relationship with Indira Gandhi a decade after the Indian PM was given a cold welcome in the White House by President Nixon. Gonsalves revealed nearly three decades later that it was he and Vernon Walters who had worked in the back channel to facilitate Prime Minister Indira Gandhi's visit to Washington DC in 1982.

8

'WILFRED MUST GO'

'How is it that you remember my father?' asked a faint voice on the other end of the telephone. 'Are you Christian?' she asked, trying to make sense of the phone call that revealed a sudden interest in the life and work of her father who passed away in the 1980s. Shanthy Pragalsingh is a devout Christian, and her coreligionists and those congregating with them form a big part of her life, but she was not expecting another devout Christian to call her to enquire about her father Santosham John Wilfred. 'In fact, I am happy that you are not a Christian,' said Mrs Pragalsingh[1] as she discovered that the caller was not in search of spiritual connection but was genuinely interested to discuss the life of S.J. Wilfred, as Santosham John Wilfred was known.

S.J. Wilfred was born in Nazareth in Tirunelveli, in Madras State on 11 July 1911. The year was a landmark in the history of India, as on 12 December India's capital was shifted from Calcutta to Delhi, which back then was just being reimagined as a centre of British imperial power in South Asia. Wilfred was born a Tamilian in one of the southernmost parts of the British Empire. He had no major connection with the bureaucracy, yet such would be his destiny that he, like many others, would gravitate towards the new capital at a certain stage in his life. Indeed, Wilfred was part of the cadre of stenographers and clerks collected by the new post-Independence Government of India. As the idea of forming a solid bureaucracy for foreign affairs took shape in the backdrop of intense political discussion within the national leadership and the team led by Lord Louis Mountbatten, the rich collection of stenographers and clerks found a new opportunity. India's clerks were famous within the colonial set up for the immaculate notes that helped the colonial administration and trained a generation of bureaucrats to the power of language and communication. Foreign affairs depend on structured communication, and skilled stenographers are essential to the maintaining of official records and dictation. As a former stenographer who joined the service in the last years of the Nehru-era recollected, taking notes was the most vital part of official communication, as official orders could only be written and issued after that. Without it, India's foreign affairs would be handicapped.

In response to government advertisements, stenographers poured in from all corners of the fast-disintegrating Empire. The fine stenographers of the Raj transitioned from the past to the future. Wilfred came from Vellore, where the Christian Medical College (CMC) had made a name for itself already by the 1940s. There were many like him.

The 1905-born stenographer Lalla Chunni Lall came from Insein in Burma. He was born and educated in Burma. Sudhir Chandra Nandy came from Paikpara of Dhaka which became the administrative capital of East Pakistan in 1947. Walter Edward Eling (born in 1908), one of the seniormost stenographers in service at the time of Independence, came from the Nilgiris and before being posted to the Ministry of External Affairs had served in British outpost in Waziristan and the summer capital Shimla; between 1939 and 1947, he served as an 'assistant'—a stenographer in the office of the viceroy. Jagdish Lal Malhautra came from Gujarat in west Pakistan; Ramkrishna Sakharam Chavan came from Akola in Bombay Presidency. Keki Darashah came from Bangalore. Gopal Das Seth came from Lahore. Axel Khan Roy spoke Pashto and joined as the clerical officer of the Indian Supply Mission in London which had an all-important status as the centre, from which the essential stationery and household supplies for the staff of the ministry were disseminated in Europe. Wilfred was one of them—the first stenographers.

The clerks of the Ministry of External Affairs were part of the lowest rung of officials in the official bureaucracy. They were part of the essential structure, but they were not always expected to be in the limelight. They were part of the invisible crowd who were witness to historic moments but were rarely in focus. Wilfred's career was not meant to be in the shadows. He began as a clerk in the accounts office in May 1934 and served in the same position without any growth till November 1947, but his destiny would change once he joined the MEA.

India was in the midst of a political typhoon that was reshaping its political geography and demographics. The stormy winds of change were lifting communities from one part of the subcontinent and depositing them in another. It was traumatic as well as exhilarating. It was in this backdrop that Wilfred came to Delhi to join as a clerk in the Accounts Office and was transferred to the Ministry of External Affairs as a superintendent.

There was a great deal of fear about the work of the ministry in the early years, as families feared that their sons would be sent to unknown countries, and that was a factor that often influenced the final decision.[2] Wilfred was already in his late thirties and had a small family of his own. A few years earlier he had married his wife Flora Harris and out of the union were born three children, including Shanthy. Shanthy was a toddler of four when the order to relocate to Delhi came. For a small family located far away from the capital city of Delhi, the move was an adventure. The mothers of Flora and Santosham John Wilfred were both widows and dependent on Wilfred, but they readily agreed saying, 'You must go. Have faith in God and He will guide you.' Armed with nothing but this faith in God, and without any social capital, S.J. Wilfred arrived in Delhi with his small family in tow. The journey was long and arduous. They boarded a train from Vellore, were driven in cars and reached Delhi in seven days. But the arrival was more traumatic than the journey. The capital was enveloped in frenzy, and the Tamil-speaking family was shocked by the violence unfolding all around them.

Shanthy and her parents were walking outside one day, when suddenly, out of nowhere, a knife-wielding man emerged and proceeded to stab a pregnant woman. It was a sight that the family would never forget. Then, on another occasion, Wilfred's young son, displaying a feat of a prank, threw a shoe out from the balcony of the small house that they were allocated, and the shoe landed near a passerby who was a Sikh. The commotion triggered by the incident frightened the family. Those were times of great communal tension, and little incidents had the potential to trigger bigger fights. The all-round fear reached its peak three months after the arrival of Wilfred in Delhi when the son of a neighbour ran to their house and excitedly informed them that Mahatma Gandhi had been shot. '*Gandhi ji ko goli maar di* (They have shot Gandhiji),' he said. It was in this traumatic moment of India's history that the family got accustomed to their life in the capital.

In these new surroundings, the family experienced many hardships while living in Delhi during the late 1940s. Wilfred was not getting younger, but his work was supported by the love and affection of his wife Flora and their three children. It was at this time in Delhi that India realized the need for bringing more staff to its embassy in Kathmandu, the Hindu kingdom to the northeast of India. Nepal was a land of mystery, inaccessible by modern roads. Nepal's kings lived in luxury, and poverty was rampant. The region was rich in customs and cultural artefacts, but the traditional way of life was predominant. In Nepal's cities, people and large forests competed for space, and beauty reigned amidst peril. Cobras and other wild animals often intersected with human habitation, and after sundown, people could hear the howling of wild animals at a distance.

Mountain peaks and the beauty of the wilderness, however, did not mean the politics of the country was any less simple. Nepal was governed by traditional kings, but the real power was in the hands of the Ranas, the powerful elite who dominated the affairs of the durbar. The power of the Ranas was an irritant for many, and disenchantment was brewing over many years as winds of change began to sweep South Asia with the establishment of the modern Indian state in 1947, when the princely states joined India and formed the Indian union. With many of the north Indian kingdoms having family ties with the royals of Nepal, there were also matters of sentiment that were linked to the Himalayan country. Jawaharlal Nehru's government was acutely careful of the sentiment of Kathmandu and the crucial role that this could play in India's relations with the northern neighbour, China. Nehru had appointed Chandreshwar Prasad Narayan Singh—C.P.N. Singh—as the Indian ambassador to Nepal. C.P.N. Singh was famous for his support for the freedom movement as well as for his service to public affairs. In 1935, he was conferred a Commander of the Order of the Indian Empire (CIE). He was a man of letters and eminence and just before Independence, the British rulers honoured him with knighthood. The stint as the ambassador of India was a unique service that C.P.N. Singh was asked to take on for the Government of India.

It was sometime in 1949 that the Ministry of External Affairs suggested that S.J. Wilfred be sent to the Indian Embassy in Kathmandu under the command of C.P.N. Singh. Shanthy recollected that Singh wrote back in an authoritative manner that posting a Christian in the Indian Embassy in Nepal may not be a good idea, considering the conflicted nature of the Nepalese state structure, which viewed New Delhi's new ruling class with some suspicion. India was still reeling from the effects of the devastating communal violence of 1947, and Nehru was not in favour of allowing communal sentiment creep into administrative affairs. He wrote back saying, 'Wilfred must go.'[3] That was the end of the debate on whether Wilfred and his family should travel to Kathmandu or not, and it also marked the growth in career for S.J. Wilfred, who was no longer the clerk that he once was in the Accounts Department. By the time of his posting to Kathmandu, Wilfred was designated vice consul in the Indian Embassy in Kathmandu.[4]

South Asia was awakening from centuries of slumber, and India and Indian officials were discovering the country as well as the neighbourhood for the first time. But Nepal was a complex country, connected to India through geography, history and recent political developments. The landmark event that Wilfred would witness during his stay in Nepal would be the abolition of the Rana regime and the shifting of power from the Ranas to King Tribhuvan. But the policy for Nepal was not singularly focused on Nepal. The new diplomatic team of Delhi was viewing Nepal through the prism of a 'hands off Asia' policy.[5] According to one of the tallest first-generation Indian diplomats, Triloki Nath Kaul, from the beginning, the bulk of foreign policy focus of India has been Asia or the immediate vicinity of India in Asia.

At the time of its freedom, India was among the largest free states in the world, and as a large state with a colonial history, India was interested in ensuring the exit of the colonial powers and their allies from Asia. Long before zeroing in on Nepal, India's focus was on Indonesia, and it was here that Nehru's foreign policy machine sharpened its arguments for taking on Nepal's pro-imperialism monarchy, which was known for its *Ranashahi*, because of the dominance of the powerful Ranas. The Gurkha soldiers of Nepal are feared for their ability to fight, and they used some of that to take on the Indonesians while serving in the British Indian army. One of the major aims of Nehruvian diplomacy, therefore, was to remove the recent memories of bitterness that Asian people had inflicted upon each other while safeguarding the interests of the colonial administration and create new bridges based on mutual respect. In the words of P.R.S. Mani:

> The Gurkhas whose home is in Nepal were part of the Indian Army and some Gurkha battalions under British officers had also been involved in the fighting with Indonesians in West and Central Java where they had established significant bridge heads for later use by Dutch troops. The Gurkhas were reputed for their ruthlessness in hand to hand fighting with their kukris (curved knives) and the Second World War had witnessed their prowess against the Germans and Japanese. To the Indonesians who hated the armed forces opposing them, the distinction

between the terms Gurkhas and Indians was not known and hence every Indian was classified as a Gurkha.⁶

The role of the Nepalese aristocracy in quelling the freedom struggle in Indonesia was taken up by Nehru in November 1945, when he slammed the monarchy of Nepal for siding with the British rulers and for sending its troops to Indonesia (Dutch Indies), where the Nepalese/Gurkha soldiers acted on orders of the British government to restore supremacy of the Dutch rule over Indonesia. As mentioned earlier, the Indian soldiers in Java during the 'Battle of Surabaya' were deeply influenced by the political developments back home and the news of impending independence of India, but the soldiers from Nepal did not have such an orientation and carried out the orders of the British commanders forcefully. This affected the image of the Indian soldiers in Java too, as the locals used the term 'Gurkha' to refer to all South Asian soldiers. Nehru questioned the British duplicity of fighting World War II in the name of freedom while launching a military crackdown against the freedom-loving people of Indonesia who, like the British people, aspired for freedom.⁷ The spirit of the Quit India Movement, for which Nehru was imprisoned in 1942, was still very strong in India, and Nehru for one last time—before becoming the Prime Minister of India—showed the strain of militancy that he had witnessed in India during his younger days. On 9 November 1945, the British forces had ordered the Indonesian leaders to surrender, failing which military means would be adopted. Nehru came out in support of the Indonesian leaders and slammed the European powers as well as Nepal's monarchy. 'I admit that at present we are not prepared to do much, but I wish to sound a clear warning to the imperialist powers of Europe that if they do not quit Asia quickly and without any obstruction, it is clearly inevitable that there will be a gigantic conflict involving the whole world,' he said at a speech in Bombay that same day. For the King of Nepal (who was a puppet in the hands of the powerful Ranas), Nehru had to say this: 'The Maharaja of Nepal must be told that the use of his troops in resisting the freedom movement of the people of Indonesia is against our national respect and heritage and that it is fraught with serious consequences. Nepal, which is said to be a free state should be ashamed that its ruler, claiming to be independent, has obliged the British Government by sending his troops to Indonesia. It is amazing that the Government of Nepal has not spoken out in this respect. I want to tell Nepal that this is a matter which will affect adversely the reputation of Nepal. It will also affect adversely the friendly relations between Nepal and the rest of India.'[8]

In July 1947, the Dutch started a full-scale military offensive against the Republic of Indonesia, whose de facto power they had already recognized. India rushed to the United Nations Security Council arguing that the campaign endangered the maintenance of international peace under Article 34 of the UN charter. An early lesson was learnt when the UN called for peace in Indonesia, but the Dutch Government did not pay attention to the call for peace. India took the initiative in convening a conference involving the 'States of Asia', Australia and New Zealand in New Delhi in January 1949. The meeting demanded complete withdrawal of Dutch authorities by 15 March 1949 and transfer of power over the entire Indonesian landmass by 1 January 1950.

The Asian landmass—including South, Southeast, Far East and West Asia—was part of India's concern, and colonial powers and their former allies in these regions were under pressure from India.

'WILFRED MUST GO' 195

The clock was ticking for Nepal to climb up in the list of priorities for India.

Launching the Indian diplomatic game plan regarding the Rana rule in Nepal, Nehru was far more careful with his words. He said, 'Nepal is almost a part of India, although she is an independent country.'[9] Nepal's identity was defined by its monarchy which was linked to many ruling and erstwhile princely families of the India of the 1940s. The policy for Nepal had to be shaped in a way that would nurture India's continued links with Nepal without undermining Nepal's status as an independent country in any way. India's other concern centred on the fact that India could not 'tolerate'[10] the invasion of Nepal by a foreign power.

Travelling to Nepal was an ordeal, and the family from Vellore took up the challenge. Wilfred reached Kathmandu first during the end of 1949 and asked the family to join him after he had established himself in the new environment. For a journey that was to take them across the border of the Hindi belt of India, the family travelled to Calcutta and from there took a train to Patna. From Patna, a narrow-gauge train took them to Raxaul, the last border town on the Indian side. From Raxaul, they reached Birgunj, from where a journey on dandy and vehicles commenced first on the plains and then through mountain roads. Shanthy recollected that the journey was possible because a large number of Nepalese workers helped travellers negotiate the roads and the risk of travelling.

The travel from Chennai to Kathmandu took seven days for the Wilfreds. Within days of his arrival in Kathmandu, Wilfred became a favourite of C.P.N. Singh, the zamindar turned diplomat and administrator. Though Wilfred was in a clerical position, he became much sought after in the working of the embassy. The

Wilfreds had spent three difficult years in Delhi, and just as they were settling down into the familiar surroundings, they came to Nepal. It was the first time that Wilfred and his family were introduced to the eternal truth of diplomats: that diplomats have to be veterans at parting.

In Kathmandu, Wilfred, the former clerk in the accounts division in Madras state, was introduced to the diplomatic community, the community that floats across borders effortlessly and is never allowed to grow roots anywhere. In Nepal, Wilfred had the first experience of handling an international crisis. The king of Nepal, Tribhuvan Bir Bikram Shah, had a difficult relationship with the Ranas, the powerful courtiers who controlled the destiny of Nepal and played a key role in world affairs. Nepal had been a supplier of soldiers to the British war efforts during World Wars I and II; the issue of supplying soldiers was a difficult matter, over which the king and the Ranas clashed. The Ranas wanted to join the British war efforts during World War I, but the king was not in favour of sending soldiers. This bitterness lingered and would erupt whenever there was a decision to be taken on any crucial issue. The Ranas enjoyed unparalleled power in the Himalayan region during the heyday of the British Empire, and as a dependent class, their stature was weakened with the departure of the British authority from India. During the time that Wilfred took a mid-career jump and joined the Indian Foreign Service, powerful forces were working to redesign the Himalayan region, and Kathmandu was a city of great intrigue that attracted its own share of interesting persons.

One such person, unknown to Wilfred and his family at that time, was a German nurse and physiotherapist, Erika Leuchtag. On the Christmas Eve of 1948, Leuchtag received a letter from a European doctor asking if she would be willing to be a masseur for the Senior Queen of Nepal married to King Tribhuvan. It was an irresistible adventure. Nepal was a forbidden, mysterious kingdom, and Kathmandu was its even more mysterious capital. Leuchtag's family and friends advised her not to venture out. But she persisted and undertook the difficult journey to Kathmandu as was carried out by Wilfred and his family a year later. So, armed with her luggage, her spaniel dog Peepchen and helper Gorkhi Ram, Leuchtag walked and drove through Chandragiri pass and entered Kathmandu.

Leuchtag's first job was to serve as a masseuse and physiotherapist for the beautiful queen who required daily care from a well-trained physiotherapist. Leuchtag's family had fled Germany following the arrival of Hitler in the 1930s and came to Shimla, where she was hired by the maharaja of Patiala to serve as a physiotherapist for the maharani. This time, the assignment was different, as she had to leave the comfort of the Punjab plains and move to the wonders of the Himalayas.

Unknown to herself, the German nurse was venturing into territories that were fast becoming the playground for new major powers. Kathmandu was the abode of a king, and she expected to be greeted by the splendour of a secret world. Instead, the world that the nurse saw left her mystified and drew her deeper into the secrets of the kingdom.

Initially, Erika Leuchtag did not understand what really the truth behind the crowns and tiaras was. She had heard that the king was a debauch and that he loved alcohol. On this count, she was sort of disappointed as the king was married to two queens who shared his home peacefully. Senior Queen Kanti and junior Queen Ishwari and several princes and princesses filled the household. King Tribhuvan turned out to be quite unlike the reputation that Erika Leuchtag had heard. He loved to take care of his health and dressed tastefully. As Leuchtag walked the streets of Kathmandu, she saw ancient temples with deities that were unknown to her. The beautiful Himalayas at a distance, framing the valley, were mesmerizing and reminded her of Europe, but there was more to the physical appearance that would slowly appear before her. Initially, the dynamics of power did not make sense to Leuchtag, but as days passed and as she visited the king's residence, 'Happy Cottage', on the complex of the Narayana Hitty Palace, here was one thing that probably struck Leuchtag as odd: The king was expected to be powerful but, in case of King Tribhuvan, he appeared to be less powerful than the hereditary prime ministers, the Ranas. She walked to Singha Durbar, the centre of power in Kathmandu, and understood that the real power was wielded by Mohan Shumsher Jung Bahadur Rana. He was part of a lineage that had taken charge a century ago through a violent insurgency in which the rivals in the durbar were eliminated. During this period which began in 1846, the monarchy of Nepal was eclipsed by the rule of the Ranas. The arrival of this oligarchy was dependent on internal intrigues, but it also was linked with wider developments in the rest of South Asia, such as the Sepoy Mutiny of 1857 and the establishment of the rule of the British Crown in India. Because of their pro-British policy, the Ranas enjoyed the support of the British monarchy, which provided the Ranas with the political patronage and prestige required on the regional and European stage. During the subsequent century, the Ranas were the executives while the kings served as mere figureheads. This unique oligarchy has few parallels across the world. It ruled Nepal with an iron hand and kept the country closeted from the rest of the world, while providing unquestioning support to the British empire. A westerner fleeing authoritarian rule in her country was not expected to like the authoritarianism of the Rana rulers in Nepal, and it did not take long for Erika Leuchtag either, to understand what was really happening all around her. Leuchtag met Mohan Shumsher Rana, and the interaction made her understand the power dynamics better. The king of Nepal was considered the incarnation of Lord Vishnu, but in fact, he was a prisoner in his own palace and required permission of the Ranas to venture into the land that is governed in his name. The more Leuchtag understood, the more sympathetic she was to the charismatic and handsome King Tribhuvan.

How the queen of Nepal developed the requirement for a physiotherapist and why of all the physiotherapists, only a German woman was found to be fit for the task are questions that will probably have no answer, but Ramesh Nath Pandey, Nepal's long-time foreign minister who served from the late 1960s till the early 2000s, believes that Erika Leuchtag was somehow co-opted into India's plans to end the Rana rule in Nepal and that this was part of an elaborate plan made by the new decision-makers in Delhi.

It was on 6 November 1950, a year after his arrival in the Embassy of India in Kathmandu that Wilfred went to his workplace and found the embassy premises swamped with local people. He pushed through the mass of humanity and reached his office to discover that in his absence, King Tribhuvan and his eldest son Mahendra along with his eldest grandson Birendra had driven into the premises and sought shelter in the embassy. The king had run into trouble once again with the Ranas, and this time he took full advantage of the new Indian state and drove into the embassy. A crisis was thus thrust on to the Indian Embassy in Kathmandu. Turning away the king could have made him a lifelong enemy, and by hosting him, the Indian state was deepening enmity with the paranoid and powerful Ranas. King Tribhuvan, however, had no plan to go elsewhere, and the Indian Embassy and the ambassador had to take a decision right then and there. The situation was high-tension as the supporters of the Ranas mobilized a crowd and threatened the Indian mission while the Indian officials had to take on the responsibility of ensuring the safety of King Tribhuvan and his son and grandson, Mahendra and Birendra. As dusk fell, Ambassador Singh smuggled the king and his son and grandson from the embassy to the residence of the Indian ambassador at Sital Nivas, a beautiful white building in the middle of greenery. It was Wilfred who looked after them during this time. The guests gave him a list of items that were required for daily usage and the embassy decided to procure them from India. Within a short while, India dispatched a special aircraft carrying food items, fruits, nuts and carpets that were to be used to make the king's stay comfortable till further plans were made.

This unimaginable situation was, however, the result of some careful planning. For the previous several months, Erika Leuchtag had been in contact with the Indian ambassador Singh and probably his staff members, including Wilfred, as her daughter Shanthy recollected that the ambassador trusted Wilfred with important assignments. What had happened is that soon after she understood the problems between the Ranas and the king, Leuchtag gained the confidence of the king, her employer, and began to serve as a secret courier between the king and his potential allies, the Indians. India was a democracy, and the king was bent on freeing his monarchy from the clutches of the Rana oligarchy and in this venture his best chance of friendship was with his enemy's enemy—post-1947 India. The relationship between the two countries can be understood by the fact that despite being an immediate neighbour, Nepal had not hosted the next-door Indian PM till the explosion of the political crisis in November 1950.

The king was in a unique position till that time as he was forbidden from stepping out of his palace, but the places where he could not go were accessible to Erika Leuchtag, who could venture anywhere in Nepal, including to attend meetings with the ambassador of India—Chandreshwar Prasad Narayan Singh and his predecessor Surjit Singh Majithia (1947–49). During the stint in Kathmandu, Erika Leuchtag and King Tribhuvan exchanged thoughts through code words. According to this secret code of communication, 'serpent' meant a Rana and 'big snake' meant Prime Minister Mohan Shumsher. 'Bird' meant the Indian ambassador; 'flowers' meant letters; 'kites' meant aircrafts. The last of the code words was the most significant one as that required careful planning. It was the code word 'storm', which signified the final evacuation of the king from Nepal to India. The king was a captive but, once in a while, he was allowed to go hunting in the forests near Kathmandu, which hosted rich wildlife. Erika Leuchtag had been in continuous consultation with the Indian ambassador C.P.N. Singh, and during one such meeting near the beautiful temple of Budhanilkantha, which is located near a hill, the ambassador said that he did not promise to fly the king of Nepal out of Kathmandu, as India wanted to know what the king wanted. The conversation led to the brief exile of the king from Nepal.

The commotion in the Indian Embassy that Wilfred had witnessed thus began a fire that quickly engulfed the Himalayan kingdom. The king as an institution, and especially Tribhuvan, was widely loved by the people as that is what the Ranas wanted. The oligarchy ensured the people loved their king but never allowed that love to become a tool of power in favour of King Tribhuvan. The king was aware of the adulation that he enjoyed among the people. So, the plan was to escape from the Ranas for a while and take refuge in New Delhi to ensure that he returns with as much power restored to himself as possible. The king refused to return to his palace, and the Ranas tried to convince him by providing various options. But King Tribhuvan refused to leave the Indian Embassy. After a day of trying to safeguard the continuity of the state, the Ranas swore in Tribhuvan's youngest grandson Gyanendra as the king and minted coins in his name. This move, with its basis in the medieval past, however, did not get any international recognition and Nepal continued to remain in a non-state form.

After a brief stay at the residence of the Indian ambassador, King Tribhuvan, his son Mahendra and the eldest grandson Birendra were airlifted from Kathmandu's airport by an aircraft sent by New Delhi. The king was welcomed to Delhi, his first political visit abroad, by Prime Minister Jawaharlal Nehru.

Back in Nepal, the escape of the king triggered a major crisis as people were divided along pro- and anti-Rana lines. For over many decades, the masses had got used to the rule of the Ranas, but the monarchy still symbolized what Nepal stood for. The absence of the benevolent ruler was a major problem in the face of the law and governance of the realm. It was at this time that, as the vice consul, Wilfred had to travel across Nepal and assess the public mood and bring news of the public sentiments back to the ambassador and for the decision-makers in Delhi. In various places, the supporters of the Ranas would be waiting for the vehicles of the Indian Embassy, and they would pounce on the road and toss stones at the Indian officials. Wilfred survived such attacks on the roads as he travelled across the nook and corner of the mountainous country.

Wilfred never maintained a diary of his daily activities in Nepal or in subsequent postings through Pondicherry, Southern Rhodesia and British Guyana, but his daughter Shanthy, who lives in Bengaluru, says that they led exciting lives throughout their father's career, which lasted till the late 1960s. In the early 1960s,

Wilfred was posted to Central Africa as India's commissioner. He had to represent India in three regions that were undergoing decolonization—Southern Rhodesia, North Rhodesia and Nyasaland. These three regions subsequently became Zimbabwe, Zambia and Malawi, respectively. Representing India was a challenging task in these regions because of the anti-colonial and anti-racist struggles that the people there were leading at that time. One day, Wilfred took his family to meet a young leader who was involved in fighting for the freedom of North Rhodesia—a tall young man named Kenneth Kaunda, who at that time lived with his small family in a hut in the congested part of Lusaka. In 1964, North Rhodesia became independent, and Kaunda became the President, leaving his humble home for the presidential palace. It was here that the Wilfreds attended a get-together which was attended by Robert Mugabe. Soon he too became the leader of his country—Zimbabwe.

One day, Wilfred took his family on a tour of a copper mine in Zambia. After the visit, he suggested that India could consider sourcing copper from the rich mines of Zambia, which were some of the largest in Africa. President Kaunda gifted a small copper table to Wilfred as a token of appreciation for his role in starting the copper trade between India and free Zambia. Shanthy, his daughter, has preserved that table in her home.[11]

In March 1967, Santosham John Wilfred was appointed as the first Indian high commissioner to British Guyana, where he served till June 1969. During this time, Prime Minister Indira Gandhi visited British Guyana and attended a diplomatic get-together at the residence of the high commissioner. Gandhi was impressed by the hibiscus that Flora had grown in her garden and asked for a sapling for her garden in Delhi. After his retirement, Wilfred met Indira Gandhi at her residence in Delhi and the Prime Minister took him to her garden where the hibiscus from Guyana was in full bloom. She offered him a senior position in the Indian Embassy in Kathmandu as Wilfred had the valuable experience of handling Nepal. Wilfred politely declined. His daughter says that he did not want to go anywhere without Flora, who had passed away by then.[12] Santosham John Wilfred's career stands out among the first recruits because of the way he rose from the position of a clerk in 1947 to become an Indian Envoy in the 1960s.

The year was 1967. Satish Chandra Gauba and his young wife were staying in a hotel in Moscow as per the official requirement of the time. They had arrived a few days earlier, and as per existing norms, the Indian Embassy instructed him to stay in a hotel for the first few days while it arranged an official accommodation for him. It was the first foreign posting for Gauba and his wife Shashi, who got married just months earlier and were excited as this was the first time that they were travelling in a foreign land.

Moscow was a friendly city for Indians in the 1960s, but in the background of the Cold War, the Soviet capital had its share of intrigues. The Gaubas, however, had little idea of that side of the city till they found it out for themselves.

During the first fortnight, Gauba familiarized himself with his official tasks in Moscow, leaving his wife alone in the hotel room. In the meanwhile, the wives of the embassy staffers got to know about Shashi, and they started interacting with the new couple from India. A fortnight later, Shashi and Satish left the hotel for dinner at a colleague's residence in the city. After dinner, the host said they should sleep over in their spare bedroom, and the two happily spent the night away from the cold hotel. The next morning, they had breakfast and came to the hotel to find there was a manhunt underway for the 'missing' Indian diplomat and his wife.

The hotel manager had been harassed since the previous night by the officials of the KGB, who wanted to know the whereabouts of the Gaubas. On their arrival, the manager finally heaved a sigh of relief and said that they are heavily tracked and should thus inform the front desk about all their movements without a miss. The manager said that there is a security officer who always relays his movements to his counterpart stationed near the Indian Embassy, and they track and match movement of all Indian staffers who stay in the hotel. Any inconsistency could be a cause for trouble. Gauba was told that the matter was stopped from escalating as they had turned up on their own without causing any further embarrassment.

It was a tough lesson for Gauba, who had taken Moscow for granted for a fortnight. The Soviet Union was in the midst of the Cold War, and India was an important partner country. But the security requirements for diplomats of friendly countries were not relaxed, as there are always risks that diplomatic staff have to live with. The extra caution, therefore, was something to be welcomed and not abhorred, Gauba was told.

At the time of Gauba's arrival in Moscow, India was represented by Kewal Singh, a former ICS official who would go on to be the foreign secretary during 1972–76. Singh had hosted Prime Minister Indira Gandhi when she had visited Moscow on her way back to Delhi from a visit to the United States in 1966. Only the topmost diplomats got the Moscow assignment, and Gauba soon began to respect Kewal Singh for his abilities. He grew in his role in Moscow as a stenographer and over time came to handle almost all aspects of the embassy's functions—from visas to the purchase of household items and office stationery, events and everything else in between. 'I learned that as a stenographer my work could take me from writing notes to handling any other official assignments that the head of mission could give me,' Gauba said during an interview for this book.[13] In fact, that was a correct description of the role of a stenographer in the MEA. Stenographers were taken on board based on their typing speed and skills as a stenographer, but after joining the service they underwent a training and orientation that would allow them to branch out into various directions, like the visa section or trade division. The political situation in South Asia, in the meantime, was changing, and India was getting closer to the Soviets.

'One day, I saw an elderly person climb the stairs of the embassy alone, and I confronted him saying that the embassy had closed for the day and that he was late for official business. The gentleman said, "*Main kal se yahaan naukri kar lunga* (I will start working here from tomorrow)",' Gauba said recollecting how he met D.P. Dhar, successor of Kewal Singh. The next day, the stranger began working as the Indian ambassador to Moscow.

That new ambassador turned out to be a political appointee, a Kashmiri politician handpicked by Indira Gandhi to serve in Moscow at a critical time in her political career. As a special gesture, Dhar was allowed to have his own private secretary, whom he brought from Kashmir. The private secretary, Triloki Nath Fotedar, was the brother of Makhan Lal Fotedar, who was close to Indira Gandhi. The team worked in close coordination with the Prime Minister herself. The embassy under D.P. Dhar was to play an important role as Indira Gandhi sealed the Indo-Soviet Friendship Treaty in August 1971. Gauba would be present in the Embassy of India till December 1971 and returned to Delhi for a home posting the next year.

Gauba was born in Lyallpur in western Punjab, and his family had come to Delhi after the Partition. Speaking about his memories in Lyallpur, he said that the situation was serious as communal killings had started and the radio station from Lahore was announcing the timings of trains and names of missing persons. It was in that chaotic situation that he came to the refugee camps of Delhi, where his parents and other siblings also came to stay. They led a middle-class life in west Delhi's Janakpuri till 1963, when he joined as a stenographer thanks to a neighbour who had urged him to apply for the job, which had been advertised for in a newspaper. Soon after his joining in the MEA, he was assigned to work with Harivansh Rai Bachchan, who was in charge of the Hindi division of the MEA from 1955 to 1965. It was during this period that he became proficient in Hindi typing, which would help him in multiple assignments during the subsequent decades. As India's diplomatic footprint expanded, Gauba was among those early recruits who experienced the 'temporary postings' that became necessary as Indian prime ministers from Indira Gandhi onwards began to travel to areas that did not have an Indian diplomatic presence. Gauba travelled to places like Fiji, Nairobi, Somalia, Ivory Coast and other destinations during the years of Indira Gandhi as the MEA officials were sent out on short postings to lay the ground for important visits from India.

The stenographers were not entitled to undergo the kind of training and orientation that an A Class diplomat got soon after being recruited, and Gauba and his colleagues never received that kind of exposure. Yet they are a rich repository of stories about the bureaucratic machinery that spread so far apart from each other in different corners of the world. In the pre-internet and pre-long-haul flights era, travel abroad was viewed with anxiety.

'Foreign postings would be preceded by at least two months of preparation. We would purchase supplies of the items that would not be available in our postings. We were also allowed to carry more kilograms per person [and] that would allow us stock up for the period of posting,' said Gauba who served in Hong Kong, Ethiopia, Senegal, New York City and Dhaka during his tenure.[14]

In Hong Kong, India used to maintain a commission as Hong Kong, as a Crown colony, was entitled only to a commission; the High Commission was meant for London. During the posting to Hong Kong between 1980 and '84, Gauba's responsibilities included interacting with the local Indian population. The early 1980s were known for the proliferation of smuggling in narcotics in the Southeast Asian region. In a short while, he understood that the drugs menace was a residue of the Vietnam war. The US marines who fought in Vietnam gave birth to a culture of recreation in Southeast Asia, and the narcotics were part of that generation of violence. Gauba soon sensed that Hong Kong was a major transit point of drugs in Southeast Asia and sensed that some of the prominent members of the local Indian community could also be part of that international network. He felt a lot of money was being made by a few individuals in Hong Kong out of the drugs trade. One such Indian businessman, who belonged to a Sindhi family of Hyderabad, caught Gauba's attention, given his enormous wealth. The businessman had gold items scattered across his house. Gauba visited his house and felt that the wealth on display could not possibly come from his business. He suspected there was a backstory to the gold-plated doorknobs and faucets in the Sindhi businessman's mansion in Hong Kong. The Indian mission was not interested in carrying out investigations into the local population's activities unless there were cases in India that possibly could link them with individuals in Hong Kong. As a result, the Sindhi businessman never got investigated, though Gauba continues to have an odd feeling about the gentleman's wealth. A few years after Gauba's retirement in the early 2000s, the businessman visited India and was bestowed with a top honour meant for diasporic Indians. He passed away later.

Sometime after his return to Delhi after the Hong Kong years, Gauba was considered for a posting to the Indian Embassy in Kabul. He sought an appointment with Foreign Secretary A.P. Venkateswaran to seek his advice. Considering the age of his children, who were getting into high school, Venkateswaran asked him to reconsider the stay in Kabul, which did not have suitable schools at that time. Instead of Kabul, Gauba settled on Addis Ababa, which he remembers till now as the most peaceful and pleasant of his foreign stints. 'Addis Ababa has the best weather in the world,' Gauba said to me.

The stay in Ethiopia was the opposite of his stay in Dhaka when Bangladesh was entering a phase of tumult. 'We had just arrived in Dhaka a few days earlier, and we were planning to attend the programme in the Indian High Commission on 15 August, and in the previous night, Sheikh Mujibur Rahman was assassinated with his entire family,' Shashi Gauba recollected. During their stay in Dhaka, the Gaubas witnessed the period of military takeover following the assassination of Sheikh Mujibur Rahman and the killing of other prominent Awami League leaders in a Dhaka jail. 'Those were very intense days, and security instructions had to be followed. We were told to avoid windows at all costs even at home,' said Gauba.[15]

Satish Chandra Gauba's accounts, which begin from the Nehru era, continued till the end of the Vajpayee years and covered four decades of diplomacy. They indicate that despite not being involved in the teams of actual decision-makers, stenographers and office assistants, members of the Branch B of the IFS, were significant recorders of diplomatic history. In the conventional writing of diplomatic accounts, the stenographer cadre is never included but the 'assistants' or stenographers, a few of whom went on to become ambassadors like Santosham John Wilfred, are important witnesses of India's diplomatic history. They are the ones who do the physical work in missions and outside, and they were noted for their importance from the very beginning. In his 'Preface' to the *History of Services*, K.P.S. Menon (Jr) wrote, '...until the Branch (B) of the Service was constituted, any history of Services of officers of the Indian Foreign Service would have been incomplete.' The publication of the directory was prompted, Menon said, as 'Recruitment to Branch (B) of the Service' was 'nearing completion' and it has 'therefore, been possible to bring out' the statement. What distinguishes the IFS–B is that it grew more like a collection of people with diverse sets of skills—starting with typing, translation, literary writing and radio communication but going all the way to military information and even intelligence requirements. Therefore, Harivansh Rai Bachchan, Madanjeet Singh who is celebrated through the annual UNESCO Madanjeet Singh Prize, former wireless operator Seshadri Krishnaswamy and several others were hired under this segment.

9

REBELS AND PRINCES

THE NEWSPAPERS CARRIED EXPLOSIVE HEADLINES announcing the arrest of a deadly insurgent.[1] The Kerala police had arrested a major ideologue of the underground Maoist movement, they said. This catch was different. The man was sixty-two years old. Murali Kannampilly was a legend among the Maoists; he had mentored dozens of Maoist cadre over the decades, beginning his first brush with extremist ideology in the Emergency days when he participated in attacks against local police in Kerala. How a diplomat's son became a Maoist leader was a matter of speculation. Twenty-first century readers were reminded of Karunakara Menon Kannampilly in this way, decades after his demise, as the father of one of the legendary Maoist leaders of modern India.

Karunakara Menon Kannampilly, the diplomat father of Murali, would have been proud of his son because in his lifetime, his own exploits pitted him against the colonial Raj when he carried out anti-colonial activities in Myanmar before joining the foreign service.

Karunakara Menon Kannampilly draws attention in the *History of Services* as his career details stand out among the rest. The directory says that just before Independence he began as a secretary in the History Committee of the I.N.A. of Netaji Subhas Chandra Bose. His career also contrasts with that of P.R.S. Mani. Mani was an employee of the British Indian government and was disappointed with the turn of events and therefore joined the national movement. Kannampilly, in comparison, was a rebel from the beginning. According to the Kannampilly family, a year before Indian Independence, it was Jawaharlal Nehru himself who suggested that K.M. Kannampilly should lead the History Committee of the INA to record the epic battle that it had waged in Southeast and East Asia during the early 1940s for India's liberation. 'He led the team for seven to eight months and then gave up saying that it was not possible for him to write history of INA in an objective manner as it was all too recent for him,' said one of the sons of Ambassador Kannampilly.[2]

K.M. Kannampilly was much more than that, and it was probably not possible for the MEA to publish his legendary exploits in the *History of Services* because of lack of space. The 1912-born Kannampilly was a wanderer from the beginning, and his life was full of accidental developments. It is said that Kannampilly's father was disappointed by the personal and political choices of his two elder sons and had blamed education for their rebelliousness. His father thereafter came up with the idea that his next son, Karunakara, would be allowed to be educated only till the tenth standard and then would be dedicated to look after the land holdings of the family. Legend in the Kannampilly family has it that it was a school headmaster who prevailed upon his angry father and helped Kannampilly complete his school and college education.

Soon after his post-graduation at the Annamalai University in Chidambaram (Tamil Nadu), Kannampilly proceeded to Singapore to teach English literature at a YMCA school. During this time, he began playing an active role in the Malayalee association, the Indian Youth Association and the Indian Association. During this time, Kannampilly also began to mobilize the Indian workers in the rubber estates in South Johor of Malaya. In short, driven by the nationalist storm, Kannampilly reached out to Indians in Southeast Asia and earned a name for himself. Within the Indian community in Southeast Asia, Kannampilly became well known because of his essays and writings in *Kerala Bandhu* and *The Indian* which were published from Singapore and Kuala Lumpur respectively.

The roots of his activism lay in the Indian Independence League (IIL), which was started by Rash Behari Bose. After Singapore fell into Japanese hands, Kannampilly became one of the first organizers of the Indian Independence League in Singapore and became the secretary-general of the Malaya territorial branch of the IIL. When the IIL headquarters were moved to Rangoon in keeping with the developments within the region, he was called by Netaji Subhas Chandra Bose to take over the Independence League Organisation in Burma and ultimately became the secretary-general of the Indian Independence League in Southeast Asia. As the war drew to a close in Southeast Asia, he was placed under house arrest when he began publishing a political magazine called *Rangoon Review*. The magazine was supportive of the movement for independence of Burma championed by General Aung San and India–Burma cooperation. The close cooperation between Kannampilly and General Aung San was a problem for the British authorities who deported him to Singapore.

The year 1946–47 marked a great transition in South and Southeast Asia. In March 1946, Nehru carried out a pan-Malaya tour to look into the condition of Indian nationals who had suffered a great deal during the time that the Japanese ruled over the region. The visit was a landmark because of the huge welcome that Nehru received from the local population. Kannampilly was one of the few who worked on the ground to make the visit a success. Kannampilly was banned from entering India by the British authorities. But after Nehru headed the interim government, the ban was lifted and he was allowed to come back to India.

The long stay in Burma had brought Kannampilly close to General Aung San, who was already a legendary figure in Burma in the 1930s. After he came back to India he was asked to be the secretary of the INA History Committee. A few months later, as mentioned earlier, he gave up that job because he felt the events were too recent to be recalled dispassionately. But his years in Southeast Asia and extensive interactions with expat Indians provided him with a wide network of nationalists in Thailand, Burma, Malaya and Singapore. Hence, he was made the organizing secretary of the Asian Relations Conference hosted in Delhi in 1947. Nationalists and leaders from twenty-five countries came to New Delhi that month to participate in the brainstorming session—the biggest multilateral discussion held in Delhi months before Indian Independence was declared. K.M. Kannampilly had a brief interlude after the Asian Relations Conference when he planned to join active politics and was about to contest the election on a ticket from the Praja Socialist Party in Kerala. His plans, however, were disturbed when Praja Socialist Party joined hands with the Congress. 'He did not want to be a part of the Congress,' said one of the sons of Ambassador Kannampilly. Kannampilly planned to return to Burma and join the upcoming Aung San who was the 'equivalent of Netaji in Burma'. The nationalist movement in India had triggered a cascading effect, and all the British or European possessions in Asia were pushed into the circle of instability. The Burmese general, often credited with setting up the Tatmadaw in today's Myanmar, was a known socialist who believed in a Burma that would be based upon inter-ethnic harmony and development of the country's economy. Powerful international and financial forces at home were aligned against General Aung San. In the meanwhile, Aung San took over power in Burma and the restriction on his entry into Burma was removed. But his future in Burma was disrupted at the last moment.

Merely minutes before Kannampilly boarded the aircraft in Delhi on 19 July 1947, the political situation in Burma changed. An airport staffer rushed towards Kannampilly carrying a message from the office of the Prime Minister. The message revealed that General Aung San had been assassinated just minutes earlier. Kannampilly's strength lay in his wide knowledge of Southeast Asia which he gathered during his long years in the Indian Independence League and was to prove to be useful to Jawaharlal Nehru in the early years. His son says thereafter his father began to work with Jawaharlal Nehru and joined the Indian Foreign Service. Both Kannampilly and P.R.S. Mani belonged to a group of specialists on Southeast Asia who came into prominence during World War II. While Mani was a rebel from within the ranks of the British Indian military, Kannampilly came from a privileged Nair family but became a rebel. Kannampilly's secularism was complemented by his anti-caste stance. For instance, he would not emphasize his middle name—Menon—as it would give away and unduly emphasize his caste identity. 'He always introduced himself as K.M. Kannampilly, without highlighting the middle name,' said the son.

As the Indian government led by Nehru moved towards recognizing the Indonesian government, N. Raghavan (formerly the finance minister in Bose's Indian government in exile) was sent as the envoy. Kannampilly was sent there as an attaché and served as the first secretary from October 1947 to February 1949. Raghavan served in multiple missions subsequently, including China, France and Switzerland, and retired in 1961, but the *History of Services*, which chronicled several INA veterans who joined the IFS, did not include Raghavan's name. This appears to be a significant omission.

The situation in Indonesia or the Dutch Indies was complex. During World War II, the entire Indonesian landmass, barring small parts, was under the rule of Imperial Japan. This changed dramatically after the defeat of Japan as the Indonesian nationalists declared the independence of the Dutch Indies on 17 August 1945. But the process of gaining independence could not be completed for four more years as the former colonial power tried to roll back Indonesian history and revive colonial control. It was in this condition that Kannampilly was stationed in Jakarta. Indonesia would leave a lasting impact on Kannampilly's career as it was here that he would return to in 1971 to serve in his last posting as the ambassador of India before retiring.

As a veteran of the Southeast Asia, Kannampilly already had the shape of his foreign service career in independent India carved out. The *History of Services* records that his first appointment at Batavia was followed by his stint in the Indian Embassy in Rangoon where he served as deputy secretary from May 1950 to March 1954. Southeast Asia was marked by the unfolding war in Indochina which was a destabilizing factor for the entire region apart from the post-colonial difficulties that major countries like Thailand, Burma and Indonesia were faced with. The presence of Kannampilly on the ground provided a continuity as he had widespread network in the region, stretching back to more than two decades. Fresh recruits in the early days of the Indian Foreign

Service were sent to universities in the UK, France, Germany and the United States for training, but with those like Kannampilly, Mani and M.R.A. Baig, the officers came with their own national and international social capital which was highly useful in actual problem-solving on the ground. Appointments of this kind were an innovation that served well as the new recruits were not yet equipped to deal with the social and diplomatic requirements that the societies in the region were undergoing.

After the assassination of General Aung San, Kannampilly stayed back in Delhi mobilizing the remaining members of the INA, who helped in ensuring law and order in Delhi, which was facing riots. His son recollected that his father was fiercely secular and so were his ex-INA colleagues, who were therefore trusted by Nehru in dealing with the communal situation prevailing in the capital at that time. After his first stint at Jakarta from October 1947 to February 1949, Kannampilly went on to be one of the main experts working on the problems of the Southeast Asia during the next two decades. He served as deputy secretary in the Indian Embassy in Rangoon from May 1950 to March 1954. Next came the big role that India had to play in Southeast Asia as the chair of the International Commission for Supervision and Control (ICSC). The ICSC was an amalgamation of three ICSCs that were meant to supervise the implementation of the Geneva Accords of 1954, which ended French control over the Indochina. The three international commissions were meant for Vietnam, Laos and Cambodia. India was drawn to the Indochina theatre. All the three ICSCs had India as the chair. This interesting development was a sign of India's neutrality and the credibility that Nehru's diplomatic machinery had acquired immediately after Independence. In his own words, these were all 'difficult problems'. 'We are naturally interested in peace in Indochina, but why should we, with all our problems, seek to carry other people's burden? That question my people ask me. Why did we do it? Not willingly, but circumstances compelled us, and we feel that if we had refused to undertake that burden, well, there might have been greater trouble in Indochina. When the two conflicting parties asked us—both of them asked us—we just could not say no, it would have been escaping from our duty and obligation. So we went there, and there we are.'[3] Karunakara Menon Kannampilly became the deputy secretary-general of the ICSC-Laos and served in that position from September 1954 to November 1955. In between, on 20 May 1955, he was confirmed as an IFS officer under the Senior Scale.[4] He started the Indian mission in Denmark in 1962 and stayed on till 1965. Before that, he was a counsellor in the Embassy of India in Beijing from 1958. Soon after his return from Denmark, he would be dispatched to North Vietnam to explore conditions of peace and dialogue.[5] North Vietnam's position on India had been impacted after the 1962 Sino-Indian war, and New Delhi was not in regular contact with the Government of Ho Chi Minh, who wanted to unite South Vietnam with North Vietnam and create a single communist state. Given the situation and assertion of Chinese power, North Vietnam supported Beijing's version of what transpired along the Himalayan borders between India and China in 1962. Kannampilly's visit to Laos and North Vietnam, which took place three months after Indira Gandhi became PM for the first time, was therefore of good use to the Indian government as it once again revived political connections between the two sides. This little window of warmth with North Vietnam would help India in the coming years as its ties with the Soviet bloc would be helpful in reclaiming its regional dominance. It was during this phase of Kannampilly's career that he got the chance to leave a lasting imprint on India's diplomacy with the

Southeast Asian region as he headed the Indian delegation that negotiated the border agreement with Burma, signed on 10 March 1967, demarcating the difficult border between the two sides. Kannampilly was a joint secretary-level officer at that time. He retired from the IFS in 1970 after having served as the Indian ambassador to Indonesia.

After clearing the civil service examination, a bunch of young probationers were waiting at the Gate No. 5 in South Block one morning in 1964 when they caught a glimpse of the Prime Minister of India, who had been at the helm for seventeen years. As Jawaharlal Nehru saw the young officers dressed in the formal official attire, he turned at them and smiled saying, 'Oh, what a peaceful invasion!'[6]

The officers did not get a chance to meet Nehru formally. That chance meeting for the batch of 1964 took place as they were called for the last interview that the Ministry of External Affairs used to hold for the young recruits before finally letting them come on board. Former ambassador of India K.P. Fabian recalled during an interaction with this author that the interview was not meant to eliminate any of the selected candidates but was aimed at ascertaining the suitability of the candidate from the point of view of the serving officials. The practices of the Ministry of External Affairs had become established by the time Fabian joined the fledgling team of Indian diplomats. Nehru passed away soon after that chance meeting with Fabian and his batch of officers. The foreign service of India that he had set up with existing available talent had established itself by that time with its own traditions, and there was no looking back thereafter. Nehru departed from the scene on 27 May 1964, but the officers whom he had taken to create the foundation of the service in the late 1940s would continue to tower over the young recruits for many years.

One of them would meet Fabian when he was posted to Madagascar for his first foreign posting, which came a year after Nehru's demise. Fabian would serve in the Indian Embassy in Madagascar under Ambassador Cyril John Stracey. The posting in Antananarivo was pleasant and the task involved taking care of the Indian migrants—mostly Gujaratis—who had made Madagascar their home. Many residents had arrived in Madagascar during the British era and had not returned home since—which made them stateless as they lacked documentary evidence. One of the main tasks for the Indian Embassy was thus to ensure that the Indians in the country were assisted with official documents so that they were not inconvenienced. Cyril John Stracey towered over the rest of the staff with his presence. An Anglo-Indian by birth, Stracey maintained an air of formality. Fabian remembers him as an officer who would prefer a long table when he asked his staff to meet him for a personal meeting, just to make sure that the air of formality prevailed in the meeting. That apart, he was highly particular about courtesy for his guests. Stracey had a love for the good things in life, maintained his attachment for Paris, where he was posted before being sent to Madagascar, and often managed to get a nod from the Ministry of External Affairs for items for the mission from Paris. Fabian was just beginning his career and Stracey was going to retire soon, but the enigmatic ambassador was a subject of interest for his younger colleagues because of his cosmopolitan personality and lifestyle. Over time, Fabian would find out that the ambassador's driver, Ganesh Singh, had worked as the cook for Netaji Subhas Chandra Bose. Nehru's recruits for the foreign service were like him in many ways. They adapted to the new circumstances that they had created, but they also carried a bit of India's past with them. Ganesh Singh and Stracey were those Indians who were part of the new India, but below the surface, they also carried the history of India's past with them. Stracey's next posting was in Finland, where he would retire, ending his career in the Indian Foreign Service, in which he was appointed on 1 September 1948.[7]

Before his postings to Paris and Madagascar, Stracey had served as secretary of the Indian Goodwill Mission to Ethiopia (1948) and as second secretary of the Indian High Commission in Karachi (November 1948–June 1951), Bonn (1952) and Indonesia (starting from 1956). Fabian, as a direct recruit, would have a thirty-six-year long tenure as a diplomat, but Stracey barely had a two-decade long stint. From Finland he returned to his home in Bengaluru (then Bangalore). But he ensured that Ganesh Singh would continue to be the chauffeur of the Indian ambassador in Finland. Fabian would be posted as the Indian ambassador to Finland in the mid-1980s, and he was happy to meet Ganesh Singh in Helsinki. The nearly-sixty-year-old Ganesh Singh had fallen in love with a Finnish lady, who also had a flourishing catering business. Together, they had a happy family in Helsinki and maintained the bond between Stracey and Netaji Subhas Chandra Bose that was forged during the high point of India's rebellion against the British Empire.

Stracey's presence evoked mystery as the Anglo-Indians, once the chosen ones in the official ranks, were a rarity after the departure of the British from India. Stracey was, of course, different as he had proved his patriotism in the battlefield.

Stracey had not signed up for a life in diplomacy. He had aspired to be a soldier.

In the first week of January 1935, Mrs Churchill, the wife of Winston Churchill, arrived in Chennai, then Madras. She was accompanied by a few other passengers who had left the United Kingdom in December 1934 for a pleasure trip on board a luxury yacht, Rosuro.[8] The yacht had travelled through the Mediterranean and stopped at Aden before reaching the southern shores of India. It was to proceed to Rangoon in Southeast Asia and the Far East. In Madras, she was surrounded by the press, which wanted to know her opinion about Indian affairs as that same year, the Government of India Act was to be a reality, laying the path for self-rule for Indians. Mrs Churchill expressed her interest in Indian affairs but avoided commenting on political issues as she was on a personal trip.[9]

That same week, the results of the competitive examination held in October 1934 for entering the Indian Military Academy in Dehradun were announced. Cyril John Stracey of nearby Mysore was one of those who cleared the test.[10] The Straceys were the descendants of John and Edward—two Irish brothers who came to India during the early days of the British East India Company. The brothers came from Cork in Ireland and arrived at a time when the East India Company was conquering the Indian princely states, and the local royals hired western assistants liberally to draw from the resources that they had to offer. John Stracey worked as a British commercial agent representing the west Indian interest of the company while Edward worked for the company in Madras. Both married Portuguese girls from Kochi. Subsequently, the two brothers began to work for the Nizam of Hyderabad while their children began serving the British rulers who had come to overpower all Indian princely states after the mutiny of 1857. It was from this lineage that Ethel and Daniel, parents of Cyril John Stracey, had emerged.

Cyril John Stracey was born in Kurnool a year after World War I began. Anglo-Indians were a community that came up during the centuries' long interaction between India and Europe, and this community lived in proximity to the centres of the administration and the military. One such location was Richmond Town of Bangalore, where a concentration of the community lived close to the military facilities. Like several other first-generation Indian diplomats, Stracey too had not gone to college as he cleared the competitive examination to join the Indian Military Academy in Dehradun even before completing his intermediate. The period was not easy as the Stracey family underwent a lot of hardship to ensure he completed his training. Daniel Stracey passed away just before Cyril Stracey could clear his admission test for the IMA, and his mother, Ethel Stracey, sold the house in Bangalore and went to Rangoon to stay with her brother-in-law. Cyril Stracey had an artistic bent of mind, and he was given to drawing and designing—both skills he would use much later during his time in the INA of Subhas Chandra Bose.

After completing his training at the IMA, Cyril John Stracey's first posting was at Bannu in the Northwest Frontier, which was the training ground of many officers of the Indian Political Service, some of whom would go on to join the Indian Foreign Service with Stracey. After the beginning of World War II, the battalion was sent to Burma, where Cyril confronted military duties at the battlefield.

He was taken prisoner by the Japanese on the Jitra front close to the Thai–Malaya boundary. It was here that an Indian officer of the INA came to meet five Anglo-Indian Prisoners of War (POWs), including Stracey. The meeting had a transformative effect on Stracey. He joined the INA, a force aligned with the Japanese, at great personal risk; he could have been court-martialled if captured by the British Indian forces. It was this phase of Stracey's life that gave him an eternal place in the annals of Indian history, as he was one among the last comrades of the INA to interact with Bose in Singapore during those fateful last days of World War II.

On 15 August 1945, Netaji decided to erect a memorial on the sea face of Singapore, so that it could deliver a statement of defiance to the British forces who were expected to arrive soon after the surrender of Japan. Stracey, who had a gift of designing and drawing, arrived to meet Netaji with a few models and rolls of papers containing designs of the memorial. Netaji made his selection from the designs and said, 'Colonel Stracey, I want this memorial to rise on the sea face of Singapore before the British make a landing there. Do you think you will be able to do it?' 'Certainly, Sir,' was Stracey's reply. He then proceeded to build the structure bearing the motto of the INA—'Unity, Trust and Sacrifice', or 'Ittehad, Itmad aur Qurbani'.

On 6 and 9 August 1945, the United States dropped two atomic bombs on Hiroshima and Nagasaki, hastening the end of the war's front in Asia. Hours after Netaji had given perhaps one of the last orders of his life—to Stracey—Japan surrendered, and with it was lost the cause that the INA had sacrificed so much for since being launched on 10 August 1942.

On 5 September 1943 the memorial greeted the British soldiers—most of whom were Indians under the command of Lord Mountbatten. Three days later, they dynamited the memorial. That act of vandalism could have ended a physical memory of a proud episode of the Indian freedom struggle, but it only added to the legend of Netaji Subhas Chandra Bose, in which Stracey was a significant witness.

One of the young recruits for the year who stood at Gate No. 5 was K.P. Fabian, who went on to be India's ambassador to Italy and played the leading official role in South Block during the airlift operation of Indians from Iraq in 1990.

'What! Come to your temple where even Hindus of other castes are not permitted entry, not to speak of members of other communities who are all equally near and dear to me. No, Sir, definitely not,' Netaji said, rejecting the Dussehra invite from the head priest of the Chettiyar temple in Singapore.[11]

The head priest of the Chettiyar temple in Singapore had planned a special Dussehra festival for Netaji Subhas Chandra Bose. It was a grand occasion for the Indian community, and he wanted Netaji to be the chief guest. Word had spread that Netaji was in Singapore and the head priest arrived to invite Netaji. The Indian National Army had thought of the appointment as a courtesy call by the orthodox priest and had not anticipated the invite. Netaji, however, was in no mood to accept the invite.

Word had gone out that the temple in Singapore was not open to all Hindus and that people of other communities were not allowed entry. The previous few years were tumultuous in the life of Subhas Chandra Bose. Staunchly against the idea of Indians fighting for the British rulers, Netaji quietly left Calcutta on the night of 16–17 January 1941 for a journey that he had carefully planned. From Calcutta, Netaji reached Germany where he launched the Indian Legion with the help of the Indian POWs who were arrested by General Rommel's forces. Hitler's war machine, however, was past its peak by the early 1940s, when Japan scored a big victory against the British in Southeast Asia and captured Singapore. The Indian community in Germany reached out to Netaji during his stay in the country and provided him with the support he required. Netaji spoke German well, but he also required local Indian German speakers for his larger engagement; among such speakers he found a worthy friend in an Indian student, Abid Hasan Safrani, who was one of the civilians to join the Indian Legion. Safrani's association with the charismatic Indian leader increased as Netaji grew disillusioned with the German war against the Soviet Union, as both Germany and the Soviets were potential supporters for India's liberation. Safrani was the only compatriot to join Netaji on the epic journey in a German U-boat in 1943. Netaji was a symbol of communal amity in India and wanted to take a Hindu, a Muslim and a Sikh aboard on the German submarine, but on being told by the German naval officials that he could take only one assistant, he chose Safrani. Netaji and Safrani, despite being untrained civilians, travelled half the world in the U-boat to a rendezvous point over the Indian Ocean near Madagascar. Here the two men were transferred to a rubber dinghy that carried them to a waiting Japanese submarine that had surfaced earlier. Netaji was given a hero's welcome in Tokyo, where Hideki Tojo honoured him as the leader of India. It was against this backdrop that British-governed Singapore was conquered in February 1942 by the Imperial Japanese Army, which, after consolidating their presence in the region, helped Netaji come to Singapore too in July 1943. In Singapore, Netaji was given a rousing welcome by the large Indian population. On 21 October in the same year, he launched the Provisional Government of Free India or Azad Hind. The Azad Hind government was unequivocal in declaring that India would be freed of British rule through an armed struggle. Throughout this period, Safrani remained with Bose and chronicled the epic adventure.

The India that Netaji wanted to build with the blood and sacrifice of the soldiers of the Indian National Army—INA—would not have any place for any of the divisiveness that permeated Indian politics in the early 1940s. Comrades of the INA knew Netaji was a religious person and would have felt it odd had he gone to the Chettiyar temple and offered his prayers.

Closer to Dussehra, the head priest returned to meet Netaji once again. This time, he did not seek appointment and simply arrived with a steely determination in his eyes. Abid Hasan Safrani, the close associate of Netaji, had many responsibilities, and one of those was to decide who could meet the legendary leader who was providing leadership to the INA while in exile in Southeast Asia. Safrani met the head priest and was struck by the 'look of his eyes'.[12] There was a marked difference in the way they approached Netaji. Unlike the last time, they stood straight, without bending, and said, 'Sir, tomorrow evening I am holding an Indian national demonstration in my temple. I shall be grateful if you would preside over it.'[13]

The next day, when Netaji arrived at the temple, he found the temple was filled to capacity with men wearing the uniforms of the INA and the fez worn by Indian Muslims, indicating the composition of the audience. The priests came to welcome Netaji reverentially and led him and his companions to the sanctum sanctorum, where Netaji performed a puja and submitted the offerings to the deity. Safrani stood a few steps behind Netaji initially, but the priests pushed him to proceed and join Netaji, and there the two—one a Hindu and the other a Muslim—offered the puja and accepted the tilaks that were placed by the head priest. Exiting the temple a bit later, Netaji gently wiped the tilak from his forehead and Safrani followed his leader. Netaji did deliver a speech on that occasion of visiting the temple, but the interaction with the head priest had filled Safrani with such a headiness that he could not register anything. That feeling of oneness that was created by the gesture of the priests pushing him to participate in the rituals had filled Safrani with 'an invigorating music'.[14] It was probably this feeling that filled Abid Hasan Safrani when he, with 1,000 other soldiers and high-ranking figures of the INA, marched through the forests and hills of Burma and proceeded to Manipur at a time when defeat was staring the INA in the eye.

Abid Hasan Safrani, Karunakara Menon Kannampilly, N. Raghavan and Cyril John Stracey were part of a small group of unique diplomats with their past in the INA of Subhas Chandra Bose which Jawaharlal Nehru recruited to be a part of the new diplomatic brigade of India. Apart from the four, the list included Madan Mohan Khurana, who joined the IFS on 1 October 1948, and Mahboob Ahmed, who joined the foreign service on 1 April 1949.[15]

The 1960s was the decade of war for Asia. The South Asian region was left shaken by the wars of 1962 and 1965, and nearby, in Southeast Asia, the Vietnam war raged, casting a long shadow on India's present and future. The demise of Lal Bahadur Shastri in January 1966 pushed India into mourning, but there were more pressing problems than the death of the Prime Minister. Indira Gandhi had become the next Prime Minister, but the economy and diplomacy were in tatters. War and famine had both hit India, and after the 1965 India–Pakistan war, relations with the United States had nosedived. India required massive agriculture support to avoid domestic unrest, but that could come from the United States only if India extended its diplomatic support for the US war in Vietnam.

The Vietnamese crisis was not new to India as the Nehru government had been part of the negotiation to enforce the 1954 Geneva Accords in the region. For several years during the conflict, India did not have full-fledged diplomatic relations with North Vietnam though it engaged both North and South Vietnam as a sign of its neutrality in the conflict. It served as the chair of the International Commission for Supervision and Control (ICSC), which was constituted after the Geneva Accords of 1954 for peace building in French Indochina. In the early days, India maintained consulate-level relations with North and South Vietnam and later upgraded its relations to include ambassadors on 7 January 1972.[16] The phase of 1965–72, though, was particularly crucial for Vietnam, and Indian leadership had to do a tightrope walk to deal with the biggest military crisis. The difficulty of the Vietnam policy was evident soon after the 1962 Sino-Indian war, when Foreign Secretary Y.D. Gundevia was passing through Hanoi. A North Vietnamese official had confronted Gundevia saying that the war was triggered by India's military actions. Reporting on the matter a decade later, *The Times of India* recollected that the exchange soon turned into an 'unpleasant argument'.[17] Finally, K.R. Narayanan, who was the consul general of India to North Vietnam at that time, intervened saying that the foreign secretary was getting late for a lunch engagement. Gundevia, who began his career as an ICS officer in 1930, quickly recovered, and the Indian and the North Vietnamese officials had a cordial lunch after that as Narayanan, the future President of India, ensured peace. But nothing prepared the Indian side for what followed—a diplomatic scandal of sorts was inflicted by India's consul general on South Vietnam's capital, Saigon.

The two consuls—K.R. Narayanan and Pradyumma Sinhji Kotda Sangani—were poles apart in every aspect. Kocheril Raman

Narayanan was born into a Dalit family in Travancore and received his BA from Travancore University before proceeding to get a BSc (Economics) from the London School of Economics with a specialization in political science. He became a lecturer in English literature at the University College of Trivandrum in 1943 and joined the editorial department of *The Hindu* in Madras in 1944. A year later, Narayanan shifted to Mumbai where he joined *The Times of India* and was one of the first IFS officers to be recruited on 19 April 1949. His first posting was at the Ministry of External Affairs, where he served as attaché, followed by a posting to the Indian Embassy in Rangoon, from July 1949 to November 1950. His next foreign posting came in Tokyo where he served from 1951 to 1954. In 1955, he was posted to the Indian High Commission in London.

The consul general in South Vietnam hailed from the princely state of Kotda Sangani, one of the Rajput princely states of Kathiawar. Pradyumma Sinhji was, in fact, the ruler of Kotda Sangani, a fourth-class princely state of the British era. Pradyumma Sinhji's youth was spent far from the public service of the post-1947 India. His circle included the likes of the rulers of Indore, Mysore and Gwalior. A strikingly handsome prince, Pradyumma Sinhji married the daughter of the maharaja of Mysore, Vijayalakshmi. Narayanan and Pradyumma Sinhji reflected two facets of the new India. Narayanan was taught by Harold Laski, the great political theorist in the London School of Economics and married Ma Tint, a Burmese national. (The *History of Services* makes the reference that Ma Tint had adopted Indian nationality after marriage.) The period beginning with the arrival of Indira Gandhi as the Prime Minister was particularly sensitive also from the point of view of India's foreign policy as the issue of India's unwillingness to support the American war effort in Vietnam became tangled, not so surprisingly, with India's dire agriculture situation as well as New Delhi's concerns about US arms sales to Pakistan. In 1969, India held out a threat to upgrade the mission to North Vietnam after the United States insisted that it was free to give weapons to Pakistan.[18]

Indira Gandhi chose the United States as her first foreign destination in 1966, and she struck up a rapport with President Lyndon Johnson. She agreed to the American demand to open an educational foundation called USEFI in India and indicated that India 'understood' why the US government was waging the war in Vietnam. Back home, she faced a terrible backlash for the steps, and it was suggested that the devaluation of the Indian currency was carried out at the behest of the US government. Partly as continuation of the hard-line policy and partly to pacify her domestic critics, Indira Gandhi, soon after her return from the US, made a U-turn and 'deplored' the war on Vietnam. The US imposed a heavy penalty and delayed the food aid that was promised during her visit to the US.

It was in this backdrop that Pradyumma Sinhji made a diplomatic faux pas that was remembered for many years. Pradyumma Sinhji issued a public statement in his name declaring that the government of Indira Gandhi should change its policy on Vietnam. The real reasons that prompted the former ruler of a well-regarded princely state from Kathiawar to rebel against the official policy of the day was not known. But it caused deep embarrassment to the South Block, which urged him to disown his own statement by blaming the press for misrepresenting facts. However, Pradyumma Sinhji announced that he had no intention of backtracking and would repeat the plea to the government 'however painful the process'.[19]

The royals had a special place in India's diplomatic history, and it was natural that several found place in the newly formed Indian

Foreign Service. Kotda Sangani, for example, was classic princely India where the princes lived lavishly in the company of European administrators, who hunted tigers in their moments of leisure. On other occasions, the guns would be turned on the 'dacoits' and 'bandits', who abounded in princely states.

The Independence of India did not automatically lead to the merger of the princely states in the new state to be led from New Delhi, and in many cases, protracted negotiation ensured the desired result. Kotda Sangani was one of the twelve Kathiawari states that were acutely aware of the rights of the princely states, as promised by the outgoing colonial administration. In 1945, Kotda Sangani was part of the group of the eleven royal families of Kathiawar that kept a list of 'minimum demands' before the upcoming administration. These states opposed the 'attachment scheme' and formed what came to be known as the 'anti-attachment states' bloc', which began to consult the veteran lawyer Dr M.R. Jayakar. These states wanted to ensure the continuation of some form of control even after the merger with the Indian union. They also insisted on ensuring consent before the merger became effective. The rulers of Lakhtar and Kotda Sangani—both Rajput domains—led the formation and the group that also included estates of Jasdan, Virpur, Lathi, Vala, Muli, Mansa, Bajana, Vadia, Manavadar and Sayla. The inclusion of the likes of Pradyumma Sinhji was, therefore, indicative of the evolving Indian state's internal dynamics, which were best on display at the time of the merger of Hyderabad in 1948. The embarrassing incident triggered by Pradyumma Sinhji over India's Vietnam policy, therefore, cannot be viewed as just an outburst of a diplomat who did not agree with his superiors but also as a member of the traditional Indian elite of the early twentieth century who probably felt that he did not belong to the new India that was emerging under their watch. Sinhji did not last in foreign service and resigned soon after this incident. In the case of Vietnam, in particular, his criticism of the Indira Gandhi government's leftist policy, however, did not pass the test of time. The humiliation of India by Lyndon Johnson left a deep mark, but India did not change its policy on Vietnam. The hard line on Vietnam strengthened India's friendship with the USSR, which went on to help New Delhi in the war of 1971.

The princely states would be tested repeatedly by the Indira Gandhi government, and the outburst by Kotda Sangani's former ruler on the topic of Vietnam was only a symptom of the larger problem that erupted when the Indira government launched the wider structural reform.

Pradyumma Sinhji's sudden outbursts had been noticed in July 1967, when Sri Lanka and India were in negotiation for the repatriation of 'stateless' people of Indian origin residing in Sri Lanka. The issue was an obvious irritant for India as it involved the fate of Sri Lankan Tamils. Sri Lanka was also facing a foreign currency crisis at this time. At a press conference organized to discuss these issues, a journalist asked Pradyumma Sinhji, who was then the deputy high commissioner, if India would extend Sri Lanka a loan. The deputy high commissioner retorted: 'Why don't you ask China?'[20] The diplomatic *faux pas* ruffled quite a few feathers, and the High Commission of India in Colombo had to issue a clarification later.

Similar circumstances surrounded the service of Surendra Sinh Alirajpur. Alirajpur, presently a part of the state of Madhya Pradesh, was under the Bhopawar Agency in central India. The state assumed prominence during the time of Surendra Sinh's grandfather, the maharaja of Alirajpur, who was a good polo player as well as a *shikari* (hunter). The maharaja also helped substantially in raising the fortunes of his state. Maharaja Sir Pratap Sinhji passed away at the age of sixty-seven on 10 June 1948, months after abdicating the throne in favour of his grandson, Surendra Sinh, who joined the Indian Foreign Service in 1949 like Pradyumma Sinhji of Kotda Sangani. While the world was at war, India was dealing with changes within. One of the changes that India had undergone was that two decades after Independence, a new generation of voters had emerged and Indira Gandhi represented that new restless generation, which was supported by the Communist Party of India (CPI). The government campaigned on abolishing the privy purses of the former princely states, arguing that privy purses were not equivalent to right to property, which was enshrined in the Constitution, and that they represented a political settlement that had to change with the changing times. The former princes tried their best to stall the move, and the maharajas of Rewa, Indore, Jambukhoda, Aundh and Vadia opposed the planned abolition of the privy purses and privileges. Pradyumma Sinhji Kotda Sangani had left the IFS by that time and joined the maharajas to oppose the move.

One of the former rulers suggested that the government should put the proposal for a referendum in the areas that previously constituted the princely states. The idea was radical and threatened to unravel the Indian state as the former princely states once governed nearly 46 per cent of the landmass which became part of India after the Partition of 1947. The princes campaigned for solving the difference through 'a spirit of cooperation' and pleaded that the government should respect the 'sanctity of the pledged word'. These arguments did not help bridge the gulf between the Indira Gandhi government and the princes.

On 3 September 1970, the Lok Sabha passed the Constitution (24th Amendment) Bill that abolished the privy purses and privileges of the former princely states. In a symbolic move, the last remnants of the princely states, which were part of the political culture of India for hundreds of years, were done away with. There was, of course, an economic reason behind the move, but more important was the political impact of the bill, which was viewed as a statement by the evolving Indian democracy that was unwilling to have any more links with the princely states of the past. While the Congress and the leftist forces supported the bill, the Congress (O), the Swatantra Party and the Jana Sangh opposed the move. The bill went down in Indian history as one of the major steps taken by Indira Gandhi to cement her image as a powerful leader. The bitterness of that time cast a shadow on the relations between the new Indian state and the former rulers. Surendra Sinh, at that time India's high commissioner to Singapore, opposed the abolition of privy purse. He issued a formal statement and urged the government to reconsider the move. The Ministry of External Affairs took note of the scandalous situation, where a prominent diplomat on an important foreign posting declared his opposition to one of the landmark decisions of the Government of India. MEA asked Surendra Sinh to explain his remarks, and he responded saying that the remarks represented his personal opinion and had no bearing on his professional responsibilities. The matter ended at that point, though it did not endear him to the leading members of the bureaucracy.

Apart from the likes of Pradyumma Sinhji and Surendra Sinh Alirajpur, other notable princes in the diplomatic service of the 1950s and the 1960s included Narendra Singh, former diwan of Sarila in central India, and Shardul Bikram Shah, who was the maharajkumar of the Tehri Garhwal. The elegant and scholarly Narendra Singh Sarila served as the aid-de-camp to Governor General Lord Mountbatten in 1948. He was appointed in the IFS on 22 August 1948 and went on to train with the probationers of the 1948 batch.[21]

There were also the likes of Natwar Singh who, however, fell in a different category as he came through the competitive examination. The connection between the princely states and diplomatic service was not new and went back to the days when modern India was emerging from the cocoon of colonial administration in the backdrop of the defeat of imperial Germany by the Allied powers in World War I.

India had become a stakeholder in the future of post-WWI Europe, but there were doubts about how and in what capacity would India participate in the settlement of a war that was fought among the European powers. But then there were precedents already which showed that India had been part of several international agreements with the western powers long before World War I.

A representative of India had signed the Berne Convention in 1874 which made India a member of the Universal Postal Union. In 1890, India took part in the Conference of the International Union for the Publication of Customs Tariffs. India under the British rule signed the International Wireless Telegraph Convention in 1912. India had a representation at the International Radiotelegraph Conference in 1912. By the end of World War I, India, despite being under foreign rule, was party to 150 multilateral treaties and 44 bilateral treaties.[22] India also took part in the International Alliance of Women to promote universal suffrage. The anomaly of India in a global platform was, however, difficult to erase because of the complexities involved.

The Europeans got to know India as the biggest overseas colony of the British empire. But the reality was somewhat mixed. The Indian Empire of the British Crown, in fact, consisted of the territories that the Crown ruled directly in addition to around 562 kingdoms and principalities spread across South Asia. While the international domain had got familiarized with the British-ruled India, they were also familiar with princely states of the Nizams of Hyderabad, the Rajput rulers of Jaipur, the royals of Saurashtra and Kutch, the nawabs of Dhaka and many other such territories. In a strict sense, this meant that the resident of one kingdom was in fact a foreigner to another kingdom. The legal definition of an Indian citizen was not yet settled in the early twentieth century when India acquired an international presence.

To the world, India was defined as per the Interpretation Act, 1889, which refers to India as British India. According to the Section 18(5) of the Act, India included 'British India, together with any territories of any native prince or chief under the suzerainty of His Majesty.' Accordingly, the princely states did not have any right to conclude treaties with other foreign powers and that power laid exclusively with the British government.

The Paris Peace Conference regarded India as a 'composite character'.[23] This meant that India attended the international conference of nations as a new and unique entity. Because of this composite nature, one member representing the princely states participated in the delegations that were sent to the League of Nations. Precedents and India's growing relevance in issues like narcotics smuggling and supply of manpower and increasing military importance gave India an identity of its own, but it took some concrete developments for India to acquire that voice.

First, the British public opinion was swayed in favour of the Indian subjects of His Majesty after India provided support to Britain in World War I. On 22 September 1915, Mian Muhammad Shafi floated a resolution in the Legislative Council demanding invitation to India in the future Imperial Conferences. This found a sympathetic hearing from Viceroy Lord Hardinge. It was followed by a decision of the war cabinet in January 1917, according to which India would be included in the next conference. The war cabinet met in March 1917 when India was represented by James Meston, Satyendra Prasanna Sinha and the maharaja of Bikaner, Ganga Singh. It was at this conference that a resolution was passed for the Dominions and India to confer 'a right to an adequate voice in foreign policy and foreign relations.'

The moment of birth of Indian foreign policy had finally arrived and Maharaja Ganga Singh of Bikaner was present there at this landmark moment. Given the long history of state-to-state relations that the princely states maintained with Great Britain and the association of these entities with the post-colonial Indian state, it was natural that some of them were inducted into the Indian Foreign Service—probably as an inducement by the new Indian state to ensure cooperation and harmony.

10

THE FIRST WOMEN RECRUITS
LEILAMANI AND VIJAYA LAKSHMI

ONE PLEASANT MORNING OF MARCH 1934, the district administrator's office in Fatehgarh was shaken up with the news of an impending sati. The practice of Hindu women burning themselves at the funeral pyre of their husbands had been outlawed by Lord Bentinck in 1829; yet, a century later, like a stubborn disease this social evil would show up. Sub divisional magistrate Yezdezard Dinshaw Gundevia rushed from his breakfast table to the house of the deceased Siaram, a petition writer in the local court who had died that morning. Gundevia had not prepared himself for the sight that greeted him. Son of an art gallery owner, Gundevia had trained as a barrister in London and had joined the Indian Civil Service in 1930. A Parsee with a young wife, Gundevia was well-liked by his British as well as Indian colleagues who confided in him like one of their own. Despite his popularity, the sight in the house of the late Siaram traumatized Gundevia. The police officer had narrated that soon after Siaram's demise, his wife had announced her plans to perform *sahagamana* or sati.

The neighbourhood was naturally buzzing with the prospects of witnessing a sati event.

As he stood transfixed at the entrance of the funereal house, he saw an absurd drama being enacted with the dead man's wife, Kalavati, who was dressed like a new bride with gold jewellery and saree. In the middle of all this, beside the dead body of her late husband, Kalavati was performing a ritual shaking her head wildly from side to side as she repeated mantras that a sadhu and a priest chanted. Gundevia took a few moments to gather his wits and decided to use some strong-arm tactics to stop the performance of the illegal ritual, which involved the burning of a widow alive while the entire community would watch as if they were witnessing something divine. Gundevia felt that there is nothing divine if society allowed the suicide of a helpless widow. He confronted the sadhu, who appeared to be the biggest proponent of the sati present on the spot, and asked him who he was and what was he doing in his district. The sadhu said that he was overseeing the process and proudly announced that his entire *akhada* (party) would soon be arriving to ensure the performance of sati by Kalavati. Gundevia first targeted the sadhu with, 'Darogaji, take this *badmash* (scoundrel) away and lock him up.'[1] The sub inspector accompanying Gundevia promptly arrested the sadhu for encouraging an illegal action. Next, he asked the priest if he was complicit in provoking Kalavati to commit suicide, and the priest meekly said he was there only to recite the mantras. Gundevia was determined to prevent the sati from taking place in the area under his command. He next held on to Kalavati by the wrist and locked her up in a room while she wailed in protest. Within a short while, with her main provocateurs locked away or removed forcibly, Kalavati calmed down as her husband's pyre was lit under the watchful eyes of the local police. A terrible tragedy was averted because the chief official in charge of governance in the region held on to his modern convictions and was not swayed by the display of support or curiosity that the locals had put up. Finally, the official machinery won the day.

India, by the 1930s, had emerged as a land of extremes. On the one hand, the country had made progress and had a class of civil servants who were steeped in modern values, but on the other hand, there were those who felt strongly about continuing the past practices that gave India a reputation of being a land of superstition and dark practices. Gundevia, who had a name as an upright official, served as the additional collector in Gorakhpur in the late 1930s, followed by administrative stints as collector and magistrate in Mirzapur and Farrukhabad. His more than a decade of service in the heart of the Gangetic plains gave him exposure to the real India as it lived and evolved. Just before India attained independence, Gundevia was appointed as secretary to the representative of the Government of India in Burma during 1945–47 and began his career as a diplomat for India.[2]

Gundevia's tenure in the Hindi heartland of the Raj coincided with the landmark changes that were underway. After three rounds of failed Round Table Conferences in London, the Government of India Act, 1935 began a process of uncertain transition. In the provincial election that were held in 1937, Congress came to power in the all-important United Provinces, where Govind Ballabh Pant became the chief minister and Nehru's sister Vijaya Lakshmi Pandit became a member of the ministerial cabinet. On the one hand, there was the India where sati was still being attempted and women were confined to homes and on the other, there was a section within the nationalist circle that wanted women to forge ahead and take positions of power. It was from the latter section that the early female recruits of the Indian Foreign Service would spring.

On page number nine of the *History of Services* debuts Leilamani Naidu. Naidu was born in 1903, which made her one of the seniormost diplomats of India at the time of the birth of the IFS. She was three years younger than Vijaya Lakshmi Pandit, who also happened to be an official diplomat at the birth of India. The two, however, differed from each other. Leilamani Naidu joined the Indian Foreign Service and served as a professional diplomat for many years. Vijaya Lakshmi was a diplomat, but she fell under a very special category of diplomats who were put together by Nehru himself to work as his 'foreign policy advisors'.[3]

In the infancy of the IFS, the service had to contend with a certain number of informal and irregular features, and it was in this non-bureaucratic nook that the role for women first came up. One has to give credit to Vijaya Lakshmi Pandit for creating that space in India's diplomatic brigade. Diplomacy was one of the several things that Pandit did in her career, and that is why this monograph will take up her section after Leilamani Naidu, who in fact transitioned from a pre-Independence activist-academic career into a diplomatic career.

Like the careers of many of those who joined the Indian Foreign Service in 1948–49, Leilamani Naidu's choice of careers had also been influenced by the epic scale of events unfolding in the country at that time.

Her grandfather, Aghorenath Chattopadhyay, was the first principal of Nizam College in Hyderabad. Her mother was the eldest child of Aghorenath—Sarojini Naidu. The Chattopadhyays and Naidus were caught in political and diplomatic web of the emerging India by virtue of their very location in Hyderabad, which had a strong nationalist current even when it was under the rule of the Nizam. Winds of change had begun to blow with the enactment of the Government of India Act, 1935. In 1936, the

Nizam's Government set up a large Reforms Office with Mirza Aliyar Khan, director of the State Information Bureau, as its head. This office was to act as an extension of the political department of the Nizam's government. Naidu was appointed as part of this Reforms Office. This was an important initiative and provided an early training for Naidu in public affairs. But Naidu's core training was at home; she and her siblings Jayasooriya and Padmaja Naidu were the 'products of the composite culture' that existed at that time in Hyderabad.[4] As per the accounts of those who met her, she was absolutely non-communal.[5] Apart from Hyderabad, her other training was at home, which was radical in comparison to other households of that time.

She, however, made a mark as a teacher of English literature in the Osmania University's College for Women (1941–47). She briefly was the head of the Philosophy Department in the same college in 1947 before joining the Indian Foreign Service on 11 September 1948, when she was posted as the OSD in the Ministry of External Affairs. That technically made her the first female Indian Foreign Service Officer. But it was in her years as an academic in the strongly anti-colonial climate that Leilamani Naidu made her mark and created her own legend. The story was recounted by one of her students in the philosophy department, Shiva Dua, who went on to be one of the legendary teachers in Miranda House in the University of Delhi in the twentieth century. Dua was a young student aspiring to be a teacher in a government college in the early 1940s when she agonized over the possibility of becoming a teacher in a college in British-ruled India. During one of Leilamani Naidu's lectures, she opened the door and found the principal standing there, obviously eavesdropping on Naidu to see what she was teaching her students. She banged the door and said, 'If this lady thinks that I'm preaching sedition and she's trying to eavesdrop, she's mistaken. If she thinks that because I'm the daughter of my mother, I am preaching sedition, she's wrong. But children, don't be surprised if you don't find me here after the summer vacation. If I can't have freedom of conscience in teaching, I shall not serve the government.'[6] The fiery temper was not unexpected of Leilamani Naidu, who had both soft nationalists like Sarojini Naidu and as well as her maternal uncle Virendranath Chattopadhyay in her family. Virendranath was famous for his international networking among the German and Russian groups which he carried on for nearly four decades till he was killed by an order of the Soviet leadership because of suspected espionage on 2 September 1937. Her personal and professional backgrounds and commitments obviously proved to be helpful as India began to make its first stirrings to form a foreign service. There can be doubts about the way these early recruits—including Leilamani Naidu—were taken on board, but there was no doubt in their commitment to the new state that had emerged from a rule that they so despised.

In March of 1947, with barely a few months before the final Independence, India's emerging leadership invited delegates from twenty-five countries to what would be known as the Asian Relations Conference. India had spent the previous century under the control of the United Kingdom. Its worldview as well its relations around the world were shaped by the primary impulses generated by the administration of the United Kingdom. As a new nation, India would need to have new friends and partners in the commercial and political domains of the world. Countries had to be invited to participate in the making of the new country. The conference was aimed at providing a platform to India and its partners across the world. It was not expected to provide a definite template for India's diplomatic and economic future and would be a 'preliminary and exploratory' exercise only.[7] The most important function of the conference was that it would introduce all the leaders of the participating countries and help them connect with each other—not as heads of colonies but as leaders of independent countries. The conference, which was described as an expression of 'Asian consciousness', would take up matters like immigration and racial discrimination persisting in the world, in addition to economic and trade possibilities.[8] The Indian Council of World Affairs, a red and white structure built and funded by the nationalist princes, lawyers, business houses and bureaucrats, had emerged as the most important centre for policy analysis and interaction, and invites were sent from here to around thirty-three countries, out of which twenty-five responded.

Every participating country was asked to send a maximum of twenty representatives in each delegation; that meant four observers on behalf of the representative government and sixteen delegates from other parts of their government. On an average, each country was to be represented by five or six members. Delegates were expected from countries like Philippines and Indonesia, from Southeast Asia and Afghanistan. Japan too was invited through the American authorities as Tokyo was yet to emerge out of the shadow of the destruction of World War II. Apart from the delegates from the Asian countries, the United States, the United Kingdom and Australia sent observers to the conference.

There were to be fifty participants on behalf of India representing 'a complete cross section of the highest elements in the national life of the country', reported *The Times of India*.[9] Leilamani Naidu debuted at this landmark conference as a member of the Indian delegation. The leader of the Indian delegation was none other than her mother, Sarojini Naidu. The Asian Relations Conference was the first international conference on foreign affairs that was organized in New Delhi under the aegis of the nationalist leaders. The arrival of Leilamani in those early days to Delhi ensured that she would be present in the South Block even as the idea of a professional foreign service was germinating.

The foreign affairs of India was to be more focused on the needs and aspirations of the Indian masses, and one of the first items on the agenda was to ensure the comfortable travel for Indian tourists and pilgrims who wanted to visit abroad, especially to Saudi Arabia for Hajj. Hajj was and remains one of the largest logistical operations undertaken by the Government of India annually. With the advent of the new government in India, there were expectations for helping the bulk of pilgrims with better accommodation during their stay in Bombay before their departure for Jeddah. It was Leilamani Naidu's job to ensure that there were sufficient number of *musafirkhanas* in Bombay to house the pilgrims and ensure there were decent arrangements on board the ships that would take them to Saudi Arabia for the annual pilgrimage. Over the subsequent decades, the facilitation of Hajj would grow to be a major operation undertaken with the support of multiple agencies and ministries and the Ministry of External Affairs would play a crucial role. Hajj was to be an important issue for post-1947 India because of the Pakistan factor. The new nation to India's west had emerged as the self-proclaimed custodian of Islam in South Asia and had begun to use the issue of Hajj as a tool to allege discrimination against the Muslims in India. India had just been through the harrowing phase of the Partition and had witnessed communal riots, and the government of Jawaharlal Nehru, therefore, treated the Hajj division with care. Another first recruit who had joined the Indian Foreign Service's Branch A was Mohammed Yunus. When Pakistan alleged that the Hajj pilgrims were being tormented by India, the Nehru government summoned him to the South Block to look after the Hajj affairs. Yunus had already served in Jakarta, Ankara and Baghdad since joining the IFS in October 1947. He expected greater freedom in the headquarters but in South Block he was appointed as a deputy secretary between October 1952 and September 1954. But in the politically important issue of Hajj, it was Leilamani Naidu who commanded the affairs, and Yunus was to serve as her assistant during the 1950s. Significantly, Leilamani Naidu was present during the important internal arguments in the Ministry of External Affairs in the late 1940s, when the official debate about recognition for Israel took place. Israel came into existence a few months before Naidu joined the IFS, and, soon after, she had to deal with the question of whether to recognize the new state, which had come up in parts of what was historically known as Palestine.[10] While the discussion was ongoing, Secretary-General Girja Shankar Bajpai settled the matter saying that there was not much of a difference between 'de jure' and 'de facto' recognition.

Exactly, two years after Naidu's arrival in the IFS, India recognized Israel as a state on 15 September 1950. Though India did not open an outpost in Israel, the 1953–54 annual report of the Ministry of External Affairs recorded that an Israeli consulate had come up in Mumbai in the previous year. Naidu did go abroad as a member of the Indian delegation—notably the one to China in 1952—and did handle politically sensitive wings like the Hajj, but she was not posted abroad unlike the foreign service officers of latter decades or her contemporary Vijaya Lakshmi Pandit. In 1958, she was granted an extension of service till September of that year.[11]

Vijaya Lakshmi Pandit was not recruited as a diplomat through her competitive examination; nor was Leilamani Naidu. Therefore, neither fell strictly in the ambit of professional diplomats as mentioned in the *History of Services*. Yet, Leilamani Naidu found a mention in the directory as she had formally joined the Indian diplomatic service after Independence. Naidu served at the headquarters while Pandit served in important missions like Moscow and Washington DC. Both were extraordinarily successful in professional terms and were examples for the post-1947 generation. But Leilamani Naidu was a rare female in the nearly absolute maleness of the South Block in the early years of the IFS.

The first decade after Independence would witness several women joining the IFS followed by hundreds of others during subsequent decades, but what distinguished the generation of Vijaya Lakshmi Pandit and Leilamani Naidu was their strong anti-colonial sentiment, which they blended with their strong social and diaspora contacts in the West. Pandit overall was a special case as without her, India's diplomacy in the global high table would be incomplete in the 1940s and the 1950s, and therefore, she is essential in any writing on diplomats in the early years after Independence. It's her unpredictable career, personal tragedies and unconventional life choices that continue to give her a larger-than-life profile.

After the 1937 election, Mrs Pandit, as she was better known, was sworn in as the minister of Local Governance and Public Health in the United Provinces and became the first Indian woman to hold a public office during the British colonial era. Her experience in governance would prove to be valuable, and she, with her paternal as well as personal social network, would prove to be of great help for India's emerging global posture a decade later. But in 1937, India's future looked uncertain.

Starting with 1937, the political process at home and abroad spiralled at a fast pace, and the government at home was overwhelmed by global developments as World War II began in Europe. Upset at India being hurled into the second big war in two decades, the Congress governments resigned. As the war intensified and spread, drawing Indian cities within the range of Japanese bombers, London sent the Cripps Mission to convince Congress leaders to support British war efforts. The mission failed, paving the way for the Quit India movement launched on 9 August 1942. The political leadership of free India was almost entirely imprisoned during the rest of World War II while Subhas Chandra Bose continued the struggle for freedom abroad.

Following the end of the provincial governments in 1939, Vijaya Lakshmi Pandit, now a former minister with nationwide fame, became the leader of the All India Women's Conference. Her married life with scholar, lawyer and later Congress activist Ranjit Pandit had begun in 1921, with a wedding where she had worn a khadi saree spun by Kasturba Gandhi. Following the wedding, the couple left for Calcutta, where Ranjit practised law, and the two began to attend the British Club and went to the weekend horse racing. But with the political agitation not showing any sign of slowing down, the couple returned to Allahabad, which had become the centre of Congress' political activities. Starting with the onset of World War II, the entire political leadership of India and their associates were frequently in and out of prison as the British rulers navigated the waters of national struggle for independence. One of the impacts of frequent imprisonment was on the health of Ranjit, and he succumbed to pleurisy on 14 January 1944.

The period presented Vijaya Lakshmi Pandit with the most volatile phase of her life. With her brother in jail, she was the only Nehru who was in the political and administrative world of India. With three growing up daughters, Pandit had to reinvent herself and her family. There was little time before the world could overwhelm her. At this time, she took a series of unusually bold decisions that made her indispensable for India's diplomacy later in the decade. There were substantial reasons that prompted Pandit to move heaven and the earth to emerge from the shadow of grief and financial insecurity that she suddenly discovered herself in. To make matters worse, she realized that Ranjit Pandit had passed away intestate, and as a result, his property and earnings went to his elder brother's family.[12]

At this time, Vijaya Lakshmi Pandit went back in time to draw strength from a friendship that had earned herself the 'bad girl' epithet in Allahabad[13] of 1919, when India was in the midst of the Khilafat movement and Anand Bhavan was being visited by many nationalist figures. One of the new visitors in the house was a strikingly handsome journalist and political activist named Syud Hossain. Hossain was from a prominent Muslim family of Calcutta which was linked to the nawabs of Bengal. Hossain was, however, not an unwanted stranger in Anand Bhavan and had a legitimate reason to be present there as he was hired by Motilal Nehru to be the editor of his newspaper, *The Independent*, which was a hugely popular publication during those days.[14] The striking Sarup Kumari Nehru and Hossain fell in love.[15] The 1888-born Hossain was twelve years older than Sarup, and he in fact was a year older than Jawaharlal too. In youthful rebellion, the two eloped and became the talk of the town. The scandal was short-lived but hit Motilal Nehru, who had a number of colleagues and friends in Kolkata. The marriage was conducted according to Islamic rules and was not recognized by the Nehrus, who sought intervention even from Mahatma Gandhi to convince the young Sarup to change her mind. Syud was sent off to London to campaign for the Khilafat movement, and Sarup was sent to Sabarmati Ashram to 'purify her mind and soul'.[16] Two years later, Sarup was married to Ranjit Pandit in a flower bedecked ceremony in Anand Bhavan, and she took a new name—Vijaya Lakshmi—and started a new journey. Hossain did not return to India till much later, but as Vijaya Lakshmi Pandit's marital life ended tragically with the demise of Ranjit Pandit, she reached out to Hossain, who had by then become one of the most important ambassadors of the Indian freedom struggle in US media and the academia. Hossain visited India infrequently after this period, but he did return to Dhaka, his motherland, which was undergoing serious changes in 1937, when the Salimullah Muslim Hall Union of the University of Dacca (Dhaka) described him as the 'Marvel of the Orient'.[17]

In a bold move, Vijaya Lakshmi Pandit wanted to reincarnate her political life and take control of her life as well as the lives of her three daughters. With obvious support from Syud Hossain and his National Committee for Indian Independence, the former minister of UP decided to earn a living by lecturing across the United States.

In the midst of the war, grief and famine that ravaged Bengal, India's relations with the United States began to undergo widespread changes mainly because of the large presence of American military personnel and top military leaders who dealt with the war's India–Burma–China theatre. The United States was critical of the British rule over India and agreed to give her a visa. During her visits to Calcutta, Vijaya Lakshmi Pandit had met one of the leading military figures of the Allied powers, Lt General George E. Stratemeyer, and he offered her a bucket seat on a military transport aircraft that operated out of India. This gesture helped her as she had no money for the ticket.[18] Pandit thus flew to San Francisco, where after more than two decades, she met Syud Hossain. Within the societal context of 1919, the Islamic marriage between the two presided over by a Maulavi was a scandal that was erased from public memory, as it was politically inconvenient for the Nehrus who, despite being of a secular and progressive orientation, had to conduct themselves as per the orthodox sentiments prevailing within the larger Hindu society and the Congress.[19]

In the subsequent two decades, while Vijaya Lakshmi Pandit became a mother as well as the first female minister of the United Provinces, Syud Hossain campaigned for India's freedom in the United States and became a powerful force in the intellectual circles that included the likes of Pearl S. Buck, who was a prominent champion of India's independence.

Vijaya Lakshmi Pandit's emergence as the voice of India was not, therefore, an officially sanctioned move, nor was she chosen by the jailed national leaders. It was the result of her personal decision, prompted by a mix of personal circumstances and choices. But it was the San Francisco conference of April 1945 which gave Vijaya Lakshmi Pandit the ultimate opportunity to emerge as the voice of India. The official delegation to the global conference was led by Sir Firoz Khan Noon and Ramaswami Mudaliar, but the Indians in the United States firmly supported Vijaya Lakshmi Pandit to represent their country. She, therefore, got a 'self-appointed role' in San Francisco.[20] Pandit's public meetings were packed, and though India became one of the founding members of the United Nations, which was born out of the deliberations at San Francisco, the official delegation's task was performed by Vijaya Lakshmi Pandit and not by Noon and Mudaliar. The Indian side had by then realized the mistake of not utilizing her skills in public speaking and political sensibilities. As the New York session convened for 1946, Lord Wavell, the viceroy, recommended Vijaya Lakshmi's name as the leader of the delegation.

Why of all countries she chose to go to the United States to reinvent her career remains an enduring mystery, because the Nehru family had extensive contacts, especially in the underground revolutionary network and academic circuit in Europe; they were not known to have similar network in the United States. The credit for having such a network goes to Syud Hossain who, for reasons best known to him, allowed Vijaya Lakshmi Pandit to engage that network. The world was in transition, and the centre of the world was shifting from the eastern coast of the Atlantic Ocean to the western coast, where the United States had emerged as the formidable leader of the Allied powers or the western democracies, and it was Syud Hossain who, for nearly two decades, campaigned in almost all the major university campuses and town halls in the United States demanding independence for India. Syud Hossain did not return to Allahabad again, but he did return to Calcutta in 1937, the year Vijaya Lakshmi Pandit became minister, where he met with Netaji Subhas Chandra Bose. Following Independence, both Vijaya Lakshmi Pandit and Syud Hossain were recruited by Jawaharlal Nehru to serve as India's ambassadors in Moscow and Egypt respectively. Syud Hossain died in Egypt in 1949, and the Government of India looks after his grave in Cairo till date.

The years of 1944–46 were years of transformation. World War II was drawing to a close, but along with that, this phase also brought the desire to bring in a more long-lasting order of things that would serve India and other emerging actors on the world stage. While Vijaya Lakshmi Pandit toured in the US with the melancholic Syud Hossain, dramatic changes were taking place in Asia and Europe. In the United Kingdom, the Labour government of Clement Attlee was elected, and with it came the last phase of the freedom struggle. In the newspapers of the United States, Vijaya Lakshmi Pandit read that her brother had been released after more than 1,000 days in various jails of India. But by then, Vijaya Lakshmi Pandit, through her public pronouncements, had articulated India's position and allegiances under the upcoming world order, where the big blocs would play a role.

In Pandit's opinion, India and the United States followed the 'same ideals'[21] and were closer than they were to the United Kingdom. She highlighted the common colonial past of the two countries and the requirement of anti-poverty measures where the US could be a great partner of India in the way it had emerged as a force in support of liberating Europe from Nazi control. While appealing for closer India–US ties, she also made the point that there are a large number of Asians who were suffering because of Japanese occupation—a chord that struck strongly because of the war in Asia.[22] Vijaya Lakshmi Pandit was modifying India's foreign policy consciousness, which had emerged in the previous century and come into the focus of the Congress during the inter-war period. Her Asianism[23] was part of the modern consciousness of India. This tradition found support from Keshab Chandra Sen and his Brahmo Samaj of the nineteenth century and the Indian National Congress, which announced in 1928 that 'India should develop contacts with other countries and peoples who also suffer under imperialism and desire to combat it'. Subsequently, the Working Committee of the Indian National Congress convened the first session of a Pan-Asiatic Committee in 1930 in India.[24]

An agenda for India's diplomacy—liberal, modern and progressive—that was synergized with the greatest western power of the time emerged as Vijaya Lakshmi Pandit spoke in public meetings that were organized by the Indian friends and American sympathizers, who often described her as the 'sister of India's imprisoned leader' and 'one of the most notable women of our time'.

Perhaps it was to Vijaya Lakshmi Pandit's credit that even before Jawaharlal Nehru had become the single-man think tank that he was for India's foreign affairs beginning with 1947, his sister had created a playing field where her role would be sought after singularly, because she had taken the front row seat in the theatre of the world and saw the emergence of the new world. Vijaya Lakshmi Pandit, by her determined rebellion to the men of her life, became one of the first woman diplomats that Jawaharlal Nehru's diplomatic machinery would have to hire, and she was sent for the most important diplomatic assignments to Moscow and Washington DC as India attained independence. But before that of course, India created the agenda that it was going to pursue as an independent country.

11

FROM HANUMANNAGAR TO TASHKENT

CHANDRA SHEKHAR JHA

THE BIGGEST IMMEDIATE BENEFICIARIES OF Indian Independence in the Asian and African continents came from Indonesia, then known as the Dutch Indies. Indonesian Nationalist Party (Partai Nasional Indonesia) leaders were dealing with a difficult situation. They had been promised independence during World War II by the colonial ruler, the Netherlands, but soon after the end of the war, the colonial hold regained strength. Prime Minister Jawaharlal Nehru expressed wholehearted support to the Indonesian freedom fighters and these initiatives soon turned into a conference of Asian and African countries in Delhi during January 1949 which was attended by nineteen Asian and African countries. The meeting ended with the delegates expressing 'unanimous' support for the freedom of Indonesia and demanding the exit of the Dutch from the largest Southeast Asian country. It was understood that as the largest country of South Asia, India had set the norms for its region, and as the equivalent of India in Southeast Asia, Indonesia would similarly deliver the norms for its region and guide the struggle for self-rule which was at a critical stage there in the late 1940s. This conference was, in fact, the first in the series which ultimately led to the Bandung Conference of 1955.[1] Between the 1942 movement to overthrow colonial rule and the blood-drenched independence of India, the world had changed, and the realization had descended in Delhi that India would have to play a role in the dramatic transformation sweeping the world. The foreign policy had to honour the sacrifices that Indians had made over the past four decades of nationalist non-violent and violent struggle but also balance India's fast-evolving diplomatic and economic requirements. This called for establishing new official links and commercial contacts. The outreach to the largest Southeast Asian country's popular struggle was based on Nehru's personal friendship with Dr Mohammad Hatta, Dr Koesno Sosrodihardjo Sukarno and Dr Sutan Sjahrir. The foreign policy moves ranged from political–diplomatic to economic initiatives, and accordingly, the Nehru government built relations with the freedom struggles of Asia, Africa and Latin America while maintaining relation with the Commonwealth and balancing the two major Cold War blocs. The combination of initiatives was a major departure from the steps that India was allowed to undertake till a few years ago when the Soviet Union was not allowed to have a full-fledged diplomatic mission in British-ruled India, and political radicals of Southeast Asia would have found no official welcome in South Block. The policy mix was driven by Nehru's own 'One World' concept, which he had been championing since his inauguration as the Prime Minister of the interim government of India on 7 September 1946. Nehru wanted the world to represent unity of purpose and address the issues facing the majority of humanity.

He mentioned the same topic a year later during the 23 March 1947 Asian Relations Conference. The result of these interactions led to a close association with a number of leaders from India's neighbourhood.

Along with the trio of Sukarno, Hatta and Sjahrir of Indonesia, he also became close to S.W.R.D. Bandaranaike of Sri Lanka during the very early phase of prime ministership. This networking came naturally to Nehru and perhaps was the easier part of his foreign policy set-up, as he had been in charge of the Foreign Affairs department of the Indian National Congress for years and had built contacts across continents as the trend of public movements was clear to him. By welcoming political radicals of Nepal and freedom-seeking political leaders of other countries, the new leadership created a new order. At the same time, they also set up the official structure. At the time when ideals like 'One World' were being shaped by Nehru, the opposite was happening on the ground, and it was one such development in East Africa that would bring spotlight on one of the longest serving foreign service officers of the Nehru era in South Block.

During the colonial period, the administrative and financial requirements enhanced the movement of Indians abroad. Indian labour introduced changes wherever they were sent. In South Africa, Indian labour was used in the development of sugar plantations, and similar sugarcane farming was intensified in Fiji and Mauritius when Indian labourers reached there. From Malaya (Malaysia) to Burma (Myanmar), similar agriculture and infrastructure building initiatives were implemented by the Indians.

One of the places where Indians found official support and local acceptance was East Africa. But with the end of World War II, change began to sweep Africa, and new immigration regulations hitting the Indians residing in the region were proposed. The proposed regulations in the colonial governments in East Africa, covering Kenya, Uganda and Tanganyika, thus created a furore in India. The interim government in India found itself in the spotlight due to the new regulation and was forced to address the concern despite being powerless. So, they sent a fact-finding mission to the region during August–September 1946. The tension between the local Indians and native Africans was unfortunate as the fates of African national movements and India were intertwined, as the Gandhian school of struggle actually arose in South Africa and became an accepted model inside Africa even before the Gandhian struggle became known in India. Besides, there was nothing wrong with the Africans being eager to control their fate, and controlling immigration from other countries was well within their rights. African nationalists were simply trying to assert control over their land and economy, and in that India, the newly independent major power of Asia, was naturally expected to support the African position. But the challenge in this case was posed by reports of discrimination and intimidation of local Indians circulating at the same time as the changes were introduced. The incoming government of India had to be seen as fair, and just not to the anti-colonial Africans but also to their own people, who were watching to see if they would be capable of looking after their interest in different parts of the world.

Accordingly, Sir Maharaj Singh, a retired bureaucrat with a deep experience of the problems of overseas Indians, was dispatched as the leader of a fact-finding three-member team to East Africa to deal with the situation. The other two members of the team were Sarwar Hassan, secretary of the Indian Institute of International Affairs, and Chandra Shekhar Jha, member-secretary. The report created by this team was one of the first reports submitted to Jawaharlal Nehru, who at that time was the head of the interim government of 1946. The document highlighted the commonalities between two sides and said that Indians and Africans always handled political challenges together and that there was no difference on that front. The Maharaj Singh mission to East Africa made a series of suggestions to strengthen relations between India and Africa, and ultimately, it was this step that led to India announcing a series of scholarships for African students—which went on to be the foundation for India–Africa academic, science and tech cooperation decades later.

Jha was still in Nairobi when Nehru's name was announced as the Prime Minister of the interim government. In his memoir, Jha wrote, 'I was thrilled at the news. I felt proud to learn that Nehru would be minister in charge of the Commonwealth Relations Department, to which I belonged.'[2] The freedom struggle had ended and the leaders who had spent their youth fighting for the elusive independence of India had now acquired the difficult task of governance. Chandra Shekhar Jha, who had joined the Indian Civil Service in 1932, had spent his early years reading about the agitations shaped by the national leaders.[3] But till 1946, administrative officers and anti-colonial national leaders had little or perhaps no chance to meet each other. At the time of arrival of Nehru as the Prime Minister, Jha wrote, 'I had never met Nehru.'[4] Yet, during the subsequent seventeen years when Nehru would be the Prime Minister of India, Jha would work with him in South Block for seven years and represent him on many platforms, including in Paris 1948, when he was the secretary-general of the Indian delegation to the UN General Assembly that year. He would be a joint secretary in the Ministry of External Affairs during 1954–57—a phase well-remembered for the Bandung Conference and the beginning of a new world order. Under Nehru, the External Affairs Ministry had thinkers and institution builders like the troika of Girja Shankar Bajpai, Subimal Dutt and V.K. Krishna Menon, and then there were the likes of C.S. Jha, who were career bureaucrats serving in important positions and delivering on the diplomatic front.

The troika of Bajpai–Menon–Dutt is known to be the primary continuous presence in the foreign policy domain of the Nehru era, from the mid-1940s till the 1962 war. But Jha was present next to Nehru during the 'creative period of Nehru's career', which included the landmark Bandung conference, the pinnacle of Nehru's Afro-Asian diplomacy that defined the agenda of the Global South.[5]

According to Jha, the creative phase of Nehru's diplomacy began with Indian support for the UN initiatives in Korea in 1950, when Delhi sent an Indian ambulance unit to the region followed by India's success in bringing an end to the Korean war. This phase also included the first phase of India's nuclear diplomacy covering the disarmament and abolition of nuclear tests and weapons. But Jha found himself a place in the history of post-1947 diplomacy by being a participant in most of the steps that led to the Bandung Conference of 1955.

The final plenary session of the Bandung Conference was held on 24 April 1955. Nehru spoke eloquently about the condition facing Asia and Africa in the backdrop of the Cold War. He watched the remaining part of the session sitting with the rest of his delegation. The Indonesians had welcomed Nehru warmly and gave him a large villa for the duration of his stay which became the most frequented address as many delegates would walk in to meet and share ideas. Jha said the conference was Nehru's idea, and everyone more or less acknowledged that during the conference. Some countries like Pakistan and Turkey, which were part of western defence initiatives, already found it difficult to accept the predominance that Nehru had acquired. Nehru wanted to frame a consensus document that would echo the overwhelming concern about colonialism and the urgency of achieving decolonization quickly.

Some countries led by Pakistan and Turkey represented the group of nations that had become part of the Western alliance and wanted the conference to legitimize the membership of military pacts with the western powers 'under the cover of the right of collective self-defence'.[6] They also wanted to condemn 'all types of colonialism including international doctrines resorting to the methods of force, infiltration and subversion.'[7] This was obviously aimed at the communist bloc and the non-aligned countries led by India, and Egypt opposed this as much as China and Burma. Finally, after an all-night session during 23–24 April 1955, an agreement was reached, and the famous Bandung Declaration was unanimously adopted. The final communiqué and the Declaration on the Promotion of World Peace and Cooperation marked a historic moment as it was the first time in the modern era that the countries of Asia and Africa joined hands to condemn colonialism 'in all its manifestations' as an 'evil which should speedily be brought to an end'. The impact of the Bandung text can be measured by the fact that it amplified the opinion of the bulk of the global map on the issue of colonialism. What was even more significant was that by referring to the right of self-defence from the point of view of the African and Asian nations, it gave anti-colonial struggles a kind of legitimacy that was to help in achieving decolonization in the years to come.

Chandra Shekhar Jha saw the entire day's proceedings sitting behind Nehru in Bandung on the historic last day and observed Nehru taking notes in between. At the end of the proceedings, Nehru showed him that he had noted down the time that each speaker had taken, and in total, the nineteen speakers had taken 102 minutes. The list made by Nehru showed that he had clocked the longest speech of all leaders at 17 minutes. At the end of the day, Nehru gifted the paper to Jha as a souvenir.

The Bandung Conference was a historic occasion and the finest hour of Nehruvian diplomacy. The conference was the first occasion in the history of the mankind when the people of former colonies had come together and the first time that an Indian leader had left such a deep impact on relations among nations. The leaders at Bandung represented 1,400 million people, or nearly two-third of the world's population. Out of the twenty-nine nations that attended the Bandung conference, twelve sent their prime ministers and six their foreign ministers, and the communiqué of the conference created an electrifying effect. Within a few months of Bandung, on 1 January 1956, Sudan became independent, and on 2 March 1956, Morocco followed. Less than a month later, on 20 March 1956, Tunisia too became free. Malaysia was also on its path to independence. Several countries that had attended Bandung conference but were not members of the United Nations had become members of the world body soon after. The defence blocs of the west, especially the Baghdad Pact, became weak, and Jordan, Sudan, Libya and Liberia had become increasingly neutral. Out of the rest, Pakistan, Iran, the Philippines, Thailand and Turkey were in the pro-west bloc, and China and North Vietnam remained in the Soviet bloc.

An even bigger achievement was the recognition that non-alignment or neutrality received in international affairs. Neutrality had become a bad word in the highly polarized society of the West, which was reeling from the bitterness caused by World War II and the Holocaust, but Bandung brought legitimacy to the idea once again. Non-alignment was not a passive position and Bandung's demands for decolonization, disarmament and a bigger share of global economic pie for Asia and Africa indicated that it was every bit a political project that sought reordering of the world. The return of neutrality got its biggest stamp of acceptance with the Austrian Peace Treaty, which was signed weeks after the Bandung summit. The treaty signed by the US, the USSR, France and the UK ensured withdrawal of occupation forces from Austrian territory, secured its neutrality and recognized neutrality as an acceptable instrument in post-World War II international relations. Finally, Bandung marked the entry of the People's Republic of China into global platforms.

The one area where Bandung fell short was on the economic front, as the economic blueprint of Afro-Asian cooperation did not take off as quickly as the political implications.

Jha had come a long way since 1932 when he had joined the Indian Civil Service in the inter-war period. Back then, freedom was widely sought after in India even though the path ahead appeared uncertain. It was in this condition that the son of a Congress politician of Bihar—Shiva Shankar Jha—decided to join the service of the colonial administration. Jha's career took him to Orissa and Bihar where he worked in administrative positions for the next decade. Bihar and Orissa formed a joint cadre at that time for the ICS, and both the provinces were caught in the vortex of the national struggle, which gave Jha plenty of opportunity to interact with both the nationalist agitators and the status quo-seekers, consisting of the landlords and zamindars who were worried about their loosening grip over the emerging Indian society. Imperial UK was pursuing a contradictory policy when it came to the Indian theatre. The modern education system, which was introduced in India during the nineteenth and the early part of the twentieth centuries, was based on the traditions of reason and rational thinking in modern Europe. It was this particular tradition that had provided inspiration to the Indian population. But faced with the nationalist clamour, the UK in the early twentieth century joined hands with feudal orthodoxy and entitlement. Surprisingly though, it was in this section of feudal entitlement that the first stirrings of Indian foreign policy were noticed in the early twentieth century.

The feudal forces, however, failed to get electoral support in the elections of 1937, which were held in the backdrop of the Government of India Act, 1935. The Congress, which won most seats after defeating the orthodox and feudal parties, wanted full power to run the popularly elected provincial governments, but the colonial administration was initially unwilling to share full authority with the elected rulers. After much consultation and negotiation, finally the first elected government of pre-Independence India took power in 1937. This particular phase was an early opening, as it gave the officials of the ICS a much-required window to work with the future rulers of India. By the late 1930s, it probably was clear that the future of India belonged to the nationalist agitators who wanted to dislodge the coalition between the Indian social orthodoxy and the colonial rulers. The bureaucrats belonging to the generation of Chandra Shekhar Jha were thus slowly accustomed to the leaders who were getting ready to replace the troubled alliance between the two fast weakening political forces.

Chandra Shekhar Jha himself came from the heart of social orthodoxy in India. A Maithili brahmin, he was born to Shiva Shankar Jha, a rebel in an orthodox Hindu household in Mithila. Shiva Shankar had travelled to Calcutta where he studied at Presidency College and returned to his home and became a lawyer. Later, he also became a prominent Congress politician. Jha, however, was not given to political protests though he indulged in student protests briefly during his days as a student in Patna which attracted negative attention from the colonial administration. His brief exposure to political agitation nearly wrecked his bureaucratic career at its birth as the local police of Madhubani gave a negative remark before his recruitment into the Indian Civil Service. Finally, it was the chief secretary of Bihar, P.C. Tallents who cleared his recruitment saying that the Jhas were known to him; that recommendation helped him overcome the objection from the police in Madhubani. Thanks to his parent cadre of Orissa and Bihar, Jha was dragged into the international relations of India much before he became a part of the Indian diplomatic brigade.

India was hurled into World War II without the consent of her people and that meant the domestic administration also had to be geared to meet the challenges facing the Allied powers. The Congress opposed the war but announced that it considered the fascists as its main adversary. That did not help it much as the setbacks in the early part of the war made the colonial government appear weak, and a weak administration quickly morphed into a repressive regime as it wanted to keep the Congress under pressure to pre-empt any chances of a popular uprising against an unpopular government.

Soon, war came closer as Cuttack, where Jha was the district magistrate became a major point in the Allied war against imperial Japan. Opposite Cuttack, near the Mahanadi (a river) in Choudwar, a major American airbase was constructed; the airbase used to host aircrafts that flew all the way over the eastern Himalayas, which formed the natural barrier between India and the Tibetan plateau.

The war brought in an action-packed period for the young ICS officer. Because of his father's stature within the Congress in north Bihar, Jha was in contact with the foot soldiers of the Congress in the region who continuously relayed to him the hardships that common people were being subjected to in the name of wartime measures. The crisis escalated when the famine broke out in Bengal, next door to Orissa, as the British administration bought out all the supplies of the private traders in Bengal. The collusion between the profit-seeking private traders and the desperate administration had to be fought. Jha was then responsible for civil supplies in Orissa, and he learnt from his sources that having exhausted the Bengal food market, the government's focus had shifted to Orissa's private traders. He sensed that the man-made famine of Bengal was about to be implemented in Orissa. He swung into action and ordered inspection of trains leaving Orissa; the administration was asked to stop trains if they were found to be carrying rice out of the state. That and other administrative steps stabilized the food situation in Orissa. This order, of course, earned him the wrath of New Delhi but there was a growing realization that it was the right thing to do to prevent another man-made famine.[8] In 1945, Chandra Shekhar Jha was honoured with an Officer of the Order of British Empire (OBE) in recognition of his administrative performance. The next year, he was transferred to Delhi and joined the Department of Commonwealth Relations, the embryonic organ out of which the Ministry of External Affairs would be born.

Jha made quick professional progress and became a joint secretary in 1947—one of the six joint secretaries in the Ministry of External Affairs. From May 1950 onwards, he served first as the minister-ad-interim, and from October 1951, became the ambassador of India in Ankara. It was his first ambassadorial posting and his first posting abroad. He learnt French during this posting. Jha was struck by the simplicity with which the Turkish political class conducted itself, with most of the top leaders choosing to reside in rented apartments instead of large bungalows with open spaces—unlike what had become the norm back home in New Delhi. Turkey was an important country from the Indian point of view as the two also shared a strong phase of common struggle during the Khilafat movement in 1918–1924, which coincided with the last phase of the Ottoman rule in Turkey. The Nehru government had sent Diwan Chaman Lal, a senior Congressman, as the first ambassador of India to Turkey. An anecdote that Chandra Shekhar Jha picked up on reaching Turkey was that Lal had once mistaken the serving Turkish President, Mahmud Celâl Bayar, as a steward in the President's house and had offered him a tip after a banquet. Jha confessed that the story was probably embellished and was a reflection of the social awkwardness of Chaman Lal. It nevertheless provided a window to the days when leaders conducted themselves without much fanfare.

The 'creative period' of diplomacy for Nehru was also the 'formative period', according to Jha. After this initial four years of 1946–50, were three phases covering the non-aligned movement's overall trajectory (1951–56) and the final two years following the 1962 war when Nehru was at the end of his political career dealing with the burden of the defeat.

The colonial state of India nurtured its own geostrategic understanding, with which it perceived India's neighbourhood in its unique manner. Some of these ideas helped the Empire to stabilize its rule in South Asia. But after Independence, the same ideas served as source of the problems that Indian foreign policy had to deal with. Olaf Caroe, the last foreign secretary of the colonial administration, had extensive experience of working in the northwest frontier during his days in the Indian Civil Service. Upon his retirement, he wrote a book, *Wells of Power,* which went on to become the defining treatise for foreign affairs. According to Caroe, the West Asian region was of increased significance because of discovery of petroleum during the early twentieth century. This implied a continuum between the 'wells of power' and the British territory in South Asia. After the end of the colonial era, the British interest was diluted and had to be reinvented. UK's policy towards Pakistan was partially shaped by this desire to strengthen links with the heart of the region of energy. According to Caroe, the gateway to the wells of power was located in Iraq's Basra, the port that connected the Persian Gulf and in turn with the western coast of the Indian Empire—now Pakistan. Jha states that the British establishment after 1947 came to believe that a strong British presence was required in the West Asian region to safeguard the strong British energy interest that grew at the time when territorial control was slipping away in the Indian Empire.

The tilt towards Pakistan was strengthened from the very beginning as Pakistan reached out to the United States, the centre of the western bloc in the Cold War. According to a report prepared by the South Asia division of the State Department in November 1949, Pakistan, soon after its inception in 1947, sought a five-year loan of $510,000,000 from the US government.[9] This outreach failed because of the India–Pakistan war of 1947, which prompted the US to impose an arms embargo on both India and Pakistan in an attempt to prevent a major escalation. The embargo was lifted in 1949, when Pakistan sent a military delegation to the US where it indicated a willingness to be associated with the US. The situation in South Asia soon worsened because of a major communal massacre in East Pakistan which stabilized with the Jawaharlal Nehru–Liaquat Ali pact of 1950. Despite the temporary truce of 1950, the two sides grew in two different trajectories. As mentioned above, Pakistan attended the Bandung conference but invested its strategic future with the American bloc. A decade later, this would trigger the first serious difficulty for India in relation to the Kashmir issue.

In the first half of the 1960s, two Harvard classmates of the batch of 1923–24, Francis Plimpton and Adlai E. Stevenson, had arrived in the United Nations. This time, they were present in the UN Security Council as the representatives of the United States. Stevenson was the ambassador of the US to the UNSC and Plimpton was his deputy. Between the two of them, the diplomats divided the responsibilities that the Kennedy administration had to deliver at the world body. The year 1962 would end up as a fateful one for India because of the Sino-Indian War of October–November, but early that year, President Kennedy called up the Irish Prime Minister and foreign minister asking Frederick Boland, the Irish ambassador to the UN, to table a resolution seeking plebiscite in Kashmir. According to Plimpton, it was the only occasion when President Kennedy had intervened to ensure that the resolution was not tabled by the US but by a third country.[10]

The resolution was tabled but India was saved by a Soviet veto. However, before that, Plimpton approached Jha, who was then serving as India's ambassador to the UN, with the proposal that a distinguished person could be the negotiator between India and Pakistan. In this regard, Plimpton proposed the name of Eugene Black, president of the World Bank. Black had acquired a great amount of goodwill two years earlier by mediating the Indus Waters Treaty, and Plimpton probably thought that Black would be the right candidate to deal with Kashmir after delivering on the contentious issue of dividing the waters of the Indus. Jha politely conveyed to Plimpton that the question of negotiation does not arise as Kashmir remains an integral part of India's sovereign territory which can't be subjected to negotiation. The resolution came to the UN on 1 February 1962. The date coincided with the general election in India. From 1962 to 1965, Pakistan would repeatedly attempt to bring up the Kashmir issue and Jha would be there to deal with the attempt. In 1965, Pakistan once again attempted the formula of sending in well-organized armed groups of Pakistani paramilitary forces disguised as mujahideen to cross the ceasefire line in Jammu and Kashmir. For a brief moment during this time, India considered taking up the Pakistani action to the Security Council but gave up considering the negative experience of the past one and half decades.

The last big transition in Delhi was in 1947, when the tragedy of the Partition cast a shadow on India's Independence. The demise of Nehru on 27 May 1964 opened the door for another political transition, and this time too the country faced another shadow—that of defeat in the Sino-Indian war of 1962. The passing away of Nehru after more than seventeen years of providing leadership to a country that had not experienced free existence before 1947 was an unprecedented jolt. India and the United States had come close after the war of 1962 and the two were in close diplomatic and military discussion at the time of Nehru's demise. Y.B. Chavan had become the defence minister after the defeat at the hands of the Chinese prompted changes at the top level and Defence Minister Krishna Menon had to resign. Chavan was not the most favoured man of the PMO, but circumstances had pushed him into the chair of the defence minister. In April, the Government of India decided to send Chavan to the United States. The welcome that Chavan received was elaborate and indicated that the Americans were willing to make the best use of the opportunity that the defeat had opened up for them to renew friendship with India. The ambassador of India at Washington DC at that time was B.K. Nehru. On 26 May 1964, the entire Indian delegation along with the Indian defence minister was in Colorado Springs. Late that night Chavan was informed that Prime Minister Nehru had passed away. From there, a US Air Force plane flew Chavan and his team, including ambassador B.K. Nehru and Avtar Dar, a first-generation IFS officer, to Delhi. The US Secretary of State Dean Rusk accompanied Chavan to represent the US government at the funeral of Nehru. Delhi was still new to the process of transition, and there were all kinds of rumours and gossip in the city.

Emotions ran high as the funeral of Nehru took place in Delhi. Krishna Menon, companion of Nehru for decades and an indispensable part of Nehru's foreign affairs team, who was once described by Plimpton as 'satanic', fainted out of grief and exhaustion. Just at that moment, an officer in uniform came to Chavan and whispered in Marathi, 'Sir, beware of deceit.' The incident was meant to illustrate the all-round air of uncertainty that the bureaucracy was dealing with in the immediate aftermath of the demise of the first Prime Minister. Chavan would later tell his close associates that the rumour was partly fuelled by the fact that the chief of Army staff, General J.N. Chaudhuri, had moved a brigade into the capital, ostensibly to aid in the funeral. However, the absence of General Chaudhuri from work had fuelled speculations that the military under his command was probably thinking of a coup. The rumour of a post-Nehru coup was mentioned by several authors, including Michael Brecher, who recorded that J.N. Chaudhuri had ordered the movement of 6,000 troops into Delhi and that they were present in prominent places across the city. The rumours swirled in the city for around a fortnight. Brecher said that the matter was not reported in the media but was discussed at the highest level of the government.[11] It was in this backdrop that power shifted to Lal Bahadur Shastri after a brief period during which Gulzari Lal Nanda served as the PM of India. Jha would be a frontline witness to war, triumph and tragedy from the front ranks of history during the coming two years.

With the advent of the Shastri era, a separate office of the External Affairs Minister appeared.

In January 1965, West Pakistan Rangers and the Indus Rangers carried out an audacious strike inside India. The forces reached two kilometres inside Indian territory on the Kutch–Sindh border near the fort of Kanjarkot. India demanded that Pakistan withdraw from the area but instead early on the morning of 9 April 1965, Pakistan's armed forces launched a large-scale attack on the Indian post at Sardar and Vigo Kot. Pakistan was emboldened by the continuous advances and claimed around 3,500 square miles of the Rann of Kutch. India was left with no option but to create a diversionary attack somewhere else in Pakistan and make Pakistan pay for the first round of aggression. This meant enlarging the war which had to be a political decision.

Chandra Shekhar Jha was the foreign secretary in 1965 and he was instructed to reach out across the world to convey the Indian position regarding the Pakistani invasion in the Rann of Kutch. Sensing grave danger of a full-scale war, the UK High Commissioner John Freeman reached out to Jha, and the British Prime Minister Harold Wilson wrote to Prime Minister Shastri and to Pakistan's military ruler, Ayub Khan. Finally, an agreement was reached, mediated by Wilson. As per the agreement signed on 30 June 1965, ministers of the two governments were to meet within one month of the ceasefire to decide on the demarcation of the border. But the agreement was of little value, in fact, as Pakistan thought India was yet to recover from the shocking defeat of 1962. Ultimately, Islamabad's military gamble would backfire, but the impression of India's military weakness tempted General Ayub Khan's forces.

Inspired by the military move in Kutch, on 5 August 1965, Pakistan launched a massive infiltration across the ceasefire line in Kashmir. The fighters were well-equipped and for nearly two days carried out sabotage and arson before New Delhi realized the full extent of the invasion. Pakistan maintained the position that it had nothing to do with the irregular fighters as they were 'mujahids'. The lies were exposed by the United Nations Military Observer Group in India and Pakistan (UNMOGIP), which had the task of watching the movements of Indian and Pakistani armed forces. UNMOGIP reports revealed that the Pakistani 'mujahids' were getting support from the regular armed forces of Pakistan.[12] The next move was to take the war into the Pakistani territory so that the pressure on the Chamb sector and Akhnoor could be reduced. On 4 September 1965, Shastri asked Chandra Shekhar Jha to proceed to New York, where he was to provide muscle to the Indian case at the UN Security Council. Shastri had decided to broaden the war and required the top diplomats of India to be present in New York. Indian troops crossing the border for Lahore and Sialkot was a 'momentous' decision according to Jha. The bold decision taken by Shastri, however, did not get support from the UK, which had been party to peace-making between India and Pakistan in the last few months. Prime Minister Harold Wilson issued a statement on 6 September 1965, in which he condemned the Indian action. Jha noted that throughout the year, the high commissioner of the UK, John Freeman, had reported the aggressive moves by Pakistan to London which, however, were ignored by Wilson while making the remarks. This was a turning point in the war as well as peace for India as neither the UN nor the UK were seen as acceptable and honest brokers who could bring the conflict to an end. Jha was present at the UN as per Shastri's order to deal with the international pressure and bring an end to the crisis, as there was a real possibility of it becoming a much bigger war drawing in China—a country that could join the conflict on behalf of Pakistan, which had been stunned by the Indian forces marching across the plains of Punjab near Lahore and Sialkot. In the UN, Jha noticed that the Western powers had more or less lined up along the British Prime Minister's remarks, and the series of meetings under UN General-Secretary U. Thant did not yield much. The outcome of this stalemate meant the war was to be prolonged.

By the time, Jha returned from New York on 21 September, India was in the middle of the war and conflict protocols like blackouts were solidly in place. The Security Council called for ceasefire from 7 a.m. GMT on 22 September. Pakistan, which had initiated the conflict, had a particularly difficult task in accepting the ceasefire, and Jha said that it was goaded into accepting the offer by the United States.[13] Without a military solution in sight, Pakistan too came around and both the parties accepted the 20 September proposal from Soviet Premier Kosygin, in which he had called for a cessation of hostilities and offered his good offices for re-establishing normal ties between India and Pakistan. The situation, however, remained tense and unresolved after the ceasefire of 22 September came into force. The two sides remained in a state of 'no war no peace' till about November 1965 when the Soviet ambassador called on PM Shastri and handed him a letter from Premier Kosygin. In the letter, Kosygin had highlighted the danger of the situation prevailing between West Pakistan and India, as the war had morphed into a shooting war without resolution and neither side had withdrawn from the territories they had occupied during the conflict. Kosygin expressed his concern and offered to host a conference in Tashkent between the delegations of India and Pakistan, where the two sides could discuss normalization of relations.

Prime Minister Shastri was not particularly keen on getting support from the Soviet Union, as in the past such summits had been infructuous. Additionally, Shastri had publicly declared that India would not withdraw from strategically advantageous areas like Hajipir Pass and Kargil, as these were originally part of Indian territory. There were reasons for not getting into a dialogue mediated by a third party, but there were more pressing reasons to do so as Shastri felt that the Soviet Union had been 'consistently friendly' to India and that rejecting such an offer from Moscow would be 'inexpedient'.

That apart, there were economic reasons for opting for peace as the nearly year-long conflict was putting a great strain on the exchequer. It was finally agreed that Shastri would go to the table from a position of power as India had captured Pakistani territories and had altered the map of west Pakistan.

The officials selected for the Tashkent summit were almost entirely from the 'first recruits'. Apart from PM Shastri, the delegation included Foreign Minister Swaran Singh and Defence Minister Y.B. Chavan. Among the diplomats there were Foreign Secretary Chandra Shekhar Jha, T.N. Kaul, the Indian ambassador to the Soviet Union, Indian High Commissioner to Pakistan Kewal Singh, External Publicity Chief I.J. Bahadur Singh, Legal Adviser Krishna Rao, Special Officer on Kashmir Affairs B.L. Sharma and Deputy Secretary Kayatyani Shankar Bajpai. From the Defence Ministry, Deputy Chief of Staff General Kumaramangalam and Joint Secretary D.R. Kohli, and from the Home Ministry, L.P. Singh, the home secretary, were among those who represented the security establishment. From the PMO, L.K. Jha and Private

Secretary of the Prime Minister C.P. Srivastava accompanied the Prime Minister.

Packed with this strong team of diplomats, bureaucrats and military men, Lal Bahadur Shastri flew to the last fortnight of his life. The Skymaster aircraft of the Indian Air Force flew out on 1 January 1966 and took a detour, avoiding Pakistan and flying over Iran and Afghanistan. A large media delegation accompanied Shastri on this trip. At the airport in Tashkent, Prime Minister Shastri was received by Premier Kosygin. The Soviet leaders did not spare any effort to showcase the importance they attached to the peace-making initiative. They had taken upon themselves the responsibility of delivering an assignment where the United Nations and the United Kingdom had earlier failed. The entire city of Tashkent had turned out to welcome Lal Bahadur Shastri and Ayub Khan, and the streets were decorated with the Indian, Pakistani and Soviet flags. The Soviets welcomed both the rival parties with equal honour and warmth. The Tashkent summit was a test also for the Soviet leadership, which wanted to prove to the world that they were a great power not only because of their enormous military arsenal but also because of their ability to be an honest broker in one of the most difficult cases.

Anticipating a long session of negotiation, the Soviets had made extensive arrangements in the city. The Indian leader was given a luxurious dacha, where Shastri and his staff members had ample space. The meticulous arrangement included an Indian kitchen. The Prime Minister's residence was connected to the Intourist Hotel, which was the venue of the negotiation. Apart from that, full-fledged arrangements had been made to help the two teams to be in contact with their teams back in Delhi and Islamabad. Equally detailed arrangements were made also for the world press that had come in full strength.

Negotiations began on 2 January 1966 in the octagonal-shaped meeting hall of the Tashkent Municipal Council. Kosygin began the discussion with his remarks, and Shastri said the discussion should look beyond solving the immediate crisis and move to the sharing of waters of the eastern rivers with Pakistan. The formal meeting was followed by a one-on-one meeting between Ayub Khan and Shastri. The Soviet delegation stayed away from these private meetings. After such meetings, Shastri and Khan would brief their respective teams about the important points. Ayub Khan addressed Shastri as 'elder brother' and sought an end to the Kashmir dispute. Lal Bahadur Shastri was soft-spoken throughout the negotiation and kept his message direct. The two qualities, combined with his physical appearance, was a potent weapon at the negotiation table. The discussion between the two leaders could not proceed further after a point, and to break the ice, a meeting between Zulfikar Ali Bhutto and Swaran Singh—the two foreign ministers—was mooted. That meeting too failed to make any headway. The Soviet representatives maintained a distance from the discussions but kept themselves informed of the developments through informal contacts. The talks continued in this manner till 7 January when it became clear that the negotiations had failed. Jha and the media secretary of Pakistan, Altaf Gauhar, briefed their respective teams, indicating bilateral discussion had failed to make progress. It was then that the Soviet leadership stepped in.

On 8 January, Kosygin along with Andrey Gromyko met Shastri and informed him that they had managed to convince Pakistan to accept the draft declaration. The Soviets also articulated the opinion of the Pakistani delegation and said the Kashmir issue should be given prominence in the draft declaration. Shastri rejected this insertion categorically. The difficult clause was regarding the withdrawal of armed forces. The main problem was that both sides had made public declarations and the Indian PM had mentioned that India would not withdraw from the areas that it had conquered. Kosygin, however, said that it was necessary for India to withdraw from Hajipir Pass to attain 'durable peace'. The Indian position was legally sound. Pakistan-occupied Kashmir was part of the Jammu and Kashmir state, which belonged to India, and the Indian forces, therefore, could not be asked to withdraw from the territories that it had restored from Pakistan. On 8 January, after meeting with his cabinet colleagues, Shastri communicated that a withdrawal from Hajipir Pass could not be avoided if a 'satisfactory joint declaration' between India and Pakistan could be drafted. Jha went to the rest of the team and informed Kewal Singh, I.J. Bahadur Singh, D.R. Kohli, Shankar Bajpai and others on the planned withdrawal. After some more discussion, they agreed to commit to withdraw from Hajipir Pass and other positions. The much-needed breakthrough in the Tashkent summit had been achieved.

On 10 January, Foreign Secretary Jha got up early and prepared a media statement that he was going to release to the press in the evening. He took the necessary permissions from the Indian PM. A grand signature ceremony was held at 3 p.m. at the Tashkent Municipal Meeting Hall later that day and neither Shastri nor Khan made any statements. The only person who spoke was Kosygin. The two leaders who signed the declaration were Shastri and Khan. Then came a moment of premonition. Prime Minister Shastri met the Indian media team informally after the signing of the agreement and sought the support of the media in communicating the details of the agreement with the people back home. At that point, a senior journalist asked in a 'perfectly friendly way': 'Mr Prime Minister, have you given away Hajipir?' That question clearly showed the Indian side what was at stake. Shastri had made public declaration about not surrendering Hajipir Pass, and now he had won peace with Pakistan but lost Hajipir Pass. The conspiracy theories ever since have failed to provide full details of what transpired subsequently, but it is quite possible to imagine that Shastri came under tremendous pressure after the signing of the deal in Tashkent. Prime Minister Shastri explained to the press that he had signed the agreement 'reluctantly' considering that the withdrawal was not a high price to pay if it could ensure peace between India and Pakistan.

After the reception that followed, Shastri left with Swaran Singh and Y.B. Chavan in his car to the dacha. Jha would not see Shastri alive after that. A little after midnight, he was roused from bed by a commotion in his corridor. He heard the agitated voices of Swaran Singh and T.N. Kaul explaining that Shastri had fallen ill. Jha arrived in the dacha with others and witnessed six Soviet doctors massaging and giving external respiratory support to Shastri. Soviet leaders Kosygin and Malinowski came in as the Soviet doctors tried to revive Shastri for the next couple of hours. After some time, they confirmed that the Indian Prime Minister had died. It was with the permission of the Soviet leadership that the Indian team sent a telegram to President Dr S. Radhakrishnan informing him of the passing away of Prime Minister Shastri. It was thus that the Indian PM who sealed a peace agreement with Pakistan died before reaping the benefits of the deal. Jha said that around a million people lined the roads of Tashkent to bid goodbye to Shastri as the gun carriage carried his body to the airport. Over the past ten days, Tashkent had lived with the news of the peace dialogue between India and Pakistan; the sudden tragedy, therefore, disoriented the population of the city. The scenes at the airport were equally spectacular. Swaran Singh, Chavan, Kosygin, Jha and Ayub Khan carried Shastri's body. Ayub Khan was genuinely distressed by the turn of events. As he boarded the aircraft to accompany Shastri on his last journey back home, he asked, 'Jha Sahab, *yeh kya ho gaya? Khuda na karein iska nateeja hamare mulko par bura ho*. (Mr Jha, what a terrible thing to happen. God forbid that the consequences of this tragedy are harmful to our countries.)'[14]

A sea of humanity had arrived at the Delhi airport in the afternoon of 11 January 1966. The Tashkent Summit and Declaration were dramatic in many respects. The dialogue had failed as the media had begun to report on 8 January, when suddenly a breakthrough took place, and the Tashkent Declaration was sealed. Then, just as the celebration was to begin, the death of Shastri gave the meeting a particularly solemn reputation. As a result, the declaration ended the conflict that Pakistan had started on 5 August 1965 and restored the status quo ante. The Indian cabinet presided over by interim PM Gulzari Lal Nanda approved the Tashkent Declaration. Only one minister, Mahavir Tyagi, minister of rehabilitation, disagreed as he believed that India had surrendered the Hajipir Pass and other areas wrongly. Tyagi later resigned from the cabinet because of this matter.

12

MIRZA RASHID ALI BAIG

THE PROTOCOL CHIEF WHO MADE ALL THE DIFFERENCE

1955 WAS THE YEAR OF Indian diplomacy. On the one hand, Bandung summit meant India had to put up its best diplomatic show abroad that year, and on the other, that also meant that New Delhi emerged as one of the most-visited capitals of the post-colonial world. This was also the year of a turnaround in India–Soviet relations. In June that year, Prime Minister Nehru had visited the Soviet Union for the first time. He had allowed the Soviet Union to open a diplomatic mission in Delhi years ago, but bilateral relations between the two were far from what it could have been because of Joseph Stalin's sceptical attitude towards India. That year, General Secretary Khrushchev, successor to Stalin, was to visit India along with Premier Bulganin. The Soviets had given a grand welcome to Nehru, and the understanding was that the Indian welcome would have to match that of Moscow. This was a difficult task. India had been hosting big foreign visitors since at least the Asian Relations Conference of 1947, but the visit by Soviet leadership was another matter. Nehru was the first major non-communist leader to visit Moscow and his successful tour proved that Winston Churchill was wrong in saying that the Soviet Union was behind an 'iron curtain'. The visit of the Soviet leadership to India was therefore going to be a momentous occasion.

The protocol division of the Ministry of External Affairs drew up plans for welcoming official guests. But the division needed to be revitalized to welcome leaders from a superpower. The task of drawing up the hosting plans thus fell on the second head of the protocol division—Mirza Rashid Ali Baig. The challenge before Baig was of a different order. The scale of the welcome often indicated the importance of the visit, and the leader of the Soviet bloc could not just be welcomed through official ceremonies—that would be insufficient. The entire capital of India had to be worked up to a festive spirit to make the effort worthwhile. M.R.A. Baig began planning the visit that would begin a festival.

A major challenge before the Indian hosts was the fact that Indians did not have a unitary culture to showcase. Soviets paid a great deal of emphasis on cultural shows for foreign delegates, and the Indians felt it was necessary to showcase something spectacular to impress the Soviet guests. The problem was, however, that India did not have one form of art, as every part of the country had something unique to offer. The responsibility of planning for the cultural show thus fell on Baig's wife, Tara.

She chose a spacious part of the Rashtrapati Bhavan, which was not hitherto used, and a large stage was erected for the performance. Earthen lamps were lit, and two performances depicted the dance forms of tribal India and classical Indian dance forms. The performance took place in the backdrop of thousands of diyas, and the atmosphere turned ecstatic as Mrinalini Sarabhai took to the stage. India was a newly independent country, and public enthusiasm was high because of the popularity of the Soviet Union; hundreds of thousands of people lined the roads across the city—from the airport in Palam to the central part of the city in Connaught Circus. People sat on the roads as they waited for the Soviet leaders and threw flowers on the way. This was the first visit to a non-Soviet Asian country by the Soviet leaders, and it was spectacular. The visit also highlighted the challenges that the protocol division would be used to deal with in subsequent years. Welcoming guests from the Palam airport required the placing of props like sofas, signboards and flags all through the 12 miles between the airport and the central location of the city where the guests would be housed. M.R.A. Baig reached out to the Public Works Department to produce hundreds of marquees, sofas and chairs for the elaborate welcome ceremonies in the airport. These props became like items of a film set and would be taken out and used by the PWD for hundreds of subsequent visits as and when requested by the Ministry of External Affairs. It was during this time that the Protocol Division and the PWD came up with the idea of floral designs to welcome the guests. Among the many ideas was one to create the flags of the guest country with flowers. Gigantic floral flags of India and the USSR were placed on prime roundabouts in the Lutyen's zone of New Delhi so that the motorcade carrying Khrushchev and Bulganin could see them. The high point of the visit was the public welcome, which was led by PM Nehru at the Ramlila Maidan, the meeting point of Old and New Delhi. The video cameras of the international press captured the sea of humanity that came out to greet Khrushchev and Bulganin. The expression on the faces of Bulganin, Khrushchev and the rest of the delegation suggests that they had never witnessed such a spectacular welcome anywhere in previous visits to other countries.

The spectacular welcome was obviously designed to serve the aims of the government of the day. Jawaharlal Nehru was, after all, from the Congress, and apart from his personal recollections of visits to the Soviet Union, there was the memory of the Congress–Communist relationship which played in the background as courting the Soviet Union became a part of the Indian foreign policy. A formal communist party was formed in 1928, but throughout the previous decade regional communist groups had functioned across India, and the unrest caused by these smaller communist movements influenced the economic and foreign policy thinking of the Congress in the early 1930s and subsequently.[1] After Independence, the communist movement posed a major law and order challenge in large parts of the country. The Soviet Union and the Communist Party of China did not regard India as truly independent during 1947–48. The Soviet Union under Joseph Stalin, together with the Communist Party of China, supported the Tebhaga and Telangana insurrections in 1948–50 led by the Communist Party of India. The uprisings were crushed by the Nehru government, but the experience showed that India's domestic arena was linked to India's foreign affairs, and the two had to be handled carefully. It was with the arrival of the Khrushchev–Bulganin era that Delhi finally convinced Moscow of its independent status. The welcome ceremony laid out for the Soviet leaders, therefore, was the need of the hour for a state that had to worry about its own survival in a difficult world. Most importantly, during his stay in India, Khrushchev spent two days in Kashmir, where he declared that Jammu and Kashmir belonged to India. The Kashmir dispute had caused a great deal of embarrassment for India since the beginning, and the support from

Khrushchev came at a crucial moment for the Nehru government. If the purpose behind the spectacular hospitality was to impress the Soviet guests and get them to sway to the Indian tune, then Baig had succeeded in achieving his goal.

The protocol division under M.R.A. Baig managed to create a name for the hospitality that the Indian royalties were famous for extending to their guests. Many of the innovations of the time, by M.R.A. Baig, like the floral carpets and portraits carrying flags of guest countries and names of leaders, continue to be in practice even in the twenty-first century as India has moved ahead in time, and this was in evidence as the G20 summit-related events that began earlier in 2023.

As mentioned before, the period of M.R.A. Baig can be credited with laying the foundation of the protocol division, one of the most important divisions of the ministry. But the period of Inder Chopra was also important, as he too had handled incoming visits. The biggest visit that he handled was that of Marshal Tito, who had paid his first India visit in 1954. The real spurt in incoming visits took place in 1955, the Bandung year. Having started, this spurt was to last for several years. Foreign visits had reduced considerably in the last months of the Nehru era, which fell like a heavy blanket over South Block after the setback in the war of 1962. But in the frenetic activities of the mid-1950s, there were no signs of the setbacks of the future. India was the leader of the decolonized world, and apart from the superpowers, smaller countries also wanted to head to New Delhi. One of the challenges that the incoming guests threw to M.R.A. Baig was that the country had to produce flags of foreign countries. This may appear to be an easy task, but it is never so. Every flag has its distinctive features, and flags of developing countries have more such features. Western flags are mostly rectangular in shape and are designed in simple colours, but flags of Asia, Africa and Latin American countries were often richly adorned. Errors in reproducing these flags could easily create diplomatic embarrassment for the Indian side. Reproducing the design and the shape of the flags on time, therefore, was an important task. Baig, in addition, had a unique demand to meet which came from President Rajendra Prasad, who insisted that khadi fabric should be used to create the flags of incoming guest countries. The first President of India, a veteran Gandhian, had noble intentions in demanding khadi flags, but it was quite a challenge—the khadi unit was not yet competent enough to produce hundreds of flags of complicated shapes and designs. Still, the organization rose to the occasion, and flags of foreign countries were produced in vast numbers for the protocol division of the Ministry of External Affairs. The flags were used to decorate routes and roundabouts in the capital with the help of the PWD's engineering and horticultural divisions.

The show put up by the protocol division under M.R.A. Baig was of such quality that the Russian movie cameramen who accompanied Bulganin–Khrushchev requested the Indian officials to send them to Moscow 'en bloc' and perform before the Soviet citizens.[2] Another significant part of the plans to welcome a national level guest was the part of the national anthem, which acquired a special significance with the spurt in new nation states. But the protocol division could not get sufficiently qualified orchestras in India that could play western music. Orchestras solved the challenge in western capitals where national anthems were played for the incoming heads of state or government. Baig came up with the solution that the choir of the Protestant Cathedral in Delhi be used to perform the national anthems. In this venture, he found support from organist and choirmaster Arthur Mahinder who trained and conducted the choir in the mid-'50s. After the visit of Khrushchev, when the singing of the Soviet anthem became a super hit with the Russians, the performance for the visiting guests became a regular feature of the protocol's tasks. After the first performance, the Protestant Cathedral's choir would be asked to perform the national anthems of foreign countries frequently. With the help of the embassies of the countries concerned, Baig used to get the musical notes of the anthem well in advance for the choir. To help with the language, diction and accent, he would ask the diplomats of foreign embassies to come and guide the choir. Buoyed by the success and recognition, Arthur Mahinder converted his choir into the Delhi Choral Society.[3] Over the years, Arthur Mahinder's team was replaced by music bands of the Indian armed forces which perform at the Rashtrapati Bhavan to welcome the guests.

Cultural programmes started by Tara Baig, however, faced a hurdle after couple of performances, as she had a full-time work in the Indian Council of Child Welfare. The evening cultural show that she had organized during Khrushchev's visit, however, became an established tradition of the protocol requirements of the Indian government and was retained. Baig chose to institutionalize this and turned to the All India Radio's vast collection of artistes who stepped in to carry forward the tradition. The All India Radio came up with a movable or collapsible stage that could be put together and dismantled quickly based on requirements, and cultural shows immediately following the state banquets became a routine for that time. During his tenure as the protocol chief, Baig hosted a great variety of the high and the mighty like Khrushchev, the Dalai Lama, US President Dwight D. Eisenhower, Chou En-lai, Vietnamese leader Ho Chi-Minh, Queen Elizabeth II, Ghanaian President Nkrumah, Egypt's Gamal Abdel Nasser, King Saud, the Shah of Iran, Crown Prince Akihito of Japan, the prime ministers of Denmark, Sweden and Finland, UN Secretary-General Dag Hammarskjöld and US Secretary of State John Foster Dulles, among many others. In the subsequent decades, the protocol division of the MEA handled many challenging visits, including mega shows like the NAM summit of 1983, all the way to the G20 summit in 2023. During the Mughal era, Delhi in its medieval avatar hosted state guests but the practice did not exist in the modern colonial era when Delhi once again became the capital of the empire—the British Empire. But what set apart the attempts of the 1950s was that the task of the protocol team was made interesting by the fact that these were being performed for the first time in the history of India, as never before in the modern era had New Delhi hosted state guests from so many foreign countries.

Baig would typically begin by consulting the resident foreign ambassadors, all of whom at that time were male. He would then advise and inform the MEA after consulting his government about the tastes and preferences of the state guest. The finalized 'tour programme' would be then placed before Prime Minister Nehru, and only after the final clearance from him would the plan move ahead and be circulated among all the stakeholders within the central government and the states. Planning for logistics for such high-profile visits required intense travel and high-tension coordination. Apart from items like flags, cultural shows and food, the protocol was also responsible for handling unique and unexpected requests from the guests and most importantly, security for the visiting guests. During the visit of Khrushchev and Bulganin, Soviet Ambassador Mikhail A. Menshikov, who would go on to serve as Khrushchev's ambassador to Washington DC, demanded that the Soviet leaders should visit the southern part of India and while being there, they should drink the milk of tender coconuts. He claimed that coconut water was a unique item that the Soviet leaders had not tasted before. Another item that gradually acquired high importance was the motor vehicle that was to transport the visiting dignitaries. A tough lesson was learned during Nikita Khrushchev's visit. Keeping in mind the warm sub-continental climate, the Soviet visitors arrived in November, which is generally an early winter month in India. However, for a Soviet leader used to sub-zero temperature, India was obviously not so cold. In Calcutta, Nikita Khrushchev's cavalcade faced an unexpected crisis when the main car, which was travelling very slowly, overheated and broke down in the middle of the road. Despite repeated attempts, the car refused to start, and the Soviet leaders were shifted from the car to a dilapidated police van, which then drove the guests to the residence of Governor Harendra Coomar Mookerjee. It was in these unhappy circumstances that Khrushchev was introduced to the difficulties that India faced in its industrial developments in the decade after 1947. The Khrushchev visit of 1955 gave a great template for subsequent big visits and taught the MEA a great deal about how to handle state guests in case things do not go according to the script. Khrushchev, for example, asked many questions on anything that he saw, beginning with cement or textiles or just a scene. Therefore, the officers on duty had to be of such calibre that they could deal with the curiosity of the visiting dignitary.

Out of all those who joined the diplomatic brigade at the inception of the Indian Foreign Service, Mirza Rashid Ali Baig was the most unique.

He was born in Hyderabad on 25 March 1905, the year when India was rocked by the biggest anti-British movement—a movement that ended the uneasy tranquillity of the late nineteenth-century colonial rule. His father, Mirza Abbas Ali Baig, was of a Turkish background, which went back to the late medieval period when the Deccan underwent political transitions with the springing up of multiple Muslim kingdoms. Thanks to his father, M.R.A. Baig began in diplomacy much before his birth.

Mirza Abbas Ali Baig, M.R.A. Baig's father, was appointed the Oriental Translator of the Government of Bombay, which constituted a vast chunk of the UK's colonial administration in South Asia and stretched all the way across the other side of the Arabian Sea. The Bombay Presidency included Sindh till the borders of Punjab and Aden on the southern part of the Arabian Peninsula. The area included hundreds of princes and kingdoms, which made administration of the region a real challenge for any administrator. After serving in the Bombay Government, he moved to Junagadh where he served as the diwan of the ruler of Junagadh. From there, Abbas Ali Baig was appointed to the newly formed Secretary of State's Council of India. The task of this council was to advise the secretary of state regarding the affairs relevant to India, and it consisted of retired governors and two Indians. Abbas Ali Baig retired in 1917. The affairs of the state, diplomacy and courtly manners were not unknown to Mirza Rashid Ali Baig because of his background which was enveloped in his old-world charm and refinement of character.

M.R.A. Baig, his elder brother Osman and younger brothers Sikander and Enver left for England in 1911, when Baig was five years old and studying at Clifton. According to a family document shared by his son Murad, Mirza Rashid Ali Baig and Osman were in the first batch of Indian officers to graduate from the Royal Military College of Sandhurst.

M.R.A. Baig's son, Murad, who now lives in the post-retirement house that his father built in the 1960s, said that Baig's journey to the UK at the age of five contributed to making him a 'brown Englishman'. It was this exposure to the UK that was to be challenged a few years later, making a rebel out of Baig.

M.R.A. Baig joined the 16th Light Cavalry in 1924. In the military stint that was to last just six years, Baig witnessed the regal days of the British Empire from close quarters. Two years after joining the cavalry, he was invited by a friend to visit Delhi, which was still being constructed by the architect duo of Edwin Lutyens and Herbert Baker. During that visit to Delhi, which took place in 1926, Baig had the fortune of witnessing not just the construction of the new imperial capital of New Delhi but also participating in the celebrations that the viceroy organized—a grand celebration for the kings and queens of India who came dressed in their finest brocades and competed with each other by wearing the most expensive jewels that money could possibly buy. Apart from the kings and queens of that time, he also came in contact with the members of the Legislative Assembly—Motilal Nehru, Pandit Madan Mohan Malviya, M.R. Jayakar, Homi Mody, Sir Purshottamdas Thakurdas, T.C. Goswami, Shanmugam Chetty and Dewan Chaman Lal.

It was also during this time that M.R.A. Baig came to be acquainted with the Nehrus of Allahabad. He had already met the Nehru patriarch Motilal during his stay in Delhi. In 1927, he had a chance to command the cavalry regiment at Jhansi, and on hearing that he would be at Jhansi, Sarojini Naidu, a family friend from Hyderabad, had written to Jawaharlal Nehru, who was then working as a general secretary of the Congress. Baig could not meet Nehru, as he had to leave for his first visit to the Soviet Union, which had just turned a decade old. Years later, Baig would be in charge when Nehru undertook his second visit to Moscow during 7–23 June 1955 and then for the landmark visit of Nikita Khrushchev to New Delhi and Calcutta.

In Allahabad, in the absence of Jawaharlal, Baig would meet with Motilal and Vijaya Lakshmi and her husband Ranjit Pandit.

His stay at Allahabad probably left an indelible imprint on the young cavalryman, who would soon be drawn to the very centre of nationalist politics but with a twist. The 'scales' over his eyes fell off with the introduction to the nationalist leaders in Allahabad and Bombay as his meetings with them made him feel they could be the political alternative that the country needed.

M.R.A. Baig was drawn towards the nationalist leaders, and his circle increasingly were filled with the likes of Sarojini Naidu, her daughter Padmaja and a host of other aristocrats of princely India who found his presence constructive. In the meantime, the nationalist movement of India underwent a major change. Mohammed Ali Jinnah, the most charismatic modern Muslim leader of the Congress, had left the party in 1920, and over the next decade, his disillusionment with the party and its tactics intensified further. In 1931, he moved to London. The Round Table Conference of 1930–32 took place in London, and Jinnah continued to remain there practising before the Privy Council.

But in early 1934, disillusioned with the situation abroad, Jinnah returned to Bombay. He had met Baig eight years earlier when Baig was meeting the nationalist leaders. But this time, Jinnah hoped to make a disciple out of him. He said, 'Look here. I know all about your views. You imagine that Hindus and Muslims can work together. I only wish they could. But let me tell you that they cannot as long as the Hindus are united and strong, and the Muslims are disunited and weak. The Hindus and Muslims are two arms of the Indian body. But what use is a body with one arm paralysed? By strengthening the arm, you strengthen the whole body. Does a giant ever marry a dwarf? You will never get Hindu–Muslim unity while the Muslims are in their present backward state, socially, educationally and politically. If you want to work for Hindu–Muslim unity, you must first work for the Muslims.'[4]

Baig had a syncretic impression of India, and Jinnah did not convince him with his arguments. He asked, '...unity is the opposite of communalism. The Muslim League is a purely communal organisation. How can you get unity through communalism?' Jinnah responded, 'My young friend, you know little yet about Muslims or politics. If you want the Muslims to come the whole way with you, you must first go half-way towards them.' Soon, Baig began to work as the private secretary of the leader of the Muslim League in Bombay. During this time, Baig saw many attributes of Jinnah that place him next probably only to Jinnah's first biographer Hector Bolitho because of the observations that Baig left behind. At the time of his recruitment as the secretary of the formidable Jinnah, Baig had mere familiarity with the future founder of Pakistan, but soon he would find out interesting details about Jinnah who from the mid-1930s unleashed the force that would divide the British Empire, leading to the creation of two separate nation-states in south Asia. There were two distinct features that stand out from Baig's recollections of Jinnah. On the one hand, Jinnah was a superbly successful barrister in Bombay, which was very much under the control of an elite cosmopolitan crowd composed of the colonial administrators, Parsi and Gujarati business communities and city notables and nationalist elite who had begun to use the city as the gateway to the rest of the world. With all his professional success and personal elegance, Jinnah wanted to stand out among them, not just as a venerated figure but he also wanted his community to be respected. Jinnah was every bit a complex character in the city of merchants where he felt that the Muslim community's grip on power was diminishing. Baig, who was already married by then to Tara, got a new life in Bombay after a brief corporate stint which saw him work for the Tatas. His future would have been entirely different had he continued with

Jinnah, but he ultimately did not. Nevertheless, his exposure to Jinnah showed him a great deal about the man and his ideas.

Jinnah was a dictator and not really a confident leader. The Muslim League Working Committee, which had powerful figures like Sikander Hayat Khan of Punjab, was nothing but a one-man show. He carried himself with an air of elegant authority that his followers and admirers could never penetrate. Enormously popular for championing the cause of the Muslim community, Jinnah was feared and respected for his debating skills, which Baig witnessed in the mid-1920s in the Legislative Assembly in Delhi. Baig would soon find out that despite the outward display of elegance, erudition and authority, Jinnah was entirely capable of making self-serving political moves while disregarding public welfare. One such occasion came when the Municipal Corporation of Bombay launched an adult literacy campaign in Bombay and established night schools for the working-class population of the city. The responsibility of running the night schools in the Muslim localities fell on Kulsum Sayani, notable Congress leader and social worker of Bombay. The Sayanis were from Gujarat, and Kulsum Sayani was known for her work, which involved reforming society through education and spread of awareness. She came in contact with Mahatma Gandhi soon after he began the national struggle. Her campaign for adult literacy in Bombay would have enormously benefitted the women who lived behind purdah, and the night schools would have helped women from less privileged sections of society.

One night, Sayani and Baig took Jinnah on a tour of the night schools in an attempt to secure support from the Muslim League. Jinnah walked with his two younger companions through congested neighbourhoods where the night schools were to operate. Jinnah quietly observed Sayani's good work and at the end praised her for it but refused to extend the support of the Muslim League to the adult literacy campaign. It was not difficult for Baig to figure out why his employer refused to support Kulsum Sayani's campaign for educating Muslim women. The Municipal Corporation was under the control of the Congress and Jinnah knew very well that the success of the adult literacy programme under the Municipal Corporation would ultimately increase the popularity of the Congress within the Muslim community. His political instincts did not allow him to extend support to a cause that deserved support across parties. Baig understood that the opening sentences that Jinnah had made to him were equivalent to a salesman's pitch in snaring a buyer and that the reality was far different from that early introduction. He tried at his own level to ensure mild language in the press statements that Jinnah brought out, and his friend, the journalist Frank Moraes, asked him to stay close to Jinnah as he could ensure a good influence on the man who was drifting towards an extreme position. His son, Murad, the current head of the Baig family living in Delhi, informed this author that much of the writing of Jinnah of this period was in fact drafted by M.R.A. Baig himself.[5] Baig was also an elegant writer, as is visible from his autobiography *In Different Saddles*.[6] Murad said that that quality was very much part of the education system of that period when elegant writing was taught at the elementary level in schools.

The extreme position of Jinnah soon became clearer to Baig when a British magazine, *Time and Tide,* asked him to write an article on the issue of Muslim representation. While preparing the article, Baig prepared a draft in consultation with Moraes which read, 'A Constitution must be evolved that recognises that there are in India two communities who must both share the governance of their common motherland. In evolving such a constitution, the

Muslims are ready to cooperate with the British Government, the Congress, or any party so that the present enmities may cease and India may take its place amongst the great nations of the world.' Jinnah took a look at the draft and scratched 'communities' and replaced it with 'nations'.

This was the time of great churning in India and abroad. Nazi Germany was changing the course of European history and in India, the first provincial elections took place in 1937. World War II began in 1939. In protest, all the Congress-led provincial governments resigned in November. The Muslim League, however, chose a unique agitation, and the subject of their agitation was not the colonial rule but the Congress party. He instructed the League to observe a 'Day of Deliverance and Thanksgiving'. Baig was asked to write the manifesto for the day. This task was given to him in the background of the Pirpur Report that the League brought out alleging that Hindu Congressmen were behind some of the recent communal riots which had taken place in the country. By this time the two had become suspicious of each other, and Jinnah, instead of relying on Baig's discretion, began to give him specific instructions about what exactly he wanted done. After working for six years with Jinnah, the moment of break arrived in March 1940, when Jinnah left Bombay for Lahore, where the resolution for the establishment of a separate homeland for Indian Muslims was passed in the annual session of the Muslim League. Baig, who was in Bombay, was shocked by the language of the resolution and resigned from the party. He wrote a letter that was published prominently in *The Times of India*.[7]

Baig continued to believe that Jinnah was sincere in his ideas when he took him as a member in his team in 1934. Jinnah, he said, believed that the 1937 provincial governments were to be formed as Congress–League governments. Jinnah believed that the Indian condition required a unique political solution that could not be fulfilled by the western model of the majority party government. He believed that the idea that the party that gets a majority of votes should get the chance to form government would automatically lead to the formation of a communal government. When the Congress formed provincial governments in 1937, Jinnah took his final step towards the formation of Pakistan. Baig's excellent reputation among the city's notables soon helped him become the sheriff of Bombay in 1942, and this leap would help him enormously later in the decade.

M.R.A. Baig, who personally laid down the tradition of the protocol division of the MEA and thereby left a permanent mark in the bearing of the Indian state, was a contrarian in relation to the dogmas of his time. As a person from the privileged section of the Indian society who had access to both the rebellious nationalists as well as the forces of status quo, he had a first-row view of history as it unfolded. The storm that he witnessed emanating from the speeches and writings of Jinnah would affect him personally as three of his brothers ultimately left India and chose Pakistan as their future home. The 1940s raced through war, communal disturbances and finally Independence and the Partition, but it also brought space for personal growth. Finally, it was out of this dysfunctional set up that M.R.A. Baig would get his next calling.

World War II was underway, and the Viceroy Lord Linlithgow had set up a non-official organization—National War Front—to mobilize and champion the cause of fighting the Axis powers. The organization soon turned into a repressive body under the leadership of an ICS officer P.J. Griffiths, who had become the central organizer of the National War Front. The war was fast coming to an end by 1944, and the political condition in India required that the National War Front reinvent itself to suit the requirements of the changing times. To help this transition, Prem Thapar, an ICS officer known to the Baigs, came to see Baig, carrying the message that the officials in the viceroy's Executive Council for Information and Broadcasting wanted him to become the director of the National War Front. World War II was going in a favourable direction for the Allied powers at that time, and Baig's arrival was part of that overall reorientation. It was here that he came in contact with the communists, who were supporting the war effort as they wanted the war in Europe to lead to the decisive defeat of Nazi Germany. The main goal of the British administration at the time was to ensure smooth functioning of the factories across the country as they played an important role in ensuring the efficient operation of the imperial war machine. Control of the trade unions in India, therefore, was an important part of this goal. It was at the National War Front that Baig came in contact with M.N. Roy, the legendary communist and revolutionary who had participated in the first international planning to overthrow British rule during World War I in Java. Baig was not the only one who had chosen a nuanced position, as is evident from the changing positions that many of the leading lights of the anti-colonial struggle of the previous decades adopted on the eve of India's Independence. Roy had come a long way too and discarded his staunch anti-imperialism of 1914 and had chosen a strategy of collaboration with the UK—temporarily—as it suited the global communist goals that were favourably aligned with the Allied powers. Baig was a nationalist, but he was against Mahatma Gandhi's call for boycott of supporting the war efforts, and he was certain that India's future would not remain secure under a world order dominated by Nazi Germany and imperial Japan. It was in this backdrop in June 1947 that Jawaharlal Nehru, Prime Minister of the interim government, urged M.R.A. Baig to be the consul general of India to Goa. The move made Baig one of the first few recruits into the IFS as the service was just coming into being through a number of decisions on recruitment and in response to the evolving situation.

His six years of work with Jinnah and the experience of being a nationalist Muslim in highly polarized pre-Partition India influenced Baig as he was asked to join the diplomatic brigade. Goa was a Portuguese colony in 1947, and the Baigs with their eight-year-old son Murad arrived in Panjim, where M.R.A. Baig became the first consul general of India. Murad remembers that the people of Goa celebrated on 15 August 1947 as India attained independence. The Indian Consulate in Portuguese-controlled Goa was located in a large colonial structure on Altinho hill in Panjim. On 15 August, Mirza Rashid Ali Baig invited notable people in Goa to be his guest. As his guests came in, they brought news that fear had gripped the Portuguese quarters of Panjim as they were worried that a public uprising was imminent following the birth of free India. He learnt that the entire Portuguese police, army and navy personnel had locked themselves up in barracks, fearing for their safety. Sensing the public mood, Baig came to his office and sent a coded telegram to Prime Minister Nehru. He advised New Delhi to declare Goa independent immediately. Sometime later, he received a message advising him to go slow. Prime Minister Nehru had come to the understanding that an operation in Goa might succeed because of public support but would have drawn international criticism. Baig would lament later, saying that Goa could have been liberated in 1947 instead of 19 December 1961. After the stint in Goa, Baig was transferred to Pondicherry, where he served as the consul general of French Establishments and Portuguese Possessions in India during 1947–49 before proceeding to serve as the Indian minister in the Embassy of India in the Philippines. Baig had an interesting encounter with President Ramon Magsaysay of the Philippines during his stint in Manila, where he served from 1952–55.

During a meeting with Philippines President Magsaysay, he asked what India was doing for the livestock sector. 'Selective breeding,' answered Baig. To this Magsaysay said his government was finding it difficult to use stud bulls as they were very expensive in the foreign market. Baig informed Magsaysay that India was using artificial insemination in the livestock sector and explained the process to the President of the Philippines. Magsaysay immediately called his agriculture minister and director of veterinary services and a few other officials. 'From tomorrow,' ordered President Magsaysay, 'I want artificial insemination introduced in the Philippines. If you know nothing about it go to India and find out. But I want a progress report in a month.'[8]

Baig also served in two predominantly Muslim countries—Indonesia and Iran. His tenure in Indonesia was brief and lasted from 1949 to 1950. In Iran, particularly, he felt the pressure that Muslim countries face from the local Pakistani missions. A large number of recently decolonized states in Asia and Africa were predominantly Muslim, like Sudan, Lebanon, Mauritania, Senegal, Mali and Sierra Leone. These countries were impressed by the socio-economic advances in India, but they were also impacted when news of communal disturbances in India reached them. Baig would experience this element during his postings in Iran and Indonesia where India's success was admired but the reports of communal disturbances back home always formed an irritant in bilateral ties.

In 1957, American adventurer Katherine Campman hit the headlines in India. India had completed a decade of independent existence, and in this duration, the interest about the former jewel among the British colonial possessions had increased worldwide. Satyajit Ray's film *Pather Panchali* was released in 1955, and West Bengal's Chief Minister Bidhan Chandra Roy organized a screening for Prime Minister Nehru. After the screening, Nehru ensured that the film entered the Cannes film festival. The film won the special jury prize for 'the Best Human Document' and added to the global buzz around India under Nehru's leadership.

Campman had driven across Europe, Turkey, Iraq, Iran and Pakistan to reach India in a Volkswagen. That a young woman could drive through challenging deserts and lonely mountain roads briefly grabbed the attention of the world, which was dealing with conflicts in Gaza, Egypt and Hungary and a brewing tension in Lebanon.

The Free Press Journal of Mumbai carried the news of Campman's adventure. On the same page, the proud news organization celebrated one of their own—P.R.S. Mani, who was now a senior diplomat. Mani had served three years in Bonn and had returned home for his next posting. On the way, he spent some time among journalists in Bombay. Meeting the reporter from *The Free Press Journal*, he recounted the good old days in Indonesia when Prime Minister Dr Sutan Sjahrir used his pen to make the offer of Java rice to Prime Minister Nehru. Mani was a changed man now. The confidence and charisma were still there, but he was now a family man with a wife and two young sons. 'There is an anxiety to know more about India—not the old and ancient India—but the modern India that we are building up,' said Mani.[9] Between his appointments in Bonn and Jakarta, Mani had served in Shanghai, Hong Kong and Goa and had grown into the service, where he was to serve for another quarter century. India had come a long way diplomatically. Apart from bilateral and multilateral activities, India began to play an important role in building peace in prominent conflict areas, and Indian soldiers became an important component of UN peacekeeping missions.

But there were problems on the horizon. South and Southeast Asia were far from attaining stability despite the presence of stable political leaders. In India, Nehru was hit by the Mundhra Jeep Scandal in 1957, and in the same year in March, President Sukarno, faced with left-wing military rebellions, declared martial law on 14 March. The violence that had existed in Indonesia in the mid-1940s had staged a return in the country, which had enjoyed a few years of stability. India was seen as an ally of Sukarno, and that was one of the reasons that prompted anti-Sukarno public anger to be directed against India. The next day, hundreds of Indonesians attacked and looted a building that was used to host staff members of the Indian Embassy in Jakarta. *The Times of India* reported that the crowd took away whatever it could carry and such was the anger that they tried to demolish the building, and when they could not do so, they dismantled the roof and carried it away.[10] The sudden explosion of fury against Indians revived memories of the hate that Indonesians in Java had displayed briefly in October 1945, when they had suspected that Indian soldiers were complicit in a western plot to sabotage Indonesia's freedom. The attack against Indians was unimaginable a few years earlier when Sukarno was honoured as the first 'chief guest' at the first Republic Day parade of India on 26 January 1950. Decolonization was a much-awaited step for these countries but without democratization, good governance and political stability, the gains of decolonization could be lost. Nearly a decade had passed since India had launched its own brand-new foreign service, and the complexities of the world were just beginning to be apparent. The trouble facing the Indians in Indonesia would soon be visible in other countries too, including in Burma, which was dealt with earlier. Indian diplomats would face the heat when the campaign to liberate Goa was launched in 1961. Non-alignment was born out of the idealistic phase of Nehruvian diplomacy, and now the hard phase of diplomacy became apparent. The general air of decline was further intensified with India's setback in the 1962 war against China. In his interview for this book, Natwar Singh recollected that for a few months after the defeat, 'no one wanted to visit New Delhi' for fear of angering China. The international arena welcomed India with open arms, but it also expected India to be strong, and a sign of weakness was not good for India's admirers. But there was no denying the fact that independent India had established its serious diplomatic presence through the ups and downs in the previous fifteen years, and the war with China was in fact an opportunity for certain other kinds of relationships that India began to nurture from this point onwards.

The Kargil conflict ended in July 1999, and in September, Brajesh Mishra left for a visit to Israel. It was reported that he would meet Israeli Prime Minister Ehud Barak and other senior leaders. It had been seven years since the two sides had established a formal diplomatic relationship. The nuclear tests were not a move to shut the doors on the biggest nuclear and technological powers in the world. There were expectations that India would reach out to the United States to convince it of New Delhi's requirement of nuclear deterrence through the friendly government of Israel. It was rumoured that Brajesh Mishra's visit would coincide with the visit of US Secretary of State Madeleine Albright to Israel. There were expectations that the paths of the two negotiators would cross in Tel Aviv. India was at a crossroad between the old and the new nuclear orders, and National Security Advisor Brajesh Mishra was building on the foundation of a relationship that was cemented during the crisis of 1962.

As the Chinese guns were turned against Indian positions in the high Himalayas of Ladakh, the consul general of Israel in Bombay arrived in Delhi and parked himself at The Ashok hotel near the residence of Prime Minister Nehru in Teen Murti Bhavan. He carried a telegrammed message from Prime Minister David Ben-Gurion in Tel Aviv:[11]

> It is indeed with grave concern that I have followed the development and the very serious situation that has arisen on your frontiers. All our efforts have been and are directed towards the preservation of peace in our area and throughout the world. Jerusalem, the name of our capital means in Hebrew, City of Peace. I am in total agreement with the views expressed by your Excellency that it is incumbent upon us to do all in our power. It is for this reason that we also proposed general disarmament in Israel and in our Arab neighbours even in advance of global disarmament under mutual supervision; in that we see the most effective way of preventing wars. Moreover, we have expressed our readiness to sign treaties of non-aggression between us and our neighbours. We believe that all states, great or small, must be assured of their sovereignty, independence, freedom, territorial (integrity).

Ben-Gurion's message was brought to Nehru by Consul General Arieh Eilan, who conveyed the Israeli government's assurance that the country would support India in its moment of crisis. While new windows began to open during the crisis, older relations refused to recover. With the India–Pakistan conflict of 1965 unfolding, anti-India sentiment returned in Indonesia and Indian-owned properties were attacked once again. On 15 September 1965, External Affairs Minister Swaran Singh told the Parliament that Delhi had taken up the reports of the vandalization of Indian-owned property as well as of the office of Air India with the Indonesian government. What disturbed Delhi was the realization that India's military tension with Pakistan had cast a shadow on one of the largest Asian nations, which had been a solid friend of New Delhi a decade earlier. India did not break its diplomatic relations with Indonesia, but Air India stopped servicing Garuda airlines' flights in Bombay, ultimately prompting Indonesia to discontinue the Garuda flights to Bombay. A critical gaze also fell on the Indian Foreign Service after India suffered the humiliating defeat in the war of 1962. In the backdrop of military tensions with China and Pakistan, diplomats were under pressure to deliver. A traumatic incident took place in China during 1967 when the second secretary in the Indian mission in Beijing and the third secretary were expelled by Mao's government. The two officials, K. Raghunath and P. Vijay, were nearly lynched as they made their way from the embassy to the airport and then in Canton before they entered Hong Kong, which was a British territory. As Raghunath, Vijay and a third colleague sat in the aircraft, slogans such as the following were raised: 'Indian spy K. Raghunath, get out of China'.[12] The real issue was with China, which was in the middle of the Cultural Revolution that had spiralled out of control, and the weakened relations with India was an easy target to channel the public anger that was building up because of other domestic factors.

It was in this backdrop of a tumultuous '60s that a new opportunity arose in East Pakistan, presenting Indian diplomats a new chance to salvage their fame. Indira Gandhi had famously said, 'My father was a saint. I am not.'[13] Nowhere did the truth of this statement become more apparent than in her pursuit of power—first inside the ruling Congress, where she established herself by eliminating all political challengers, and then during the biggest political crisis in South Asia, which reached its climax in 1971 when the military rulers of Islamabad refused to share power with the Awami League of East Pakistan.

The early phase of Indian diplomacy, where personal relationship between the leaders was prioritized over other factors, was now a thing of the past. Nehru's recruits had to frame their policies in the world that Nehru had left for them. Faced with the rising challenge from China and a double-winged Pakistan, India under Indira Gandhi planned the next move. It was clear that with its presence in both east and the west, Pakistan posed a long-term threat. The Indian realism, which grew in this background, is at times illustrated within the South Block through a unique interpretation of the character of Dronacharya, the headmaster of the Kuru dynasty and legendary warrior of the Mahabharat.

Before Drona became the teacher of the royal house of the Kurus, he spent his student days learning the art of war with the Panchala prince Drupad. The two struck up a strong friendship, and the prince promised Drona that once he became the king of Panchala, he would share his kingdom with his friend. Upon completing his education, Drona, by now a highly accomplished scholar of warfare, statecraft and ethics, reached out to his friend and sought a share of his kingdom. But by now Drupad had a change of heart and insulted Drona for daring to reach out with his request.

After this humiliating treatment, Drona, a young father of a child, went through a harrowing phase because of poverty. He often had to leave his child without milk. The world did not help him in his dark days, and Dronacharya realized that without effective strategy, his long years of training and hardship were of no use to him. Finally, he decided to pursue a path of vengeance and walked to the Kurus, the rivals of the kingdom of the Panchalas. Here, he offered to train the princes of the Kuru dynasty. Drona wanted to train his pupils in warfare so that they would become a force to challenge the nearby kingdom of Panchala and avenge the humiliation that King Drupad had inflicted on him. Drona spent his years training the princes to establish Hastinapur as the pre-eminent kingdom, making it powerful enough to decimate the power of Panchala. It was here that the eternal story of Ekalavya takes place in the Mahabharat.

In the Sambhava Parva of the epic, the prince of the Nishadas, Ekalavya, meets Dronacharya and seeks his training to learn the rules and art of using weapons. But Dronacharya, who was already committed to teach the Kuru princes, declined and asked Ekalavya to return to his forest.

Inside the forest, Ekalavya built a clay statue of Drona and practised sincerely and over a period mastered the weapons. Around this time, the Kuru princes went into the forest of the Nishadas with a fierce dog. The dog wandered away from the princes and appeared where Ekalavya was practising archery. The silence of the forest was broken by the aggressive dog, and Ekalavya shot arrows towards the dog, sealing the dog's jaws. As the muted dog returned to his shocked owners, they discovered Ekalavya practising archery before an idol of their teacher, Drona. On seeing his statue delivering better training than what he was able to provide to the princes, Drona displayed a diabolical side to his personality and demanded a fee for teaching Ekalavya. The Nishada prince, without realizing the trap that he was getting into, agreed to the condition. Drona demanded the thumb of Ekalavya's right hand. Ekalavya sacrificed his thumb and could never again shoot arrows in the way that he did before.

India's ethical discourse has been occupied by this episode in the Mahabharat, with critics of the caste system rightly pointing out that the treatment meted out to Ekalavya displayed the ruthless nature of the Brahminical system, based as it was on denying education to non-caste individuals. However, according to a particularly dark interpretation relevant to this book, the cruelty of Drona was actually a sign of his remarkable, single-minded quest for revenge and strategic foresight, where nothing else mattered. He assessed correctly that Ekalavya had become such a fine warrior that neighbouring kingdoms could easily challenge the Kurus by hiring him as their commander. He was determined to prevent any of the nearby kings, including Drupad, from acquiring a commander who could tilt the balance of power against the Kurus. Ekalavya, in short, had the potential to derail the revenge that Drona had been planning for so long and therefore had to be neutralized. Drona did not want Ekalavya's death; he wanted to take away his skills.

A similar correct assessment of the enemy and the aim of preventing them from challenging the existing status quo form the basis of diplomacy in India. And starting with the arrival of Indira Gandhi's government in January 1966, this strategy gradually found greater acceptance among Indian decision-makers. Indira Gandhi's quest for power was supported by P.N. Haksar, T.N. Kaul and Kewal Singh—all early recruits of the IFS under the Nehru era. Steered by these key officials, India would pursue power single-mindedly and re-establish the regional leadership in 1971. This time, the diplomatic dialogue was accompanied with fierce military will.

ACKNOWLEDGEMENTS

Diplomats are engaging storytellers, and this book could not have happened without the tales that I collected from them over the years. K. Natwar Singh, who shared the *History of Services* with me opened my eyes to the possibility of thinking about the diplomats of his generation as the first recruits of Nehruvian diplomacy. I am forever grateful to him for this and for opening his library to me—a privilege that he reserves only for his closest friends. Maharajakrishna Rasgotra, a few years elder to Natwar, is from the second batch of direct recruits into the Indian Foreign Service, and he has been generous with his time and spoke to me at length about his experiences in the IFS, for this book. What is fascinating is that Rasgotra, who was recruited into the IFS through a competitive examination in 1949, had struck up a friendship over literature with Hindi literary legend Harivansh Rai Bachchan even before joining the foreign service. In 1955, of course, Bachchan too joined the Ministry of External Affairs as officer on special duty (Hindi) and later in life wrote about his friendship with Rasgotra in his fascinating autobiography. I am equally thankful to the other direct recruit, Eric Gonsalves who gave me telephonic interviews on multiple occasions and helped me navigate the crosscurrents of diplomacy, politics and history.

Younger diplomats like Ronen Sen and K.P. Fabian, and academics like Professor Surinder Bhutani and Dr A.K. Pasha, have often helped with suggestions, ideas and details that contributed to my understanding of India's foreign affairs during the decades when Nehru's recruits held sway. Professor Rachana Kamtekar and her brother Professor Indivar Kamtekar sat down with me to discuss the life of their father Dileep Kamtekar and helped me understand the 1950s. I am indebted to them both for sharing details about the family life of Indian diplomats in the 1960s and the '70s. Like them, Nomita Sinha, Balachandran Kannampilly and Shanthy Pragalsingh also shared their valuable perspectives as children of early Indian diplomats. Murad Ali Baig opened his home, his computer and his photo library to me not just once, but multiple times. 'Who wants to remember Tara and Mirza Rashid Ali Baig?' he asked playfully on a summer afternoon. I am happy that he eventually came around to my point of view that many would be and agreed to sit down and share his memories of the gorgeous life of India's most charismatic protocol officer. My sincere gratitude also goes out to former Foreign Secretary Lalit Mansingh, for his early encouragement of this volume.

This book received the support it required when Swati Chopra of HarperCollins India took it up. Without the support of Swati, this journey could not have been completed. I am deeply thankful to Swati and Anju Christine for the patient editing. Saurav Das came up with a brilliant cover that captures the essence of the book—a photograph of Nehru with Mirza Rashid Ali Baig, both frozen in a moment in time. Siddhesh Inamdar deserves a special mention as he was the one who initially took the idea to HarperCollins India.

ACKNOWLEDGEMENTS

Anuj Bahri and his team at the Red Ink Literary Agency were the first to be consulted on this project, and I am thankful to them for the unwavering support that they have given this project over the past several years. There are many others especially in the Pradhan Mantri Sangrahalaya (formerly the Nehru Memorial Museum and Library) who have helped me while I worked on the lives of Nehru's first recruits. My experience, as a writer and reporter on foreign affairs, has been enriched by some of the most amazing journalists and editors, whom I had the fortune to encounter professionally. The late Sachidananda Murthy is someone I particularly remember for the support that he extended to me. His spirited encouragement to do 'organic reporting' was vital to my understanding of my subjects. Similarly, my former editor at *The Week*, Philip Mathew, and *Malayala Manorama*'s legendary editor, Mammen Mathew, were among those who made it possible for me to consistently work on ideas that were close to my heart. I am thankful to Dr Malini Parthasarathy for giving me a chance to report for *The Hindu*, where I started working in 2015. I am grateful to my current and former colleagues at *The Hindu* especially Amit Baruah, Suhasini Haidar, Varghese K. George, Anuradha Raman, V. Sudarshan, Srinivasan Ramani, Mini Kapoor, Dinakar Peri, Tom Cijo, Rajeev G.R. and Vikas Dhoot, all of whom have often collaborated with me during this time and enriched my understanding of the Indian state. I am grateful also to Rahul Rawat of JNU, Prem Shankar Jha and Satish Chandra Gauba for the support they have often extended to me.

I am thankful to Professor Heather Goodall of the University of Technology Sydney for guiding me on the P.R.S. Mani collection. Among the many who helped with ideas and suggestions, I am particularly indebted to Dalvinder Singh at the Ministry of External Affairs.

Finally, this work was made possible because of the support and blessings of my parents—Amita Chakraborty and Keshab Kanti Bhattacharjee. This book is dedicated to both of them. The support and blessings of Arunamoyee Dida have helped me stay on course while pursuing challenging assignments. During the writing of this book, Didibhai and Shripad brought great cheer to my life, which helped enormously.

Finally, I must acknowledge that over the years I have interacted with many serving Indian diplomats, who have helped me understand the behaviour and choices they represent. I hope *Nehru's First Recruits* will bring greater understanding—and spark renewed discussions—about Indian diplomacy and what it represents in the twenty-first century.

NOTES

1. MILITARY MEN, RADIO ANNOUNCERS, ICS OFFICERS

1. 'Funeral of Mahatma Gandhi', Akashvani, All India Radio, https://www.youtube.com/watch?v=X6rhCsogIeY.
2. This committee was formed by Indian students and activists in Berlin. Led by Virendranath Chattopadhyay and Abinash Bhattacharya, the committee was the first anti-imperialist organization formed in Central Europe that targeted the colonial masters of India.
3. Supplement to application for job in IFS, P.R.S. Mani Collection, University of Technology, Sydney.
4. *Ibid*.
5. P.R.S. Mani, *The Story of Indonesian Revolution: 1945–1950* (Madras: Centre for South and Southeast Asian Studies, University of Madras, 1986), p. 2.
6. Speech of Akbar Makarti, Indonesian vice consul in global accessibility launch of the P.R.S. Mani Collection, 29 September 2014.
7. *The Story of Indonesian Revolution*, p. 8.
8. 'Cannibalism in Jap army: International problem', *The Times of India* (Mumbai edition), 6 November 1945, p. 5.
9. *The Story of Indonesian Revolution*, p. 8.

10. Supplement to application for job in IFS, P.R.S. Mani Collection, University of Technology, Sydney.
11. *The Story of Indonesian Revolution: 1945–1950*, p. 32.
12. Sukarno's letter to Jawaharlal Nehru, P.R.S. Mani Collection University of Technology, Sydney.
13. *The Story of Indonesian Revolution*, p. 67.
14. Letter from Jawaharlal Nehru to P.R.S. Mani, 17 June 1946, P.R.S. Mani Collection, University of Technology, Sydney.
15. Supplement to Application for job in IFS, P.R.S. Mani Collection, University of Technology, Sydney.
16. *History of Services of the Officers of the Indian Foreign Service (Branches A and B)* as on the 1st September 1958 (New Delhi: Ministry of External Affairs, Government of India, 1959), p. 18. (Hereafter *History of Services*.)
17. *Ibid*.
18. *Ibid*.
19. P.R.S. Mani Collection, University of Technology, Sydney.
20. 'India could call together the world's radio chiefs', *The Times of India*, 22 August 1954, p. 2.
21. P.R.S. Mani Collection, University of Technology, Sydney.
22. Jaswant Singh, *A Call to Honour: In Service of Emergent India* (New Delhi: Rupa & Co., 2006), pp. 116–18.
23. Oral History, 'The "Mao's Smile" revisited: Sino-Indian relations during an important period', *Indian Foreign Affairs Journal*, Vol. 1, No. 4 (October–December 2006): pp. 109–18.
24. *Ibid.*, p. 113.
25. *Ibid.*, p. 111.
26. *Ibid*.
27. *Ibid*.
28. *Ibid*.
29. *Ibid.*, p. 110.
30. *Ibid.*, p. 110–12.
31. F.S. Ajazuddin, *From a Head, Through a Head, to a Head: The Secret Channel between the US and China through Pakistan* (Karachi: Oxford University Press, 2000), p. 2.

32. A.G. Noorani, 'Brajesh Mishra & Mao's Smile', *Frontline*, 28 February 2018.
33. Brajesh Mishra, 'Foreword', in *The New Asian Power Dynamic*, ed. Maharajakrishna Rasgotra (New Delhi: Sage Publication, 2006), p. 8.
34. Natwar Singh, 'Former Foreign Minister Natwar Singh pays tribute to Brajesh Mishra', *India Today*, 30 September 2012.
35. Ibid.
36. *History of Services*, p. 44.
37. T.P. Sreenivasan and James M. Peck (eds.), *Venkat Forever: A Tribute to Ambassador AP Venkateswaran* (Delhi: Konark Publishers, 2015), p. 74.
38. 'Transcript of Special Briefing by Foreign Secretary on First I2U2 Leaders' Virtual Summit (July 14, 2022)', Ministry of External Affairs, Government of India, https://mea.gov.in/media-briefings.htm?dtl/35493/Transcript_of_Special_Briefing_by_Foreign_Secretary_on_First_I2U2_Leaders_Virtual_Summit_July_14_2022.
39. J.N. Dixit, *Makers of India's Foreign Policy: Raja Ram Mohan Roy to Yashwant Sinha* (Delhi: HarperCollins Publishers India, 2004), pp. 273–90.
40. Siran Mukerji, *Indian Foreign Service: Structure, Role and Performance* (Jaipur: Aalekh Publishers, 2000), pp. 118–19.
41. *Ibid*, p. 110.
42. Annual Report, 1958–59, Ministry of External Affairs, Government of India, p. 3.
43. *Ibid.*, p. 7.
44. Annual Report, 1957–58, Ministry of External Affairs, Government of India, p. 3.
45. Oral history record of Ambassador Eric Gonsalves, *Oral History Series*, Volume 1, Interview conducted by Ambassador Kishan S. Rana, in 2010, Indian Council of World Affairs, p. 30, https://www.icwa.in/WriteReadData/RTF1984/1497424125.pdf.
46. *History of Services*, p. 10. Indar Jeet Bahadur Singh was born on 12 June 1915 in the Caribbeans and joined the Indian Foreign Service as an attaché in Shanghai where he served from January 1946 to November 46. He was confirmed in the Senior Scale of the IFS in November 1948. He served in the Indian Embassy in Washington

DC in 1950–51, and subsequently went on to serve in Beijing. He was appointed as adviser to chairman, NNRC, Korea September 1953.
47. J.N. Dixit, *Indian Foreign Service: History and Challenge* (Delhi: Konark Publishers, 2005), pp. 44–45.
48. *Ibid.* p. 50
49. Jawaharlal Nehru, 'Prime Minister's reply to the debate on Foreign Affairs in the Lok Sabha on November 20, 1956,' in *Speeches in Parliament, 16 November–7 December 1956*, NMML, p. 33.
50. Jawaharlal Nehru, 'Prime Minister's reply to the debate on Foreign Affairs in the Rajya Sabya on December 4, 1956' in *Speeches in Parliament, 16 November–7 December 1956*, NMML, p. 60.
51. 'India will take care of her children abroad', *The Free Press Journal*, Kuala Lumpur, 23 March 1946.
52. *The Free Press Journal*, Penang, 25 March 1946, P.R.S. Mani Collection, University of Technology, Sydney.

2. A FRIENDSHIP AND A CATALOGUE

1. Author's notes from an interview with Natwar Singh, June 2011.
2. 'Limaye accuses Jagat Mehta of being pro-US', *The Times of India*, 26 February 1979, p. 9.
3. Inder Malhotra, 'From soloist to conductor: second impression', *The Times of India*, 10 November 1991, p. 12.
4. K. Natwar Singh, 'No nervous nineties for veteran diplomats', *The Hindu,* 20 September 2020.
5. This is how the name appears in the History of Services, though the author feels it should be 'Lala Chunni Lall'.
6. 'Preface' by K.P.S. Menon (Jr.), in *History of Services of the Officers of the Indian Foreign Service (Branches A and B)* as on the 1st September 1958 (New Delhi: Ministry of External Affairs, Government of India, 1959).
7. Telephonic interview with Prof. Surinder K. Bhutani, October 2022.
8. Annual Report of the Ministry of External Affairs and Commonwealth Relations, 1948–49, p. 1.
9. 'Preface' by K.P.S. Menon (Jr.), in *History of Services.*

10. *Ibid*, p. 17.
11. *Ibid*, p. 48.
12. *History of Services*, p. 33.
13. Author's interview with sociologist Prof. Patricia Uberoi, December 2022.
14. *History of Services*, p. 25.
15. 'India-China Relations', Ministry of External Affairs, https://www.mea.gov.in/Portal/ForeignRelation/China_January_2014.pdf.
16. Parushotam L. Mehra, 'India, China and Tibet 1950–54', *India Quarterly*, Vol. 12, No. 1 (January–March 1956): p. 15.
17. *History of Services*, p. 25.
18. Every member of the IFS A and B had to have a 'compulsory foreign language' as mentioned in the 1958 *History of Services*.
19. 'Indians in China: The Most Honoured Guests', *Indian Foreign Affairs Journal*, Vol. 3, No. 1 (January-March 2008): p. 99.
20. *Ibid.*, p. 100.
21. Kallol Bhattacherjee, 'When Nehru wanted globe-trotting diplomats in print', *The Hindu*, 29 May 2021.
22. 'Papua New Guinea for self-reliance', *The Times of India*, 17 September 1975, p. 17.
23. Author's interview with K. Natwar Singh, 28 October 2023, New Delhi.
24. K. Natwar Singh shared this detail with the author during a 2022 interview conducted in New Delhi for this work.

3. 'EVERYONE'S TRYING TO MAKE SENSE'

1. C.S. Jha, *From Bandung to Tashkent: Glimpses of India's Foreign Policy* (New Delhi: Sangam Books, 1983), p. 53.
2. *Ibid*.
3. *History of Services of the Officers of the Indian Foreign Service (Branches A and B)* as on the 1st September 1958 (New Delhi: Ministry of External Affairs, Government of India, 1959), p. 1.
4. K.P.S. Menon, *Yesterday and Today: Collection of Articles* (Bombay: Allied Publishers, 1976), pp. 138–40.
5. *Ibid.*, p. 139.
6. *From Bandung to Tashkent*, p. 54.

7. Annual Report, 1950–51, Ministry of External Affairs, pp. 8–9.
8. Interview with Maharajakrishna Rasgotra, 21 November 2022, Delhi.
9. Harold A. Gould, *Sikhs, Swamis, Students and Spies: The India Lobby in the United States,* 1900–1946 (New Delhi: Sage Publications, 2006), pp. 40–45.
10. *Ibid.*
11. *Ibid.*, p. 45.
12. Interview with Maharajakrishna Rasgotra, 30 January 2023, New Delhi.
13. *Ibid.*
14. Amit Dasgupta, *Serving India: A Political Biography of Subimal Dutt (1903–1992)* (Delhi: Manohar, 2017), p. 110.
15. Brajesh Mishra, principal secretary to the Prime Minister was given the additional charge of National Security Advisor (NSA). This caused some controversy as a section was of the view that the two posts should have been separated. Former PM I.K. Gujral was one of those who believed that the post of NSA was a full-time job, and he expressed his opinion in 1998. Vajpayee, however, retained Mishra as his NSA.
16. Author's interview with Maharajakrishna Rasgotra, New Delhi, 30 January 2023.
17. *Serving India,* Ibid, p. 111.
18. M.O. Mathai, *Reminiscences of the Nehru Age* (New Delhi: Vikas Publishing House, 1978), pp. 198–200.
19. *Ibid.*, p. 7.
20. Josef Korbel, *Danger in Kashmir* (New York: Oxford University Press, 1954), p. 98.
21. *Ibid.*, p. 123.
22. Amit Dasgupta, *The Indian Civil Service and Indian Foreign Policy: 1923–1961* (Delhi: Routledge, 2021), p. 5.
23. Vappala Balachandran, *A Life in Shadow: The Secret Story of A.C.N. Nambiar: A Forgotten Anti-Colonial Warrior* (New Delhi: Roli Books, 2016), p. 201.
24. *Ibid.*, p. 202.

4. THE OUTSIDER BECOMES AN INSIDER: THE CAREER OF AN IFS TOPPER

1. Author's interview with Prof. Rachana Kamtekar, 18 January 2023, Noida.
2. Author's interview with Prof. Indivar Kamtekar, 20 January 2023, JNU campus, Delhi.
3. Results of IAS, IFS exams of 1951, *The Times of India*, 28 January 1952, p. 6.
4. *Ibid.*
5. Author's interview with Prof. Rachana Kamtekar, 18 January 2023, Noida.
6. *Ibid.*
7. Author's interview with Prof. Indivar Kamtekar, 20 January 2023, JNU campus, Delhi.
8. *History of Services of the Officers of the Indian Foreign Service (Branches A and B)* as on the 1st September 1958 (New Delhi: Ministry of External Affairs, Government of India, 1959), p. 3.
9. *Ibid.*, p. 5.
10. *Ibid.*
11. The first Indian ambassador to Indonesia was sent in 1949, right before the first Republic Day parade in 1950 in New Delhi which was attended by Sukarno. Between October 1947 and June 1949, Yunus was doing this job under the rank of an attache while both sides were in the process of finalizing the shape of the relationship.
12. Author's interview with Prof. Rachana Kamtekar, 20 January 2023, Noida.
13. Interview with Prof Indivar Kamtekar, 20 January 2023, JNU campus, Delhi.
14. 'India-Mauritius Bilateral Relations', High Commission of India, Port Louis, https://www.mea.gov.in/Portal/ForeignRelation/Bilateral_Brief_maurititus_2019.pdf.
15. Author's interview with Prof Rachana Kamtekar, 18 January 2023, Noida.
16. 'Envoy to West Germany', *The Times of India*, 11 September 1984, p. 14.

5. RAJ: THE ENVOY FOR 'LITTLE NATIONS'

1. 'Air link with French India: Aviator's Mission', *Times of India*, 21 April 1936, p. 10.
2. *Ibid.*
3. *Ibid.*
4. *Ibid.*
5. *Ibid.*
6. 'French Possessions in India', *The Times of India*, 3 March 1947, p. 1.
7. 'Customs Pact with French India Settlements: Termination on April 1', *The Times of India*, 19 March 1949, p. 4.
8. 'May Day in Moscow: Call to Red Army', *The Times of India*, 3 May 1949, p. 3.
9. Rajeshwar Dayal, 'Glamour of the Foreign Service: Reflections and Recollections', *Times of India*, 15 August 1969, p. 18.
10. 'ICS Examination', *The Times of India*, 15 May 1931, p. 11.
11. *History of Services of the Officers of the Indian Foreign Service (Branches A and B)* as on the 1st September 1958 (New Delhi: Ministry of External Affairs, Government of India, 1959), p. 4.
12. Alistair Cooke, 'United Nations: India deplores Big Powers' tactics. Warning note to members', *The Times of India*, 29 April 1952, p. 1.
13. Philip Roth, 'Flame of revolt in Tunisia', *The Times of India*, 3 February 1952, p. 6.
14. 'Trust France: Minister's appeal to Tunisia', *The Times of India*, 20 May 1952, p. 6.
15. 'Debate on Tunisia: U.S. Support', *The Times of India*, October 15, 1952, p. 1.
16. The name of Sushila Srivastava is printed as Sushella in the *History of Services*.
17. Zareer Masani, *And All is Said: Memoir of a Home Divided* (New Delhi: Penguin Books, 2012), p. 74.
18. Agha Hilaly became one of the prominent diplomats of Pakistan in the twentieth century and became Pakistan's ambassador to the US. He is remembered for being involved in Henry Kissinger's secret talks with China, which were conducted through Pakistani officials and President Yahya Khan.

19. Telephonic Interview with Prof. Surinder Bhutani, 22 November 2022.
20. Rajeshwar Dayal, *Mission for Hammarskojld: The Congo Crisis* (Delhi: Oxford University Press, 1976), p. 10.
21. Andrew Whitefield, 'Partition voices: Sir Ian Scott', Andrew Whitefield blog, https://www.andrewwhitehead.net/partition-voices-sir-ian-scott.html. 4:30 minute onwards Ian Scott narrated the difficulty that the increasingly 'Indianized' Indian Civil Service faced in dealing with rebellion by the nationalist leaders of the Congress.
22. Ibid
23. Dayal, *Mission for Hammarskojld: The Congo Crisis* (Delhi: Oxford University Press, 1976), p. 3.

6. *VIDESH MANTRALAYA*: THE MAN BEHIND THE TERM

1. Harivansh Rai Bachchan, *In the Afternoon of Time: An Autobiography* (Delhi: Viking, 1998), p. 363.
2. *Ibid.*, p. 380.
3. *Ibid.*, p. 382.
4. *Ibid.*, p. 382.
5. Author's interview with K. Natwar Singh, New Delhi, 7 January 2024.
6. *In the Afternoon of Time*, p. 387
7. *Ibid.*, p. 387.
8. *Ibid.*, p. 383.
9. *Ibid.*, p. 383.
10. 'Alleged plot to murder Mr Nehru: Further hearing of case', *The Times of India*, 28 September 1960, p. 9.
11. 'Austria urged to inquire death of diplomat', *The Times of India*, 7 August 1962, p. 5.
12. Anil Bhattacharya, *Bangladesher Muktijuddhey Tripura: Ojana Tathya O Ghotona* (Dhaka: Sahitya Prakash, 2019), p. 81.

7. THE FIRST EVACUATION OF INDIANS IN A FOREIGN CRISIS

1. *History of Services of the Officers of the Indian Foreign Service (Branches A and B)* as on the 1st September 1958 (New Delhi: Ministry of External Affairs, Government of India, 1959), p. 35.
2. Annual Report, 1960–61, Ministry of External Affairs, Government of India, p. 20.
3. 'The Myanmar Immigration (Emergency Provisions) (Amendment) Act 1957', Open Development Thailand, https://data.thailand.opendevelopmentmekong.net/laws_record/the-myanmar-immigration-emergency-provisions-amendment-act-1957.
4. Annual Report, 1959–60, Ministry of External Affairs, Government of India, p. 15.
5. Annual Report, 1957–58, Ministry of External Affairs, Government of India, p. 22.
6. Arunabh Saikia, 'After six decades, Manipur's Burmese Tamils get a glimpse of their ancestral places in Myanmar', Scroll.in, 24 February 2019, https://scroll.in/article/913335/after-six-decades-manipurs-burmese-tamils-get-a-glimpse-of-their-ancestral-places-in-myanmar.
7. Annual Report, Ministry of External Affairs, 1964–65, Government of India, p. 25.
8. Telephonic interview with Eric Gonsalves, 26 January 2023.
9. Oral history record of Ambassador Eric Gonsalves, Oral History Series, Volume 1, Interview conducted by Kishan S. Rana in 2010, *Indian Council of World Affairs*, p. 35, https://www.icwa.in/WriteReadData/RTF1984/1497424125.pdf.
10. *Ibid.*, p. 35.
11. *Ibid.*, p. 37. There are differing estimates of the Indian population in Myanmar/Burma of that time. Lack of a census since World War II contributed to the lack of exact numbers.
12. Telephonic interview with Eric Gonsalves, 26 January 2023.
13. Annual Report, 1963–64, Ministry of External Affairs, Government of India, p. 22.
14. Telephonic Interview with Eric Gonsalves, 26 January 2023.

15. Madhavan K. Palat (Editor), *Selected Works of Jawaharlal Nehru: Second Series, Volume Eighty-Five (1 January–26 May 1964)* (New Delhi: Jawaharlal Nehru Memorial Fund, 2019), p. 225.
16. Oral history record of Ambassador Eric Gonsalves, Oral History Series Volume 1, Interview conducted by Ambassador Kishan S. Rana, in 2010, *Indian Council of World Affairs,* p. 65, https://www.icwa.in/WriteReadData/RTF1984/1497424125.pdf.
17. *Ibid.*, p. 60.
18. Telephonic interview with Eric Gonsalves, 17 September 2022.
19. Krishna Gandhi, 'Anatomy of the Moradabad Riots', *Economic and Political Weekly,* Vol. 15, No. 36 (6 September 1980): pp. 1505–1507.
20. Katherine Frank, *The Life of Indira Nehru Gandhi* (New Delhi: HarperCollins India, 2007), p. 313.
21. Pupul Jayakar, *Indira Gandhi: A Biography* (New Delhi: Penguin Books, 1995), p. 395.
22. Telephonic interview with Eric Gonsalves, 17 September 2022; telephonic Interview with Eric Gonsalves, 26 January 2023.
23. Letter from B.K. Nehru to Congressman Emanuel Celler, 3 September 1963, Israeli Archives, Jerusalem.

8. 'WILFRED MUST GO'

1. Telephonic interview with Shanthy Pragalsingh, 6 December 2022.
2. Interview with stenographer of MEA, Satish Chandra Gauba who served from 1963, 14 December 2022, New Delhi.
3. Shanthy Pragalsingh, *Daughter of a Diplomat,* a privately published autobiography of Ms Pragalsingh focusing on her memories with her father Santosham John Wilfred, pp. 13–18.
4. *History of Services of the Officers of the Indian Foreign Service (Branches A and B)* as on the 1st September 1958 (New Delhi: Ministry of External Affairs, Government of India, 1959), p. 48.
5. T.N. Kaul, Foreign Relations, Publications Division, Ministry of Information and Broadcasting, Government of India, 25th Anniversary of Independence Series, p. 20.
6. P.R.S. Mani, *The Story of Indonesian Revolution: 1945–1950* (Madras: University of Madras, 1986), p. 9.

7. 'The flame of freedom in Asia', in *Selected Works of Jawaharlal Nehru*, Vol. 14, ed. S. Gopal, (New Delhi: Orient Longman, 1981), p. 307.
8. *Ibid*.
9. *Jawaharlal Nehru's Speeches: 1949–1953, Vol. II*, (Delhi: The Publications Division, Ministry of Information and Broadcasting, Government of India), p. 147.
10. *Ibid*.
11. *Daughter of a Diplomat*, p. 71.
12. *Ibid*., p. 94
13. Author's interview with Shashi and Satish Chandra Gauba, 12 November 2022, New Delhi.
14. *Ibid*.
15. *Ibid*.

9. REBELS AND PRINCES

1. 'Murali Kannampilly arrested: How a diplomat's son became a wanted Maoist leader', *The News Minute*, 12 May 2015, https://www.thenewsminute.com/article/murali-kannampilly-arrested-how-diplomats-son-became-wanted-maoist-leader-30268.
2. Author's telephonic interview with Balu Kannampilly on 12 February 2023.
3. *Nehru in Scandinavia*, Information Service of India, Stockholm, 1958, p. 11.
4. *History of Services of the Officers of the Indian Foreign Service (Branches A and B)* as on the 1st September 1958 (New Delhi: Ministry of External Affairs, Government of India, 1959), p. 17.
5. 'To feel the political pulse, Delhi drafts an official to North Vietnam', *The Times of India*, 1 May 1966, p. 1.
6. Author's interview with K.P. Fabian, 3 March 2023, New Delhi.
7. *History of Services*, p. 22.
8. 'Mrs Churchill in Madras: Pleasure cruise in the Far East', *The Times of India*, 7 January 1935, p. 10.
9. *Ibid*.
10. *Ibid*.
11. Abid Hasan Safrani, *The Men from Imphal* (Calcutta: A Netaji Research Bureau Publication, 1970), p. 13.

12. *Ibid.*
13. *Ibid.*
14. *Ibid.*, p. 15.
15. *History of Services*, p. 24 and 27.
16. 'India–Vietnam Bilateral Relations', Ministry of External Affairs, Government of India, https://www.mea.gov.in/Portal/ForeignRelation/Vi_Bilateral_Relations_December_2018__1_.pdf.
17. 'A Times of India Notebook', *The Times of India*, 17 April 1972, p. 6.
18. M.V. Kamath, 'US bid to checkmate India: Hanoi mission', *The Times of India*, 20 October 1969, p. 9.
19. *Ibid.*
20. 'Quip by Indian diplomat creates furore', *The Times of India*, 17 July 1967, p. 3.
21. *History of Services*, p. 31.
22. Amritha V. Shenoy, 'The Centenary of the League of Nations: Colonial India and the Making of International Law', *Asian Yearbook of International Law*, Vol. 24 (2018): p. 5.
23. *Ibid.*

10. THE FIRST WOMEN RECRUITS: LEILAMANI AND VIJAYA LAKSHMI

1. Yezdezard Dinshaw Gundevia, *In the Districts of the Raj* (Bombay: Orient Longman, 1992), p. 79.
2. *History of Services of the Officers of the Indian Foreign Service (Branches A and B) as on the 1st September 1958* (New Delhi: Ministry of External Affairs, Government of India, 1959), p. 3. He continued to serve for more than a decade in multiple important positions, including as minister in the Indian Embassy in Moscow (1950–53), ambassador to Switzerland, minister to Austria and the Vatican during 1953–54 and as deputy high commissioner in London and in Colombo, where he finally was confirmed in Grade II of the Indian Foreign Service on 9 April 1957.
3. Amit Dasgupta, *The Indian Civil Service and Indian Foreign Policy: 1923–1961* (London: Routledge, 2021), p. 223.

4. M.O. Mathai, 'Sarojini Naidu', in *Reminiscences of the Nehru Age* (New Delhi: Vikas Publishing House, 1978), p. 128.
5. *Ibid.*
6. Zareer Masani, *Indian Tales of the Raj* (Berkeley: University of California Press, 1987), pp. 89–90.
7. 'First effort to bring Asian countries together', *The Times of India*, 17 March 1947, p. 7.
8. *Ibid.*
9. *Ibid.*
10. P.R. Kumaraswamy, *India's Israel Policy* (New Delhi: Magnum Books Pvt. Ltd., 2010), p. 115.
11. *History of Services*, p. 9.
12. Vera Brittain, *Envoy Extraordinary: A Study of Vijaya Lakshmi Pandit and Her Contribution to Modern India* (New York: Routledge, 2021), p. 64.
13. *Ibid.*, p. 65.
14. Talmiz Ahmad, 'Syud Hossain: A Fascinating Footnote from India's Freedom Struggle', *The Wire*, 7 February 2021, https://thewire.in/books/book-review-syud-hossain-freedom-struggle.
15. Vijaya Lakshmi Pandit, *The Scope of Happiness: A Personal Memoir* (New York: Crown Publishers, 1979), p. 65.
16. Talmiz Ahmad, 'Syud Hossain: A Fascinating Footnote from India's Freedom Struggle', *The Wire*, 7 February 2021, https://thewire.in/books/book-review-syud-hossain-freedom-struggle.
17. J.N. Chakrabartti, *Dr. Syud Hossain: A Glimpse of His Life, Speeches and Writings* (Calcutta: P. Ghosh & Company, 2003), pp. 265–66.
18. *Envoy Extraordinary*, p. 65.
19. *The Scope of Happiness*, p. 65.
20. *Envoy Extraordinary*, p. 76.
21. *Ibid.*, p. 69.
22. *Ibid.*, p. 71.
23. Jayantanuja Bandyopadhyaya, *The Making of India's Foreign Policy: Determinants, Institutions, Processes and Personalities* (New Delhi: Allied Publishers, 1987), p. 75.
24. *Ibid.*

11. FROM HANUMANNAGAR TO TASHKENT: CHANDRA SHEKHAR JHA

1. Chandra Shekhar Jha, *From Bandung to Tashkent: Glimpses of India's Foreign Policy* (New Delhi: Sangam Books, 1983), pp. 48–49.
2. Ibid., p. 39.
3. Ibid., p. 3.
4. Ibid., p. 39.
5. Ibid., p. 58.
6. Ibid., p. 71.
7. Ibid.
8. Author's interview with journalist Prem Shankar Jha who recollected the life of his father, Chandra Shekhar Jha, for this book, New Delhi, 20 November 2023.
9. Farooq Naseem Bajwa, *Pakistan and the West: The First Decade 1947–1957* (Karachi: Oxford University Press, 1996), p. 14.
10. Dennis J. O'Brien, 'Francis T.P. Plimpton Oral History Interview – JFK#1, 10/21/1969', J.F.K. Library, https://www.jfklibrary.org/sites/default/files/archives/JFKOH/Plimpton%2C%20Francis%20T%20P/JFKOH-FTP-01/JFKOH-FTP-01-TR.pdf.
11. R.D. Pradhan, *Debacle to Revival: Y. B. Chavan as Defence Minister, 1962–65* (New Delhi: Orient Longman, 1999), pp. 205–06.
12. *From Bandung to Tashkent*, p. 207.
13. Ibid., p. 221.
14. Ibid., p. 239.

12. MIRZA RASHID ALI BAIG: THE PROTOCOL CHIEF WHO MADE ALL THE DIFFERENCE

1. Jayantanuja Bandyopadhyaya, *The Making of India's Foreign Policy: Determinants, Institutions, Processes and Personalities* (New Delhi: Allied Publishers, 1987), p. 95.
2. M.R.A Baig, *In Different Saddles* (London, Calcutta: Asia Publishing House, 1965), pp. 284–85.
3. Ibid., p. 285.
4. Ibid., p. 129.
5. Author's interview with Murad Ali Baig, New Delhi, 12 June 2023.

6. *In Different Saddles*, p. 134. (Jinnah presided over the Muslim League Working Committee like a strongman without sharing authority with any other member. Once Sir Sikander Hayat Khan and a group of Muslim League leaders from Lahore came to discuss some things in the party that they opposed as it did not take into account the condition in Punjab. After meeting with Jinnah to discuss the matter, Khan said, 'Mr Jinnah, I would like to discuss …' On hearing this, Jinnah 'slowly turned in his chair and looked at him.' Jinnah's cold stare was enough to end whatever disagreement Sikander Hayat Khan had in mind.)
7. *Ibid.*, p. 141.
8. *Ibid.*, p. 254.
9. 'Spotlight', *The Free Press Journal*, 1958, from the P.R.S. Mani Collection, University of Technology, Sydney.
10. 'Indonesians loot Indian Embassy Staff Quarters', *The Times of India*, 15 March 1957, p. 1.
11. Telegram from David Ben Gurion to Prime Minister Jawaharlal Nehru, 11 November 1962. Author's collection of documents from the Israeli Archives.
12. 'Inhuman Treatment by Red Guards: Diplomat's Account', *The Times of India*, 19 June 1967, p. 1.
13. Neerja Chaudhury, 'Indira Gandhi as a "Hindu first and Hindu last" and a grieving mother who blamed herself', *The Indian Express*, 19 November 2023, https://indianexpress.com/article/political-pulse/indira-gandhi-as-a-hindu-first-and-a-last-and-the-grieving-mother-who-blamed-herself-8868248/.

INDEX

Aam Aadmi Party, 78
Abdullah, Farooq, 56
abolition of slavery, 107
Abraham, Thomas, 97
academia, 66
Advani, L.K., 24, 33
'Afghan-led and Afghan-owned'
  peace process, 32
African forests of Congo, 128
African nationalists, 259
African national movements, 259
Afro–Asian
  bloc, 127
  cooperation, 264
  diplomacy, 261
  nations, 125
agriculture, 38
  and infrastructure building
    initiatives, 258
Aijazuddin, Fakir Syed, 30
air connectivity, 116
Air India, 113
Ajmani, Jagdish Chand, 97
Akyab, 116

Ali, Agha Mohammed, 151
Ali, Reza, 155
Allahabad Radio Station, 143
Allen, Richard, 184
All India Indira Congress, 58
All India Radio, 61, 66, 143, 288
  in Delhi, 13
  Madras, 12–13
All India Women's Conference,
  249
Al-Otaybi, Juhayman, 176
Al-Said, Nuri, 103
America(n)
  bloc, 269
  bureaucracy, 171
  capital, 171–72
  interest in China, 30
anger and youth, 5
Anglo-French aggression, 51
Anglo-Indian Prisoners of War
  (POWs), 223–24
Anglo-Indians, 222–23
Anglo-Saxon community, 90
'anti-attachment states' bloc', 232

anti-British movement, 290–91
anti-British struggle, 151–52
anti-caste stance, 215
anti-colonial, 203
  Africans, 259
  attitude, 100
  climate, 243
  movements, 6, 125
  national leaders, 260
  struggles, 124–25, 262, 299
  sympathizer, 82
anti-democratic practices, 76–77
anti-imperialism, 299
anti-racist struggles, 203
anti-US sentiment, 180
Arab League, 103
Arab nationalism, 45, 102, 103–4, 132
Arab–Soviet lines, 102–3
Arab Spring, 123, 127
Asian/Asianism, 254
  –African bloc of nations, 127
  consciousness, 245
  landmass, 194–95
Asian Relations Conference, 244, 245–46, 258, 283
assassination, 2, 5, 35–36, 80, 151, 174, 209, 217
Association of Southeast Asian Nations (ASEAN), 20
Atlantic Ocean, 253
atomic bombing of Hiroshima and Nagasaki, 123
Austrian Peace Treaty, 264
Austro-Hungarian empire, 5
Awami League, 154, 155
  of East Pakistan, 307
  leaders in a Dhaka jail, 209

Ayyangar, N. Gopalaswami, 91
Ayyar, A.S. Panchapekasa, 35, 97
Azad Hind government, 226
Azad, Maulana, 142

Babri Masjid demolition, 40
Bachchan, Ajitabh, 142
Bachchan, Harivansh Rai, 46, 61, 141, 142, 207, 210
  autobiography, 147–48
  in Cambridge and Oxford, 142
  kavi sammelans (poet gatherings), 143–44
  and Nehru's differences, 149–50
Bachchan, Teji, 144
Bagha, Jatin, 6
Baghdad Pact, 263
Baglodi, Deva Rao, 152
Baig, Mirza Abbas Ali, 291
Baig, Mirza Rashid Ali, 46, 47, 119–20, 282–309
  believe in Jinnah, 297–98
  transferred to Pondicherry, 300–301
Baig, Tara, 288
Bajpai, Girja Shankar, 21, 41, 48, 49–50, 67, 68–69, 81, 84, 86, 89, 91, 97, 247, 261
  patriotism, 81
  secretary-general in Ministry of External Affairs, 40
Bajpai, Kayatyani Shankar, 34, 97
Bajpai, Shankar, 279
Bajpai, Uma Shankar, 21
Baker, Herbert, 292
Balachandran, Vappala, 93

INDEX

Baldwin, James, 157
'Bali Jatra', 16
Bandaranaike, S.W.R.D., 258
Bandung Conference, 45–46, 257, 261, 263, 269
Bandung Declaration, 262
Bandyopadhyaya, Jayantanuja, 61
Banerjee, R.N., 87
Bangabandhu, 154
Bangkok, 116
Barak, Ehud, 304–5
Bartaman, 25
Batavia, 7
Batliwala, Soli, 94
Battle of Imphal, 7
Battle of Surabaya, 12, 13, 16, 193
Bayar, Mahmud Celâl, 268
Beijing, 27
Belgian colonizers, 129
Bells of Sarna, 159–60
Benares Hindu University, 143–44
Ben-Gurion, David, 305–06
Beria, Lavrentiy, 157–58
Bhagavad Gita, 158
Bhandari, Purshottam Lal, 21
Bhandari, Romesh, 40–41, 62
Bharatiya Janata Party (BJP), 33
Bhasha Andolan, 154
Bhattacharjea, Ajit, 73
Bhattacharjea, Mira Sinha, see Malik, Mira Ishardas

Bhattacharya, Anil, 156
Bhavan, Anand, 250
Bhopawar Agency in Central India, 233–34
Bhutan, 5–6
Bhutani, Sudarshan K., 67, 72

Bhutani, Surinder K., 67
Bhutto, Zulfikar Ali, 173–74, 176, 278
Bihar, 264
Boland, Frederick, 270
Bolivar, Simon, 3–4, 6
Bose, Khudiram, 3
Bose, Netaji Subhas Chandra, 52–53, 62, 92–93, 212, 220–21, 224–27, 249, 253
Bose, Rash Behari, 213
Bourguiba, Habib, 124, 125
Brahminical system, 309
Brecher, Michael, 272
British Central Africa, 106
British civil servants, 138
British East India Company, 222
British Empire, 61–62, 79, 289, 292
British Government, 194
British Indian police and detectives, 6
British-Indian troops, 7
British monarchy, 198
British Raj, 89, 129
  from India, 4
British-ruled India, 257
'brown Englishman', 291
Brussels Round Table Conference, 139
Buck, Pearl S., 252
Budhanilkantha temple, 201
bureaucracy, 62
Burma Bazar of Madras, 168
Burmese Army, 162
Burmese economy, 165
Burmese Immigration Act, 1957, 163

Burmese intelligence, 167
Burmese Republic, 161
Butt, Ghulam Hussain, 151

Cameron, David, 123–24
Campman, Katherine, 302
cannibalism, 11
Caroe, Olaf, 92, 268–69
Casey, William, 184
Ceauseşcu, Nicolae, 30
Celler, Emanuel, 182–83
Central Intelligence Agency, 184
Central National Organisation, 14–15
Chakravartty, Renu, 153
Chamoun, Camille, 101–02, 134
Chandernagore, 116–17
Chand, Khub, 104
Chandragiri pass, 197
Chantereine, M., 115
character assassination, 88
Chattopadhyay, Aghorenath, 242–43
Chattopadhyay, Virendranath, 244
Chaudhuri, Ajit Shankar, 147
Chaudhuri, J.N., 272
chaupai, 144
chauvinism, 14
Chavan, Ramkrishna Sakharam, 188
Chavan, Y.B., 276, 280
Chettiyar temple in Singapore, 225
'chhota Bharat', 109
Chiang Kai-shek, 49, 80
China Study Group, 71–72
Chinese economy, 72
Chinese Foreign Office, 29

Chinese leadership, 28
Chopra, Inder, 286
Choudhury, Tarek Ahmed, 154–55
Choudhury, Tarek Hossein, 155
Chou En-lai, 37, 288
Christian Medical College (CMC), Vellore, 187
Churchill, Winston, 221–22, 283
civil
   aviation, 115
   servants, 136
Clifford, Clark McAdams, 181
Clinton, Bill, 73
Coca Cola, 110
Cold War, 36, 261
   blocs, 32, 76, 136, 257
   camps, 138
   -era global politics, 24
   -era politicians, 181
collective self-defence, 262
colonial/colonialism, 262
   administration, 21, 80, 131, 136–37, 264
   ambition, 4
   possessions, 127
   rulers, 265
Commonwealth Relations, 68
Commonwealth Relations Department, 260
Commonwealth Training, 42–43, 84
communal disturbances, 301
communal divide, 2
communal riots, 2, 26
communication, 21
communist aggression, 133
communist bloc, 86
Communist Party of China, 285

Communist Party of India (CPI), 174, 234, 285
Congolese military, 129–30
Congress–Communist relationship, 285
Constitution (24th Amendment) Bill, 234–35
Constitution of Indonesia, 1945, 14
Cooch Behar, 154
Cornell University, 99
COVID-19 pandemic, 40
'creative period' of diplomacy, 268
cross-border terrorism, 38
cultural markers, 110
Cultural Revolution, 306
customs union, 118
Cuttack, 266
Czechoslovakia, 27

Damascus, 45
Damodaran, Ambady Krishnan, 62
Dar, Avtar, 272
Dass, Harbhajan, 151
Dass, Hira, 151
Dass, Pritam, 151
Dayal, Harishwar, 121–22
Dayal, Rajeshwar, 34–35, 48, 121, 125, 127, 129, 130, 131
    international peace-making, 135–36
decision-making, 17
decolonization, 45, 107, 117, 136, 161, 262, 264, 303–4
de Gaulle, Charles, 30
Delhi Choral Society, 288
Delhi–Chungking, 80

De Mello Kamath, Frederick Marion, 21
de Mellow, Melville, 1
Department of Commonwealth Relations, 267
Desai, Bhulabhai, 94
Desai, Dhirubhai, 94
Desai, Madhuri, 94
Desai, M.J., 88
Desai, Morarji, 175, 181
Devi, Rukmini, 13
Dhamija, J.N., 108
Dhar, D.P., 171, 206
    Indira Gandhi's ambassador in Moscow, 30
Dinkar, Ramdhari Singh, 144
diplomacy/diplomatic, 37, 173, 183, 242, 291
    and economic planning, 51
    history, 49
    with Israel, 38
    mission in Lhasa, 71
    relations, 45, 108
    semi-diplomatic relation' with China, 80
    subterfuge, 147
Diplomatic Bag, 113
diplomats, 22
discrimination, 259
distress rate, 167
Dixit, Jyotindra Nath, 24, 33, 36, 37, 61, 86–87
    Indian Foreign Service in 1958, 33–34
Dixon, Ian, 136–37
Doctrine, Eisenhower, 133
Donovan, Howard, 80
Dronacharya, 307–8

Dua, Shiva, 243
Dubey, Muchkund, 34, 41, 57–58
Dutch East Indies, 6
Dutch imperialism, 8
Dutch Indies, 256
Dutch policy on Indonesia, 126
Dutt, Guru, 150
Dutt, Subimal, 41, 43, 47, 49, 60–61, 62, 68–69, 83, 85, 88, 92, 101, 261

East Pakistan, 27, 154
economic/economy
    blockade, 119–20
    diplomacy, 18, 228
    hardship, 167
    and social indicators, 39
Egyptian–Syrian intervention in Lebanon, 134
Eilan, Arieh, 305–6
Ekalavya, 308–9
Eling, Walter Edward, 187–88
emergence of Israel, 102
emotions, 272
Emperor Hirohito, 8–9
Empire of Japan, 8–9
ethnic groups, 167
European development, 3
European history and economics, 84
experienced and impartial personalities, 135

Fabian, K.P., 219–21, 225
famine in Bengal, 16
Far Eastern Affairs, 81
Farrukhabad, 241
Ferdinand, Archduke Franz, 5

first women recruits, 239–55
food self-sufficiency, 45–46
foreign service, 75
Forster, E.M., 75
Fotedar, Makhan Lal, 206
Fotedar, Triloki Nath, 206
Frankfurt, 113
freedom, 2
    of Indonesia, 256–57
    -loving people of Indonesia, 193
    struggle, 260
Freeman, John, 273, 274
Free Press Journal, The, 13, 17, 302
French Indochina, 116
French territories, 118

Gaddafi, Muammar, 123, 178
Gaekwads of Baroda, 96
Gandhian freedom struggle, 41
Gandhian school of struggle, 259
Gandhi, Feroze, 40, 150
Gandhi, Indira, 26–27, 35, 40, 173–74, 179
    Emergency rule, 144
    as her first foreign destination in 1966, 231
    interpreter cadre creation, 64
    national Emergency, 76
    as Prime Minister, 46–47
    US and India political exchange, 184
Gandhi, Kasturba, 249
Gandhi, Mahatma, 1–2, 14, 80, 189, 250–51
    murder of, 151–52
Ganga–Jamuni Tehzeeb, 142
Garibaldi, Giuseppe, 3–4, 6

INDEX

Gauba, Satish Chandra, 204, 206–10
Gauhar, Altaf, 278
Geneva Accords of 1954, 217–18
German war machine, 4
Germany, 5
Gharekhan, Chinmaya, 37
Ghoshal, Jayanta, 25
Gonsalves, Eric, 41, 59, 160, 166, 170–71, 179, 181, 184–85
Gonsalves, Rose, 160
Gopal, Sarvepalli, 75–76
Gorbachev, Mikhail, 58
Gould, Harold A., 82
government jobs, 7
Government of India Act, 1935, 241, 242–43, 265
Green Revolution, 178–79
Griffiths, P.J., 298–99
Gromyko, Andrey, 174, 278
G20 summit-related events, 286, 289
Gujral, Inder Kumar, 40, 57–58
Gulf war, 169
Gundevia, Yezdezard Dinshaw, 34–35, 167, 170, 229, 239–41
Gupta, R.L., 87
Gurkha battalions, 192
Gurkha soldiers of Nepal, 192
Gurudwaras, 24
Gyanendra, 202

Hajipir Pass, 279–80, 281
Hajj pilgrims, 246–47
Haksar, Parmeshwar Narain, 26–27, 40–42, 47
Hammarskjöld, Dag, 134, 135, 138–39

'hands off Asia' policy, 192
Harris, Flora, 189
Hashemite dynasty, 102
Hatta, Mohammad, 13, 14–15, 60, 257
Hindi speeches in Parliament, 149
Hindi–Urdu dictionary, 146
Hindu–Muslim unity, 293
Hindu nationalism, 33
Hindustan Standard, 93
History of Services, 18–19, 40, 43, 62, 65, 66, 67, 73, 80, 91, 210, 212, 216, 242, 248
Ho Chi Minh, 37, 218
Holocaust, 263–64
Hossain, Malik Moazzam, 154–55
Hossain, Syud, 250–53
humanism, 14
humanity, 14, 199, 258
humiliation, 57
Husain, Zakir, 148–49
Hussein, Saddam, 112, 178

imperialism, 254
Imperial Tobacco Company of India, 152
INA History Committee, 214
Independence League Organisation, 213
Independence of Mauritius, 108–9
Independent, The, 250
India/Indian, 6
  activists and poets, 82
  citizenship and public support, 117
  community, 165
  culture/cultural, 91

diplomacy, 23, 93–94, 307
diplomatic game plan, 195
diplomatic history, 210
foreign affairs, 180
in foreign crisis, 157–85
foreign policy, 265
Independence struggle, 131
insurrection, 4
labour/labourers, 258
leadership, 94
nationalism, 3
nuclear diplomacy, 261
political geography and demographics, 188
post-Mandal, 59
social orthodoxy, 265
sovereignty, 118
-UK ties, 170
-US relationship, 170–71
India–Burma–China theatre, 251
India–China war, 182–83
India–Indonesia relations, 12
India–Indonesia warmth, 19
India–Israel relations, 182
Indian Administrative Service, 96
Indian Air Force, 277
Indian Army Observer, 7
Indian Civil Service, 66, 84, 96, 100, 136–37, 264, 266
  in 1933, 121
  in 1930, 239–40
  in 1932, 260
Indian Council of Child Welfare, 288
Indian Council of World Affairs, 167, 245
Indian Diplomatic Mission in Jakarta, 18

Indian Embassy
  in Beijing, 60, 71–72
  in Jakarta, 303
  in Kabul, 209
  in Moscow, 122
  in Nanking, 70
  of Rangoon, 63
Indian Foreign Affairs Journal, 31
Indian Foreign Service (IFS), 3, 13, 22, 38, 58, 62, 66, 71–72, 81, 108, 119–20, 171
  creation, 42
Indian High Commission in Nairobi, 26
Indian Independence League (IIL), 213
Indian Military Academy, 222
Indian Mission in Lhasa, 71
Indian National Army (INA), 227
Indian National Congress, 254, 258
Indian Political Service (IPS), 121–22, 223
Indian Red Cross, 169
Indian Revolutionary Committee, 4
Indian Supply Mission in London, 188
Indian, The, 213
India–Pakistan
  conflict of 1965, 306
  relations, 182
  war, 171, 228, 269
In Different Saddles, 296
Indonesia/Indonesian
  freedom struggle, 11
  government, 215–16
  independence, 12

INDEX

'republic', 16
rubber and oil supply, 15
textiles shortage, 17
troops in Surabaya, 10
Indonesian Nationalist Party, 256
Indo-Pak hostility, 39
Indo-Pakistan war of 1971, 31
Indo-Soviet Friendship Treaty, 27, 31
    in August 1971, 206
'Induction Training', 43
Indus Rangers, 273
industrial capability, 45–46
Indus Waters Treaty, 270
Intelligence Bureau, 66, 154
inter-ethnic harmony and development, 214
interim government in India, 259
International Alliance of Women, 236
International Bank for Reconstruction and Development, 184
International Commission for Supervision and Control (ICSC), 217, 229
international peace and security, 90
International Radiotelegraph Conference in 1912, 236
international social capital, 216–17
International Wireless Telegraph Convention in 1912, 236
Interpretation Act, 237
inter-war period, 41, 264
Iran hostage crisis, 179–80
Iraq, 103, 112
Islamic bloc, 18

Islamic Revolution of Iran, 175
Islamist-Republican Constitution, 175–76

Jaishankar, S., 47–48
Jana Sangh, 235
Jaswant Singh–Strobe Talbott negotiation, 55
Java, 6–7
Javadwipa, 6–7
Java rice supply, 17
Jawaharlal Nehru University, 67–68
Jayakar, M.R., 232
Jha, Chandra Shekhar, 34–35, 48, 81, 260, 261, 262–63, 265–69, 273
Jha, L.K., 172, 179
Jha, Shiva Shankar, 264
Jinnah, 300
Jinnah, Mohammed Ali, 46, 293–96
Johnson, Lyndon, 57, 231, 233
journalism, 7
J.P. Srivastava Group, 131

Kabir, Humayun, 142
Kalakshetra, 13
Kalavati, 240
Kalisosok prison of Surabaya, 11
Kamtekar, Dileep Shankarrao, 48, 95–97, 98, 108, 114
Kamtekar, Indivar, 97
Kamtekar, Rachana, 99, 111, 114
    to Baghdad, 112
Kamtekar, Shankarrao Anandrao, 96

Kannampilly, Karunakar Menon,
   48, 211–13, 215, 216–17, 228
   career, 218–19
Kannampilly, Murali, 211
Karaikal, 116
Kargil
   conflict, 304
   war of 1999, 26
Karna of Kurukshetra, 14
Karthikeyan, Girija, 23
Kaul, B.N., 142
Kaul, Triloki Nath, 26–27, 34–35, 192
   as Joint Magistrate, 69
Kennedy, John F., 37
Kerala Bandhu, 213
Keskar, B.V., 143
Khan, Abdul Qayum, 150–51
Khan, Ayub, 153, 273, 277, 280–81
Khan, Badshah, 137
Khan, Khan Abdul Gaffar, 137
Khan, Liaquat Ali, 151–52
Khan, Mirza Aliyar, 243
Khan, Mortuza, 155
Khan, Yahya, 30
Khan, Zafrullah, 91
Khilafat movement, 250–51
Khomeini, Ayatollah, 175
Khrushchev–Bulganin era, 284–85
Khrushchev, Nikita, 289, 290, 292
Khurana, Madan Mohan, 228
kingdom of Kalinga (Odisha), 16
King Faisal II, 103
Kissinger, Henry, 31
Kohli, D.R., 279
Korbel, Josef, 91

Korean war, 261
Kosygin, 275, 277–80
Kotda Sangani, 66–67, 230–33
Krishnamurthi, Sambasiva, 69
Krishnaswamy, Seshadri, 210
Kumar, Ajit, 147
Kurchatov, Igor, 157–58
Kurseong, 105
Kuru dynasty, 307–8
Kutch–Sindh border, 273

Labour government of Clement
   Attlee, 253–54
Lal, Diwan Chaman, 268
Lall, Chunni, 64, 187–88
Lasso, Gallo Plaza, 135
Laxman, R.K., 75
Lebanese
   constitution, 134
   crisis, 135
   foreign ministry, 73–74
Legislative Assembly in Delhi, 295
Leuchtag, Erika, 196–99, 200, 201
Lever, William, 129
liberalization, 168
Liberation War of 1971, 165, 172, 179
Limaye, Madhu, 57
linguistic disaffection, 154
Little India in 1970, 109
London School of Economics, 230
Ludhianvi, Sahir, 150
Lutyens, Edwin, 292

Madhubani, 266
Madhushala (1935), 141
Madras Presidency, 117

INDEX

Madras University, 7
Magsaysay, Ramon, 301
Mahabharat, 307–9
Mahajan, Pramod, 25
Mahe, 116
Mahinder, Arthur, 288
Majithia, Surjit Singh, 201
Malhautra, Jagdish Lal, 188
Malhotra, Inder, 57–58
Malik, Mira Ishardas, 69–70, 71, 72–73, 74
Mallaby, Aubertin Walter Sothern, 9–10
Mangharam, Bhavandas, 64
Mani, Poonamalle Ramakrishna S., 6, 7, 12, 15
   All India Radio staff members, 19–20
   death, 23–24
   Gurkhas, 192
   in West Germany as counsellor, 20
   youthful activism, 19
Mani, Rangiah Subra, 103
Maoist movement, 211
Mao Zedong, 27–30
marriages and love affairs, 69
Martial Law, 154–55
mass media, 2
masterminds, 41
Mathai, M.O., 88
Mathai, Ranjan, 23
Mathew, Philip, 123
Mauritius, 107, 108
May Day exchange, 30
McCarthy, Joseph, 157
McCloy, Jack, 183–84
media power, 21

Mehta, Jagat Singh, 35, 57
Menon, Kumar Pedma Sivasankara, 41, 49, 60–61, 65–66, 68–69, 80, 85, 92, 101, 132
Menon, V.K. Krishna, 50, 170, 261
Menon, V.K.R., 87
Menshikov, Mikhail A., 289
mental alertness, 75
Meston, James, 238
Metcalfe House in Delhi, 42
military-bureaucratic roots, 4
Ministry of Defence, 68
Ministry of External Affairs (MEA), 22, 43, 68
Mirzapur, 241
Mishra, Brajesh, 24, 25, 28, 36, 37, 40, 55, 61, 86–87, 304–5
   joined Indian Foreign Service, 26
   meeting with Haksar and Kaul, 30–31
   National Security Advisor, 37, 305
   representative of India in Beijing, 27
Mishra, Dwarka Prasad, 26
Mishra, Sudhir, 28, 30–32
Mitra, Ajai Kumar
   diplomat in Vienna, 152–53
   murder of, 152
   suicide, 153
Modi, Narendra, 33, 77–78
Mookerjee, Harendra Coomar, 290
'Moonglow', 30
Moradabad riots of 1980s, 178
Moraes, Frank, 296

Moscow, 28, 204
Mountbatten, Louis, 187
Mudaliar, Ramaswami, 252
Mugabe, Robert, 203
Mujib, Sheikh, 154–56
Mukherjee, Jatindranath, 4, 6
multi-faith prayer service, 80
Mundhra scandal, 150
Municipal Corporation of Bombay, 295–96
musafirkhanas in Bombay, 246
Muslim League, 294, 297
Muslim League Working Committee, 295
Muthamma, Chonira Belliappa, 41, 63, 69, 83

Naidu, Leilamani, 41, 60–61, 70, 242, 243–44, 245–46, 247–48
Naidu, Sarojini, 70, 242–43, 244, 245–46, 292–93
Nair, V.M.M., 59
Nambiar, Nanu, 92–93
Nanda, Gulzarilal, 178, 272, 281
Narayanan, Kocheril Raman, 63, 229–30
Narayan, Jayaprakash, 76
Nasser, Gamal Abdul, 51, 60
National Assembly of France, 120
National Democratic Alliance (NDA) government, 33
nationalism, 14, 126, 142
nationalist credentials, 125
nationalist movement, 131
nationalization of several banks, 179
National Security Advisor (NSA), 33

national security czar, 24
national struggle for independence, 249
National War Front, 298–99
Nazareth, Pascal Alan, 164, 166
Nazi Germany, 158, 297, 299
Nazi occupation, 125
Nehru–Bajpai duo, 98
Nehru, B.K., 67, 179, 182, 184
Nehru–Indira tenure phases, 40
Nehru, Jawaharlal, 2, 35–36, 40, 49, 66, 76
  era in 1955, 140
  Indonesian freedom fighters, support to, 256–57
  promotion of Hindi, 146
  revolutionaries and, 15
Nehru–Liaquat Ali pact of 1950, 122, 269
Nehru, Motilal, 250
Nehru, Ratan, 68, 88
Nehru, R.K., 72
Nehru, Sarup Kumari, 250
Nehru–Sjahrir duo, 17–18
Nehruvian diplomacy, 192, 263, 304
Neo-Destour party, 124
Nepal/Nepalese, 5–6
  aristocracy, 193
  identity, 195
  monarchy, 193–94
neutrality, 51, 263–64
Ne Win, 162, 166, 169
New Statesman, 76
Nixon, Richard, 30, 37, 171, 172
Nizam College in Hyderabad, 242
Nizams of Hyderabad, 237

INDEX

Non-Aligned Movement (NAM), 36, 108, 162–63
non-alignment, 263–64
non-Soviet Asian country, 284
Noon, Firoz Khan, 252
North Atlantic Treaty Organization (NATO), 123–24, 126
North Vietnam, 218
nuclear diplomacy, 25, 46
nuclear testing, 31–32
Nu, U., 162–63
Nyasaland, 106

Official Secrets Act (OSA), 114
oil-for-food scandal, 55, 58
oligarchy, 198
One Life is Not Enough, 58
'One World' concept, 257–58
Order of British Empire (OBE), 267
Orissa, 264, 267
Osman, 291
Osmania University's College for Women (1941-47), 243
Ottoman rule in Turkey, 268
Oxford schooling, 91

Pagoda, Shwedagon, 167
Pakistani 'mujahids', 274
Pakistani territory, 39
Pakistan-occupied Kashmir, 279
Palestine, 247
Pan-Asiatic Committee in 1930, 254
Pandey, Ramesh Nath, 199
Pandit, A.D., 121
Pandit, Ranjit, 249, 251, 292

Pandit, Vijaya Lakshmi, 67, 121, 145, 170, 241–42, 247–48, 250, 251, 254
India's foreign policy consciousness, 254
in jail, 249–50
minister of United Provinces, 252
Panikkar, K.M., 81
Pant, Govind Ballabh, 75, 151, 241
'Pantja Sila', 14
Paris Peace Conference, 41, 237
Parthasarathy, G., 29, 179
Patel, H.M., 87
Patel, Sardar Vallabhbhai, 49, 87
Pathak, R.S., 58
Pather Panchali, 302
Patna, 195
patriotism, 81
Pattar, Sardar Pritam Singh, 151
peace
  building and maintenance, 39
  -making attempts, 136
  -making initiative, 277
Peasant Tenega Rajkat, 14–15
Pehlavi, Reza Shah, 175
People's Republic of China, 71, 132
people-to-people interactions, 183
Pillai, Narayanan Raghavan, 46–47, 88
PLCA (Pay, Leave and Compensatory Allowances) Rules of 1961, 162
Plimpton, Francis, 270
POETARA, 14–15

political atmosphere of South
    Asia, 153–54
political developments, 80–81
political disturbance, 104
political independence, 49, 136
Pondicherry, 115–16, 120, 202–3
Portuguese Possessions in India,
    120
post-Babri, 59
post-Cold War, 36
post-colonial
    bloc, 127
    democracy, 52
    difficulties, 216
    India, 41, 132
    Indian state, 238
    rule, 136
post-Independence
    administrative thinking, 82
    decade, 40
    period, 151
post-Nehru coup, 272
post-war Germany, 99–100
Pragalsingh, Shanthy, 186
pragmatism, 82
Praja Socialist Party in Kerala, 214
Prasad, Rajendra, 287
pre-Independence India, 265
pre-Partition India, 300
pro- and anti-communist
    formulations, 51
pro-British policy, 198
pro-imperialism monarchy, 192
pro-Indonesian public, 17
Protestant Cathedral in Delhi,
    287–88
Protocol Division, 44
pro-west bloc, 263

public diplomacy, 48
public enthusiasm, 284
Putin, Vladimir, 58
Pyaasa, 150

Qasim, Abd al-Karim, 103
Queen of Jhansi, 3
Quit India Movement, 84, 193,
    249

racial discrimination, 110
Radhakrishnan, Sarvepalli, 76, 148
Raghavan, N., 215–16, 228
'Raghuviri Hindi', 140–41
Rahman, Mujibur, 154
Rahman, Sheikh Mujibur, 27,
    174, 209
Rajput rulers of Jaipur, 237
Raman, B.N., 153, 154
ramifications, 175
Rana, Mohan Shumsher Jung
    Bahadur, 198–99
    regime, 191–92
    rule in Nepal, 195
Ranashahi, 192
Ranbir Singh Sehgal case, 151
Rangoon Review, 213
Rann of Kutch, 273
Rao, P.V. Narasimha, 36, 57–58,
    181
Rasgotra, Maharajakrishna, 35, 59,
    81, 83–85, 87–88
rational thinking, 265
R&AW, 47
Raxaul, 195
Ray, Satyajit, 302
Reagan, Ronald, 180
realism, 51

INDEX

rebellion, 3
rebels and princes, 211–38
refugee
   influx, 150
   relocation, 169
regional intervention, 102
Registration of Foreigners (Amendment) Act, 1957, 163
representational allowance, 110–11
Republic of Indonesia, 194
Reserve Bank of India, 179
Rice, Condoleeza, 58
Rizvi, Nazir Ahmed, 151
Rohingya crisis, 164, 167
Roth, Andrew, 124
Royal Air Force Spitfires, 10
Royal Naval Volunteer Reserve, 108
royals of Saurashtra and Kutch, 237
Roy, Benoy, 174
Roy, Bidhan Chandra, 302
Roy, M.N., 299
Russian revolution, 6–7

Sabarmati Ashram, 250–51
Safrani, Abid Hasan, 46, 62, 226, 227, 228
sahagamana, 239–40
Sahib, Sheikh, 154
San, Aung, 213–15, 217
San Francisco Conference, 41, 252
Sarabhai, Mrinalini, 284
Sarkozy, Nicolas, 123–24
Sarna, Sajjan Singh, 158–59
Sathe, Ramchandra Dattatreya, 35
Saudi Arabia for Hajj, 246

Scott, Ian Dixon, 136–37, 138
Sehgal, Ranbir Singh, 150–51
self-defence, 262
self-rule, 154
Sengupta, Bhavani, 40
Sen, Keshab Chandra, 254
Sen, Ronen (Rajiv Gandhi's PMO), 40
Sethi, Ascharj Ram, 19
Shahabuddin, Syed, 61
Shah Bano case of 1986, 61
Shah, Shardul Bikram, 235
Shah, Tribhuvan Bir Bikram, 196
Shah, Zahir, 58
Shankar, Uday, 8
Shankar, Uma, 97
Sharifuddin, Amir, 11
Shastri, Lal Bahadur, 178, 179, 228, 272, 277
Shia vs Sunni, 176
Shumsher, Mohan, 201
Sichuan, 70
Sikh militancy, 178–79
Sima Shulka Sadan, 144
Singha Durbar, 198
Singh, Amarinder, 77
Singh, Avtar, 108
Singh, Chandreshwar Prasad Narayan, 201
   Indian ambassador to Nepal, 190–91
Singh, Chaudhary Charan, 175
Singh, Ganesh, 221
Singh, Ganga (maharaja of Bikaner), 238
Singh, Harjeet, 77
Singh, Heminder Kumari, 54
Singh, I.J. Bahadur, 48, 279

Singh, Jarnail, 151
Singh, Jaswant, 56
Singh, Kewal, 34–35, 36, 69, 205–6, 279
Singh, K. Natwar, 54–56, 147
Singh, Madanjeet, 210
Singh, Maharaj, 259–60
Singh, Manmohan, 34, 37, 56, 58, 59
   Dixit role as national security advisor, 87
Singh, Narendra, 235
Singh, Natwar, 33–34, 36, 37, 40, 48, 58, 62, 72, 77, 78, 236, 304
   History of Services introduction, 60
   Indian Foreign Service, 60
   liaison officer to Chinese cultural delegation, 60
   prolific writers, 48
   punishment, 75–76
   survivor, 58–59
   as undersecretary, 75
Singh, Ranbir, 19
Singh, Shailendra Kumar, 57–58
Singh, Suchittar, 151
Singh, Swaran, 276, 278, 280
Singh, Vishwanath Pratap, 57–58
Sinha, Mira, 74
Sinha, Satyendra Prasanna, 238
Sinha, Shakti, 25
Sinha, Sumal, 70, 71, 72, 74
Sinhji, Pradyumma, 66–67, 229–230, 232–34
Sinhji, Pratap, 233–34
Sinh, Surendra, 235
Sino-Indian War, 153–54, 165, 169–70, 173, 270

Sino-Soviet conflict, 27–28
Sittwe, 116
Sjahrir, Sutan, 13, 16–17, 257
Skymaster aircraft, 277
social justice, 14
social media, backdrop, 47–48
social-political fabric, 135
socio-political relevance, 35
South Asia, 5–6, 191–92
   British domination, 6
Southeast Asian conflicts, 13
sovereign territory, 119
sovereignty of people, 14
Soviet capital, 204
Soviet-China tensions, 31
Soviet delegation, 278
Soviet leadership, 277
Soviet mission, 79
Soviet nuclear weapons programme, 157–58
Soviet tanks, 50
Soviet Union, 41
Soviet veto, 270
speeches in Parliament, 149
Sri Lankan Tamils, 233
Srivastava, C.P., 276–77
Srivastava, J.P., 130
Srivastava, Sushila, 129, 130
Stalin, Joseph, 120, 285
Stalin, Vassily, 121
State's Council of India, 291
stenographers, 206–7, 210
Stevenson, Adlai E., 270
Stockholm, 94
Stracey, Cyril John, 62, 220, 221–23, 228
Stratemeyer, George E., 251
Suez Canal

INDEX

crisis of 1956, 103, 156
nationalization, 50–51
Suez Crisis of 1956, 133
Sukarno, Ahmed, 13, 19
Sukarno–Hatta–Sjahrir trio, 15
Sukarno, Koesno Sosrodihardjo, 257
Sumatra, 6–7
surgical strike, 39
Suvarnabhoomi, 6–7
Swarup, Vikas, 39
Swatantra Party, 235
Syrian Arab Republic, 45
Szochuan, 70

Tallents, P.C., 266
Tamil Chettiars, 164–65
Tashkent Declaration, 281
Tashkent Municipal Council, 278
Tashkent Summit and Declaration, 281
Tehri Garhwal, 235
territorial coherence, 117
Thatcher, Margaret, 181
Tiger Jatin, 6
Time and Tide, 296
Times of India, The, 21
Tito, Marshal, 131
Tojo, Hideki, 14–15
trans-Atlantic alliance, 119
Travancore University, 229–30
Trevelyan, Humphrey, 100
Tribhuvan, King, 199–202
'troika,' 92
Truman, Harry, 89
'Trust France', 125–26
Tulsidas, 144
Turkey, 268

Tyagi, Mahavir, 281

Uberoi, Patricia, 69
UK–France–Israel alliance, 51
Ul Haq, Zia, 176
UN Emergency Force (UNEF), 132
Union Public Service Commission (UPSC), 42–43
United Arab Republic (UAR), 45, 133–35
United Nations Military Observer Group in India and Pakistan (UNMOGIP), 274
United Nations Observation Group in Lebanon (UNOGIL), 135
United Nations Security Council, 194
United Progressive Alliance (UPA) government, 87
Universal Postal Union, 236
University College of Trivandrum, 230
University of Cambridge, 42
University of Oxford, 42
UN Security Council (UNSC), 124–25, 274
UPA government crisis, 55
USEFI in India, 231
US–Pakistan relations, 181–82

vaccine-related strength, 39
Vajpayee, Atal Bihari, 24, 40, 87, 172–73
–Advani duo, 33
–Manmohan Singh, 33
Venkataraman, S.A., 87

Venkateswaran, Ayilam
  Panchapakesa, 36, 40–41, 57,
  97, 209
  IFS officer of 1952, 35
Verghese, Samuell, 19
Verma, Siddheshwar, 141
'Videsh Mantralaya', 140–56
Vietnamese crisis, 228–29
Vietnam war, 228
Vigilance Division, 44–45
violent insurgency, 198
volatile confrontation, 177

Walters, Anthony, 184–85
Walters, Vernon Anthony, 172,
  181
War of Liberation of 1971, 171
Weberian definition of
  bureaucracy, 62
Weber, Max, 61–62
Week, The magazine, 56–57
Weightman, Hugh, 92
Wells of Power, 268–69
West Asian–North African
  (WANA) regions, 44
Western alliance, 119, 262
western bloc, 120
western capitals, 120–21, 287
Western flags, 286–87
West-Israel, 102–3
West Pakistan, 27
West Pakistan Rangers, 273

Wilfred, Santosham John, 62, 69,
  186–87
  career, 204
  as clerk in Accounts Office,
    188
  in Delhi, 195–96
  diplomatic community, 196
  family, 189–90
  Indian high commissioner to
    British Guyana, 203
  joined Indian Foreign Service,
    196
  in Kathmandu to Indian
    Embassy, 191
Wilson, Harold, 273
Woods, George, 183–84
World War II, 12, 13, 126, 192–93,
  249, 253, 258–59, 263–64, 299
  brutalities in Southeast Asia, 53
World War II years, 79–80

xenophobic rule in Burma, 53

Yanam, 116
Yangon, 116
Yugoslavia, 131
Yunus, Mohammed, 104, 246–47
  Emergency in 1975–76, 50
  as Indian consul in Jakarta, 20

Zionism, 132

ABOUT THE AUTHOR

Tripura-born Kallol Bhattacherjee grew up in the hills of Northeast India, where he got his first glimpse of India's relentless interaction with the world. In the mid-1990s, on a summer day, he boarded the *Kalka Mail* from Calcutta (now Kolkata)—a move that eventually led him to the classrooms of the University of Delhi and subsequently to Jawaharlal Nehru University, where he studied political theory, the Arab–Israeli conflict and the history of modern Lebanon. He began his journalistic career writing for *Mainstream, Seminar, The Jerusalem Post, The Indian Express* and the Iranian News Agency. Over the past two decades, he has worked at *The Week* and *The Hindu*, where he is currently a senior assistant editor, reporting and writing on international affairs. Over the years, he has reported from conflict zones around the world, including Libya, Tunisia, Syria and Iraq at the height of the Arab Spring, and from India's neighbourhood. He is the author of *The Great Game in Afghanistan: Rajiv Gandhi, General Zia and the Unending War* (2017) and *A Baloch Militant in Delhi* (2018). His social media handle at X/Twitter is @janusmyth, and he can be reached on email at janusmyth@gmail.com.

HarperCollins *Publishers* India

At HarperCollins India, we believe in telling the best stories and finding the widest readership for our books in every format possible. We started publishing in 1992; a great deal has changed since then, but what has remained constant is the passion with which our authors write their books, the love with which readers receive them, and the sheer joy and excitement that we as publishers feel in being a part of the publishing process.

Over the years, we've had the pleasure of publishing some of the finest writing from the subcontinent and around the world, including several award-winning titles and some of the biggest bestsellers in India's publishing history. But nothing has meant more to us than the fact that millions of people have read the books we published, and that somewhere, a book of ours might have made a difference.

As we look to the future, we go back to that one word— a word which has been a driving force for us all these years.

Read.

Harper Collins

4th

HARPER FICTION

HARPER NON-FICTION

HARPER BUSINESS

HarperCollins Children'sBooks

HARPER DESIGN

Harper Sport

HARPER PERENNIAL

HARPER VANTAGE

हार्पर हिन्दी